HARD TO GET

HARD TO GET

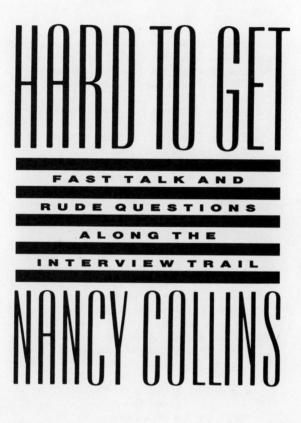

FAST TALK AND

RUDE QUESTIONS

ALONG THE

INTERVIEW TRAIL

NANCY COLLINS

RANDOM HOUSE

NEW YORK

c. 1

Some interviews included in this collection were originally
published in *Esquire, Interview, New York, Playboy,*
and *Rolling Stone.* Others are based on interviews
conducted on the *Today* show.

Grateful acknowledgment is made to the following for
permission to reprint previously published material:
Interview magazine: Robin Williams interview from the
August 1986 issue of *Interview* magazine. Reprinted by
permission of *Interview* magazine. *Playboy* magazine:
Excerpts from *Playboy* "Twenty Questions": Truman
Capote, December 1980; *Playboy* interview: Dudley
Moore, January 1983; *Playboy* interview: Joan Rivers,
November 1986. Copyright © 1980, 1982, 1986 by
Playboy. All rights reserved. Reprinted by permission.
Rolling Stone magazine: "Bette Midler: The Cheese
Bomb American Crapola Dream," from Issue 384 of
Rolling Stone magazine. Copyright © 1982 by Straight
Arrow Publishers, Inc. All rights reserved.
Reprinted by permission.

Library of Congress Cataloging-in-Publication Data
Collins, Nancy.
Hard to get : fast talk and rude questions along
the interview trail / by Nancy Collins.
p.   cm.   ISBN 0-394-57661-6
1. Celebrities—United States—Interviews. I. Title.
CT220.C58 1990   920.073—dc20   89-43417   [B]

Manufactured in the United States of America
Book design by J. K. Lambert
24689753
First Edition

FOR MAMA

"Sure, you will."

Elsie Morris Collins

CONTENTS

HARD TO GET

PROLOGUE

This is a story about high heels and low times, big risks and grand rewards, quirky dreams and pale truths, youthful stupidity and hard-learned wisdom, belly laughs and quiet tears. It's the story of a mother who dreamed out loud and a daughter who listened and came to believe that the American Dream meant life, liberty, and the pursuit of curiosity. Toward that end I've turned in some of my best—and worst—performances as a journalist and as a human being. Yet I've always tried to take both jobs seriously enough to find the humor—a philosophy honed from cocktail parties to cancer wards. This is the story of a five-foot-ten-inch blonde from Montana who takes "no" as a personal insult and hates authority as much as she loves probing those who have it.

It might be a man's world, but I never held it against them.

INTRODUCTION

I was twenty minutes into my interview with Jack Kemp and I still
hadn't asked him if he was gay.

You can't rush a thing like that, especially in a man's own home.
Kemp's wife and three of his children were standing five feet away,
directly behind NBC's *Today* show cameras. Hardly the optimal conditions for such a sensitive exchange. But when I'd suggested we talk in
his Capitol Hill office, Kemp had vetoed it.

It was no secret that the Republican congressman from New York
had been dogged by this nagging allegation throughout his sixteen-year
political career. By 1986, when we spoke, Kemp was certain to seek the
1988 Republican nomination, and the issue of his alleged homosexuality had resurfaced in *Newsweek* and *Vanity Fair*.

Kemp had yet to discuss the charge on television. Surely he expected
to be asked about it eventually, but not now, not from me. After all,

I wasn't Barbara Walters or Ted Koppel; I was "just a girl," a contributing correspondent from a morning show, there to ask the standard softball stuff. The congressman certainly didn't look worried—just a bit cranky. It was 8:30 P.M., and Kemp clearly wanted to get this little interview over with. "Let's get going," he growled.

The question had to be precisely phrased: the tougher the question, the more gentle the delivery. I couldn't appear to be bludgeoning my subject.

"Congressman Kemp," I began, "if you decide to seek the Republican presidential nomination, I'm sure you realize the scrutiny you'll have to endure. I'd like to talk to you about that.

"For years there have been allegations concerning the period when you worked in the reelection campaign of then California governor Ronald Reagan. During that campaign you were friendly with a man who was later fired for being involved in what was called a 'homosexual ring.' Although you've said you knew nothing about it, and Reagan backed you, this rumor has continued to plague you. Could you once and for all clear that up for me?"

Did I hear a pin drop? An anvil smash?

"It's impossible to once and for all clear it up because it's just a rumor," Kemp coolly replied.

But I needed the definitive denial, the answer that would publicly address the core of the rumor, preferably in seconds—in other words, the sound bite. Right or wrong, that's what TV is all about. In spite of the delicacy of the issue and the family context, both of which could justifiably cause the former Buffalo Bills quarterback to punt me through the living-room window, I had to be very specific.

"You would say, then, that, categorically, you've never been involved in a homosexual incident in your life?"

"Categorically," replied Kemp. "Absolutely."

On March 13 the Kemp interview ran at 7:15 A.M.—the section of the *Today* show devoted to hard news. Jane Pauley introduced me, I introduced the piece, and then watched, along with everyone else, on the studio monitor. I had asked Kemp the question every journalist knew had to be asked, and I'd gotten there first. That the difficult, precarious process had left me looking like Georgia O'Keeffe in her late Santa Fe period was but a small price to pay for a scoop.

In the next day's newspapers, Kemp's camp publicly cried outrage, but privately we heard that they were relieved the inevitable question had been asked and effectively addressed so early in the game.

Much more unexpected was the reaction of my colleagues in the Fourth Estate. Oh, the moral indignation that spewed from typewriters across the country! John Corry, television critic for *The New York Times,* referred to my question as "despicable." He nailed me in the same piece in which he branded Mike Wallace "smarmy" for asking Roy Cohn, the now-deceased controversial Manhattan lawyer, power broker, and former aide to Senator Joseph McCarthy, about his alleged homosexuality during an interview on *60 Minutes.* "Honey, you haven't arrived until *The New York Times* thinks you're despicable," my friend gossip columnist Liz Smith insisted.

And then there was Richard Cohen, second-tier columnist for *The Washington Post,* my own alma mater, who threw a hissy fit. Claiming to know several senators who were either homosexual or heterosexual but cheated on their wives, Cohen sniffed that he, for one, would never deign to expose them. How, he railed, could I ask such a question?

Jesus, Richard, how could I not? After all, in the winter of 1986 the rules of presidential politics were pretty clear: Running for the job meant being prepared to open up your life—and that of your family—to exhaustive media scrutiny. I scrutinized and was assailed for it. I should've expected it. It wasn't my first taste of echo-effect journalism, when breaking the story is as big a story as the story itself.

But if my colleagues had only known what we left out of the Kemp profile! To me my question was fair game. But there is a fine line between asking direct questions and staging a frontal assault, as my conversation with Kemp's wife might've been perceived had we chosen to run it.

Blond and still coed pretty at fifty, Joanne Kemp was a born-again Christian and mother of two girls. During our interview I'd asked her a rather predictable question: If one of her daughters were to be raped and as a result get pregnant, could Mrs. Kemp condone an abortion?

"Well, not really," she began, visibly uncomfortable. "But you know there are ways to prevent a pregnancy, prevent one without an abortion, even with rape."

"There are?"

"Yes," she continued confidently. "You can get a D and C."

Was I hearing right? Perhaps she'd misunderstood. "Mrs. Kemp, I believe a D and C is an abortion."

Her look of confusion told the tale: She didn't know. She panicked, sensing she'd committed the ultimate sin of the political wife: embarrassing her husband. I longed to reach out and reassure her. Why hadn't someone told her? Why did I have to be the one to explain this particular fact of life? Where was her mother? Where was her husband, for God's sake? Shouldn't a hard-line pro-lifer have enlightened his wife on the issues before subjecting her to the questions of a network news correspondent?

Ultimately, my producer and I decided not to air her interview. We didn't want to be viewed as terrorizing the Kemps, even though it was her answer—not my question—that would've gotten her into trouble.

Trouble, controversy, brouhaha, derring-do, yes, I believe we've met. If there's one lesson I've learned over the years it's this: If it doesn't make you sweat, it's not worth it. If it's not hard to get, why go for it?

True, I didn't parachute into Grenada or cover the fall of Saigon. In fact, I rarely cover a story where you can't wear high heels. Never walk into an interview under six feet—that's my motto. What God didn't give you, you buy. But, as any reporter will tell you, no matter what the story, the same tools are required: unflagging curiosity, bedrock tenacity, gumption, gall, and nerves as sturdy as a titanium hull. You can't squirm, you can't flinch, you can't run away. You can fake it plenty, but no one must know you're not in it for the distance. You go where you have to go to get the news, and you don't leave until you have it. You ask the questions that have to be asked. And you *always* accept the consequences.

For most reporters, curiosity is a genetic defect that shows itself early on. I drove my own mother so crazy with questions that one day she coined my epitaph:

"I swear, Nancy, your tombstone will read, ARE YOU SURE?"

And am I? Not unless I'm asking the questions or seeing it first-hand—a reporterly predilection that's carried me to some bizarre places.

How bizarre? Try sixty feet under water. Like many a blonde before me, I once said yes to a Hollywood producer and took a dive. The producer in question was Peter Guber, now the powerful co-chairman of Columbia Pictures, whose 1989 deal with Sony made his sidekick Jon Peters and him the highest-paid studio executives in Hollywood.

When I met him in 1975, however, Guber was still struggling to make his first million—and his first motion picture, *The Deep*, the Peter Benchley thriller starring Nick Nolte and Jacqueline Bisset that was being shot in the British Virgin Islands. Since a good part of it took place underwater, the mere notion of Bisset in a wet T-shirt was simply too irresistible for the graybeards at *Women's Wear Daily* in New York, where I was one of a gaggle of underpaid but wildly motivated young reporters. (A hundred and twenty-five bucks a week with a maximum yearly raise of $25—if, that is, you really kicked ass!)

The first person I saw when I got to Peter Island was Guber. Pumped up, hard-driving, and fast-talking, the thirty-four-year-old fledgling producer was brilliant and indisputably on his way to big things. He was also a nervous wreck, consumed by every detail as he raced around spitting out words faster than anyone I'd ever heard, myself included.

Barely had I dropped my bags when Guber swooped me into an open-air Jeep for a ten-second tour of the island, accompanied by a running (and I mean *running*) monologue on the endless perils of making a movie with a third star as temperamental as the Caribbean Sea. (At least it didn't have an agent, I pointed out.)

"When can I go to the set?" I asked.

"Tomorrow."

"Wonderful. Where is it?" I asked, scanning the horizon for klieg lights.

"Sixty feet down."

I asked Guber how we got there.

"Dive," he said.

The next thing I knew I found myself standing poolside, looking remarkably like Dustin Hoffman in *The Graduate*, my body weighted down in full scuba gear as I awaited my first—and only—scuba lesson to prepare for the following day's visit to the "set." Three hours later all I knew for sure was if I held my breath and ascended, my lungs would explode and I'd die.

"Great," my instructor enthused. "You're ready."

At dawn the next day, I was in the middle of the Caribbean, my feet dangling off the end of the *Moby II*, a converted salvage vessel that served as the movie's above-water base. I was both thrilled and scared out of my wits: torn between being Brenda Starr—who would jump fearlessly into the water and emerge with hair still perfectly coiffed— and being my mother's daughter (if she'd had her way, I'd have stayed in the shallow end of Sleeping Child Hot Springs until I was forty).

"Are you sure all the other reporters who come down here are diving down *there* to watch the filming?" I asked a scuba-suited Guber, whose feet twitched nervously alongside mine.

"Absolutely—everybody," swore Guber, exhibiting his notorious ability to talk anybody into anything. "Besides, there's nothing to worry about—I'll be there." (He forgot to mention, of course, that he was making his own first dive that day. He also forgot to mention that I was the only reporter stupid enough to actually take the plunge.)

Slowly we finned our way downward, thirty . . . forty . . . fifty . . . sixty feet, dangerously deep for a debut dive, but who knew? I had enough on my mind; I had to remember how to breathe. Suddenly a flash of light cut through the darkness. I could make out forms, figures, human beings with fins and masks and air tanks swimming and treading water around a piece of wreckage, a hunk of the R.M.S. *Rhone*, which had been embedded in the ocean since 1865.

Director Peter Yates, in blue jeans and scuba tank, was perched on top of the ancient wreckage, pantomiming to the underwater camera-man that he wanted a close-up shot. The cinematographer maneuvered his Panavision 35-mm. underwater camera (weighing 75 pounds above water, 88 ounces below, which meant that, at 137 ounces, I'd finally satisfied half of the "never too rich, never too thin" axiom) to focus on the face of a woman whose long brown hair floated around her like a mass of seaweed. As light enveloped her form, even my eyes popped out. Clad only in a bikini bottom and a white T-shirt, Bisset's voluptu-ous body would stop traffic—if, that is, there was any. Following closely behind was a towheaded Nick Nolte and a lighting man carrying one of eight 1,000-watt lights mysteriously suspended from some black snakelike cables.

Madly treading water, I watched, transfixed, as this slow-motion silent movie played itself out on the soundless soundstage. Finally, some thirty minutes later, with a languid motion, Yates indicated "cut"; the filming stopped, and, miraculously, music began. Strains of the theme from *2001* filled the ocean floor, from where I had no idea. But what did it matter? This was Hollywood! This was make-believe! This was magic!

Now all I had to do was make it back up to the surface alive.

Which, quite frankly, has been a running theme for much of my life. Just get out alive, baby. Make it back to safety before they figure out you're making it up, playing by ear, talking a good game about a game you didn't always know how to play. Particularly the First Time.

You see, it all began with Rod McKuen. I wish I could tell you I'm here today because of Jack Kennedy or Helmut Schmidt—Ringo Starr, even—but, my friends, it was Rod McKuen.

My senior year at Boston University I switched my major from theater to journalism. Endless matinees at the Roxy Theater in Hamil-ton had convinced me I was destined to act. Since I didn't believe I was pretty enough for the movies—no Sandra Dee this girl!—that meant the stage. But despite beating the boards in everything from *The Women* to *Our Town* as well as an audition for the Yale School of Drama, I had a change of mind more than heart.

"What do you want to do in the theater?" asked Delbert Mann, director of the Doris Day movies I'd grown up on, and Yale's official representative. We were sitting in the office adjacent to his elaborate home in Beverly Hills, where he had just watched me flail my way through pieces from *Twelfth Night* and *Who's Afraid of Virginia Woolf?* in my bid for Old Eli. It was my first trip to California. I'd flown in on student fare, hailed a cab at the airport, and instructed the driver to take me to Mann's address, right down the street, the cabbie assured me, from Bob Hope and Lucille Ball. As we pulled into the driveway, I felt like a tourist who'd bought a map to the stars' homes. It wasn't as if Yale had promised me anything concrete. ("Show up and we'll give you a shot," they'd said. I showed up.)

"Actually, I want to be a theater critic," I insecurely replied, hedging my bets. ("Dummy, you tell them you have to act or you'll die!" my drama teacher had groaned when I told her later.)

Yet it wasn't my talent I doubted so much as the life that went with it. An actress seemed to be the ultimate victim, an artist whose fate too often depended on people she neither liked nor respected. To me, such dependence was anathema. So, after my junior year in Europe, where I'd come to rely on *The Herald Tribune,* I decided to try writing.

My first assignment in Reporting 101 was the interview. "Talk to your aunt," said the professor, "your boyfriend, your roommate." Not for me. My definition of an interview was a conversation with Someone Famous, Someone of Import, Someone of Note. Someone like Rod McKuen, whose stickily sentimental poetry-and-song fests were selling out at Boston's Symphony Hall.

But how did I get to such a celebrity? Momentarily stumped, I fell back on my reliable stand-by: the movies. What would Roz Russell do in this situation? Why, throw on a suit, adjust the shoulder pads, grab a notebook and a sidekick, and simply show up. So I did. With my boyfriend Tom, I proceeded to the concert, and the minute McKuen moaned his last lyric, rushed to the stage door, where I blithely announced to the guard that I was from *The Boston Globe,* there to interview Mr. McKuen. The guard soon returned with McKuen's manager, who looked puzzled but interested. Five minutes later I'd sold him on my nonexistent credentials and we were being ushered into the singer's packed dressing room.

Immediately, the crowd clammed up—my first inkling of the undeserved awe the press engenders. But now what? Tom's elbow digging into my left side flicked my mental switch, and I started asking questions, frantically scribbling McKuen's every utterance in a stenographer's notebook. With each question (three into it and I still hadn't been found out!) my courage grew, and my curiosity took over. What a ride! Internally wired but externally calm, I Zenned out as the world around me fell away. It was just me and McKuen, who might as well have been Walt Whitman.

Thirty minutes later, I sailed out of that room, hooked. I'd found it. The thing I loved doing more than anything else in the world, the thing that came most naturally: talking to people about their lives. It was the perfect marriage of reality and the creative process. It was informative, it was fun, it was theatrical. Interviewing satisfied all my dramatic needs: information, communication, seduction, confrontation, concentration. Most important, however, I was *instinctively intrigued* by the choices people made. Journalism offered everything acting did with one huge plus: I ran the show.

A few weeks later the McKuen interview ran in *Boston After Dark,* a Beantown version of *The Village Voice* whose editor, on a cold call from me, barked, "Sure, kid, bring it up. I'll have a look at it." (This was too easy. Or was God simply sending a career telegram reading SEEK NO FURTHER?)

Upon seeing my byline, any second thoughts about forgoing acting were quickly dispelled. "My God, what a wonderful business," I thought. "And you don't even have to have a license." Clearly, this was the job for a maverick. All I needed was my mind and a notebook. It was my ticket to adventure, my passport to power, my visa to the most important thinkers in the world.

Like Rod McKuen.

——

If I were to sum up my career thus far, I'd have to say it's been a Heisenberg-uncertainty-principle kind of affair. This principle, a mainstay of modern particle physics, holds that you can judge either a particle's velocity or its location at any one time, but you can't judge them both at the same time. And so it's been with me. Speeding along, I always wondered whether I shouldn't stop someplace; stopped someplace, I always felt the urge to be speeding along.

Consequently, I've moved from New York to Washington to Los Angeles, tearing headlong into situations that worked—and a few that landed me flat on my bum. Still, I always managed to press on, buttressed by family, friends, and drive so huge it ought to have its own zip code. Which came in handy. For some women the career waters seem to have parted automatically; they skipped across the Red Sea of Ambition with nary a splash on their dress-for-success drabs. For me it's been like scaling K2 in Maud Frizons.

On-the-job training. Always. I'd never read a TelePrompTer until I appeared on national television and allowed four million *Today* show viewers to watch me stumble through the longest thirty seconds of my life. I didn't know steak tartare was raw until the first time I ordered it in a tony Washington restaurant and asked the waiter to "make mine rare."

Since I didn't know the rules, I never followed them. My family's values were small-town middle class. Neither of my parents went to college; when my father died at fifty-five, he'd never made more than $11,000 a year; when my mother took a job in 1960 it wasn't to "have a career"; we needed the money. Nobody I knew had ever been to New York, much less lived there, and, certainly, nobody was a journalist.

My odyssey began in Hamilton, Montana, from whence I sallied forth armed with more curiosity than judgment. That doing so was an indigenous geographical imperative never occurred to me until the day I ran into Robert Redford.

It was December 1972, and I was dispatched by *Women's Wear Daily* to cover auditions for the plum role opposite Robert Redford in *The Great Gatsby*. (The movie ended up a box-office bomb, but *Women's Wear* reported it as if it were the Paris peace talks.) Of the 150 women interviewed for Daisy, the field finally got narrowed down to Faye Dunaway, Candice Bergen, Katharine Ross, Cathy Lee Crosby,

Lois Chiles, and Mia Farrow, all of whom, except Farrow, read with Redford in New York.

Throughout the auditions, Redford, the first Big-Time movie star I'd ever seen—"Shoot me only from the left," he instructed the photographer in deference to the famous moles on the right side of his famous face—repeated the same scene with one actress after another. Since we had a lot of time to kill, Redford, like myself, took to pacing up and down the halls of the small West Fifty-fourth Street studio. On Day One, we merely smiled and nodded whenever we strode past each other, which was often. On Day Two, Redford suddenly stopped me midpromenade.

"You're from the West, aren't you?" he asked.

"Yes, how'd you know?"

"Because you walk like a western woman."

"How's that?"

"Western women cover ground."

Quite frankly, I'd had no choice. I grew up in Hamilton, Montana, an isolated village of two thousand with one radio station, one four-way traffic light, and three-digit telephone numbers. My first memories of life in the Rocky Mountains were of snow and space. Though Hamilton's physical remoteness underscored my own, it was precisely that insularity that gave perspective, providing a unique laboratory for a budding journalist. The kids with whom I started the first grade were the same ones I marched alongside twelve years later when I picked up my diploma from Hamilton High School. (Graduating class? Ninety-seven.) You knew everybody's business and they yours: You gossiped, kept track, got ensnared in life stories. In many ways, Hamilton was *Twin Peaks* idyllic: proms, boyfriends, championship football teams, and the Starlite Drive-in. Top-drawer scandal involved someone "having to get married" while the three-man police force battled to keep local rowdies from getting tanked up on beer and dragging burning bales of hay down Main Street on Friday night.

"Journalism" was *The Ravalli Republican* and *The Western News*, newspapers that ran with headlines like: BILL AND SALLY SMITH SPLIT THE SHEETS. As a result, *Time, Newsweek, Life,* and *Look* became my tutors, beginning a passionate love affair with magazines. I longed to be part of the action chronicled on those glossy pages. A tantalizing world was happening outside of Big Sky and I wanted to be smack in the middle of it. The question was: How to get there?

Enter Mama. A beautiful, five-foot-seven-inch, well-built blonde, whose shyness masked a throwaway wit and the heart of an adventuress, Mama's curiosity was high-flying and open-ended. It was her fanciful visions that laid the world at my feet. Raised in Alabama, she was the only girl among her seven siblings to leave the South and strike out on her own. Her father, Henry Morris—six feet four and as morally up-right as his size indicated—labored in the mills of Birmingham Steel, supporting his family of ten on $200 a month. When he died at ninety, "Papa" still read the Bible daily and *U.S. News & World Report* weekly.

His wife, Maggie, was an orphan Henry rescued from the cotton fields when he made her a bride at sixteen. Though illiterate, Maggie Morris imbued in her brood spunk, grit, and an unshakable ability to take what life dished out and cope with it.

At fifteen, having skipped two grades, my mother was already a high school senior, voted by her classmates the "prettiest, smartest, shyest" girl in class. But Mama had no intention of staying in Birmingham. Her senior year she eloped with a twenty-one-year-old and moved to North Carolina, where she managed a dress shop. One day, ten years later, she waited on a woman who announced she was in love—with Mama's husband. Stunned to learn of this infidelity, my mother took quick action. She flew home, threw her husband's belongings into a sheet, and tossed them on the lawn. By the time the philandering spouse pulled into the driveway, she'd changed the locks on every door.

Ignoring her father's admonitions to return to Alabama, Mama hopped the first train to Washington, D.C. Once there, she boarded a streetcar, searched for a HELP WANTED sign, and, spotting one in a dress store, talked herself into a job, ultimately working her way through secretarial school. Though her errant husband begged for a reconciliation, Mama returned to North Carolina only once—to pick up her divorce papers.

My parents met in Washington at the end of World War II, married following a whirlwind courtship, and, in 1951, moved to Montana, where Daddy was the medical librarian at the Rocky Mountain Laboratory, a branch of the National Institutes of Health, whose claim to fame was the discovery of the Rocky Mountain spotted tick vaccine. Theirs was a complicated, volatile, quicksilver union of two disparate personalities. (My brother and I honored them with NEVER A DULL MOMENT inscribed on their tombstone.) He, the son of Irish immigrants, burdened with the unusual name of Aeneas Patrick—"A.P."—was Celtic to the core: charming, bright, gregarious, witty, hard-drinking, and Roman Catholic. Like many Irishmen, his moods could be dark and melancholy.

In another life, my father might have been an entertainer or politician. But Daddy was a dreamer, better at fantasy than follow-through. Ultimately, his was a life of what-might-have-been. His frustration was palpable, spilling over onto those of us who lived with him, instilling in Pat and me a fierce determination that our own destinies not go as unrealized as had his. He was a remote father figure who left parenting largely to my mother.

Like most women of her generation and socioeconomic background, Mama was desperate for role models, and, with precious few locally available, she turned to Hollywood. One July day, seven years old and cooped up in the house with some childhood disease, I discovered a sealed carton in the basement. Exhausted from trying to keep me occupied, Mama ripped open this Pandora's box. What a treasure trove: stacks of photographs, a dilapidated rabbit coat, and a fat pile of yellowing scrapbooks. I pressed through the decaying pages plastered with grainy newspaper photos and clippings, announcements of everything from the bombing of Pearl Harbor to the engagement of Elizabeth Taylor, articles on everyone from Marie Curie to Maria Callas.

From that moment on, Mama became my own in-house version of *Who's Who*—an ongoing source of conversation and anecdotes about the talented, the accomplished, the glittering people in the World Out There, a place where, she didn't hesitate to suggest, I could belong. On long summer afternoons, with baskets of unironed shirts languishing, I'd perch on top of the refrigerator, suck on a Popsicle, and, with the radio blaring country-and-western *("Because you're mine . . . I walk the line. . . .")*, listen in rapt attention as Mama spun out her version of past-to-present fairy tales: Marilyn and Joe, James Dean, Aimee Semple McPherson, Amelia Earhart, Clare Boothe Luce. ("Now that's an interesting woman, honey. You can do that. Dare to be different.")

These interesting lives were discussed in the most minute detail. Thrillingly enough, Mama herself had had the odd brush with fame, waiting on Eleanor Roosevelt in Washington's Woodward and Lothrop stationery store, where Mama worked. The mere thought of my mother shaking hands with the first lady was dizzying, direct and living proof that Mama was as special as I knew her to be.

That specialness was deeply rooted in the Code of Southern Womanhood: You hung tough on the inside, looked great on the out, and never lost your sense of humor. "There are no ugly women—only lazy ones," she proselytized, à la Helena Rubenstein, a credo she honored even as she fought pancreatic cancer in 1985. (Having put my career on hold to care for her, I was, eight months later, racked with anguish over her inevitable death and exhausted from the sheer physical demands of nursing a terminal patient. One day, as I bathed her, Mama looked at my stressed face, untrimmed hair, and worried-thin body and said, "Honey, this is bad enough without you losing your looks over it. Go put on some lipstick.")

One month after I graduated from high school, on a warm summer evening, my father suddenly died. The week before, he'd been briefly hospitalized with his seventh heart attack in ten years. Though supposedly mild, this one finally scared Daddy into clarity. He decided to retire from the lab and join Pat, working in his first Montana congressional race, on the campaign trail. For a child of the Depression, a weekly paycheck had been necessary solace. "I've always looked forward to getting thirty years' service in the government," he said to my brother. "I've got twenty-nine plus now, but I'd rather be doing what you're doing." He told Pat of his decision the morning of July 13. At eight o'clock that night he clutched his left side and collapsed. At fifty-five, on the day my father finally figured out how he wanted to live his life, he died.

The irony of my father's death, on the eve of his new life, was staggering. But Mama remained stalwart, insisting her children follow suit. Though overnight her nest was completely empty, dreams and plans were not to be shunted aside.

By the time I graduated from Boston University in 1971, I had straddled, not always artfully, the mandates of my generation. As restless as my peers, I attended (on scholarship) three colleges in four years, including stints in England and France. Though wild for the Rolling Stones, I could sing the words to every McGuire Sisters tune and, if pressed, had to admit my favorite song was Peggy Lee's "Fever." While I marched on Washington, I also took along my electric rollers. (I wanted to end the war but look good while I did it.) I smoked dope but I didn't drop acid. Since all I had was my mind, I couldn't afford to blow it. And I didn't drop out. Drop out? Hell, I couldn't wait to drop in. I loved working—and did—every semester: seamstress, salesgirl, soda jerk. The day I got old enough, I signed on at Paul's Mall and the Jazz Workshop, a Boston jazz club, where, serving pink squirrels until 2 A.M., I picked up $50 a night in tips, sliding blurry-eyed, but rich, into my 8 A.M. classes.

Yet, by my senior year, I was still in a quandary. Despite a handful of newspaper clips and a headful of determination, I had no game plan and, certainly, no role model.

And then I read an article about Gloria Steinem.

In 1970 the women's movement was washing over America, and Gloria, its most glamorous proponent, was beginning to ride its media wave. Smart, sexy, and single, Steinem at thirty-six was indeed the "New Woman"—as *Newsweek* would knight her on its cover that summer. Moreover, she was a free-lance journalist working successfully in New York, writing what she wanted for whom she wanted and making an impact. She was doing exactly what I wanted to do someday. I had to see her.

Naturally, I picked up the phone. To my amazement, her number was in the Manhattan directory, and when I dialed it, she answered.

I asked if I might have an interview, half expecting a brush-off. "Okay," she said. "Would next Thursday in New York be all right?" I was astounded. Not only was I going to interview Gloria Steinem, I was going to New York. For the first time. Either was grounds for hysteria.

By the time I caught the train to Manhattan, I was awash in Steinemology. I'd found her aunt Sara in Ohio (phoning all of the Steinems in the Toledo phone book). I got ahold of Steinem's 1956 Smith College yearbook and traced several of the Twelve Foolish Virgins, a group who had met nightly in Gloria's dorm room. Identifying myself on the phone as a reporter, I was flabbergasted at how much people were willing to tell someone they couldn't see, much less meet.

And what thunderbolts did my sleuthing unearth? Gloria "had a great need for recognition" (yeah), "knew how to create opportunities for herself" (obviously), "had the longest fingernails in school," and hadn't always been attractive—"Gloria was almost dumpy, wore glasses, pulled her hair straight, and spent more time reading *Vogue* than Plato."

There was hope for me yet.

At 11 A.M. on the appointed day I sat at the soda fountain in the drugstore below Steinem's office, drinking coffee. On the stool next to me Ali MacGraw scarfed down a cheese Danish. (God, was New York always this exciting?) Four hours later, Ali had left and Gloria hadn't shown. When I finally reached her at home, she was mortified. She'd forgotten. Could I meet her the next morning at nine?

At nine-fifteen the next day, Steinem appeared, instantly recognizable by her mass of blond-streaked hair and blue aviator glasses. She was the most casually sophisticated thing I'd ever seen—her self-confidence fitting as snugly as her jeans. Her tiny office had only an IBM Selectric and an ashtray, the spareness an attempt at the discipline she claimed she sorely lacked. For the next four hours, we drank coffee, smoked cigarettes, and talked.

The most remarkable thing about Gloria was her candor: her willingness to trot out her insecurities and, in the process, turn them into assets. She told me about her abortion, her mother's mental illness—

neither of which she had yet revealed publicly. Most important, she treated me like a peer, a source of both exhilaration and encouragement. Maybe I had the goods after all. By the time I left her, I felt that all I had to do was get to New York and the rest would fall into place.

Mademoiselle provided my launching pad. I won a guest editorship which brought me to New York to spend the month of June at the magazine. My entry? An essay on William F. Buckley. Through a friend, I'd been invited to his house for dinner, where I discovered that Buckley called his wife "Ducky," played the piano ("Nobody Loves You When You're Down and Out"), loved wine, and was intrigued by rock music.

"How important are the Beatles?" he asked.

"They're in a class by themselves," I reported.

"Well, who do you consider important in rock at present?"

"People like Creedence Clearwater Revival."

"Who? Ah . . . I mean . . . ah, ah, what is the difference between say, the Beatles and a Clearwater Revivalist?" I turned it into my first celebrity profile.

Mademoiselle was an eye-opener. Our intimate group of twenty college girls had make-overs, traveled to Banff, Canada, and got to meet our role models of choice. So when Barbara Walters asked me what I wanted to do with my life, I told her:

"Actually, I'd like your job."

"Oh, you're too pretty to be on television."

Four weeks later I woke up to the reality of unemployment in the Big Apple. But this time fate appeared with the impossible name of Bartle Bull, the man who'd just bought *The Village Voice*. After we met at a *Mademoiselle* publishing forum, he offered me a $95-a-week job whose aim was to get the *Voice* on campuses. Not the writing slot I'd hoped for, but at least a ticket to ride.

A month later, I was ensconced in a $90-a-month Greenwich Village walk-up with the bathtub in the kitchen. I thought I'd died and gone to heaven. I had graduated college, was working for a newspaper, living in the Village, and having my burgers and fries served up at the Lion's Head, a downtown literary saloon, by a cigarette-brandishing, self-possessed waitress everyone called "Jessie," short for Jessica. Lange.

All too soon Heisenberg struck again. I still wasn't writing. Too scared to actually submit a piece to the *Voice,* I did the logical thing: I quit to free-lance. Three lean months later at a party, an unsuspecting man, whose name if not importance, I've forgotten, politely asked me what I wanted to do with my life. After an hour, staggering under the load of options I mapped out, he made a suggestion for which I'll be forever grateful: "Have you ever thought about *Women's Wear Daily?*" No. In fact, I'd never even read it.

The next morning I raced out and bought a copy. According to the masthead, the editor was someone named Michael Coady. I picked up the phone and called his office. And called and called and called and called and called, until finally he agreed to see me. Two weeks later, I had a job.

—

Women's Wear Daily was a terrific West Point. For the four years I was there, I had only one rule: Never say no to an assignment. I didn't, and it paid off. Their modus operandi was to throw reporters, raw and untested, into the ring and let them figure out the punches once they got there. *WWD* offered a crash course in power in America—from fashion and media to politics and movies. I covered it all, amassing along the way an invaluable Rolodex. My official beat was the business side of fashion, where I produced such intrepid reportage as: "Are Fur-Trimmed Sweaters Selling?" Once I got that weekly piece out of the way, I could do what I wanted, providing I could sell it to the editors: Coady; the legendary John Fairchild; and Mort Schienman, *WWD*'s unsung hero of a managing editor, whose unsentimental editing often left me, notorious for lead sentences running three paragraphs, in tears. ("The most perfect sentence in the English language has four words," he railed. " 'Jack hit the ball.' ")

One of the most important things I did at *WWD* was cover parties. I know what you're thinking—parties? *Important?* They are. A person with a wineglass in his hand will tell you things he'd never tell you holding a coffee cup. You just have to ask—a lesson I learned posthaste from John Fairchild.

Immediately after coming to the paper, I was sent to cover a cocktail party at which *WWD* favorite Jacqueline Onassis showed up. Far too intimidated to actually speak to the former first lady, I nevertheless dogged her every move, recording who she talked to, what she wore, what she drank, what she didn't eat, and what time she left. The next morning at the office I ran into Fairchild. How, he wanted to know, was the party?

"Terrific," I said, beaming triumphantly. "Jackie was there."

"Really? What'd she say?"

Say? She'd said, "Thank you," to the waiter when he handed her a drink, but I didn't think that's what he meant. "Uh, well, I didn't really talk to her," I sputtered, trying to recoup, "but I followed her around all night. I know everything she did."

Fairchild scowled in exasperated disappointment. "Oh, no, no, no, that's not enough. You must always talk to people. Get quotes. That's the point of a party. *Don't ever come back without having talked to Jackie.*"

I didn't. Whenever I covered something and Jackie was there, the woman was a goner. I'd screw up my nerve, tap her shoulder, apologize for asking, then go ahead and ask. Anything. (To her credit, Mrs. Onassis was always very gracious.) Truthfully, I never elicited anything more monumental than "I adore Billy Baldwin," but that wasn't the point. Covering social events taught me to work a room, ask provocative questions in odd places, and not be overwhelmed by anyone. If I could talk to Jackie, I could do anything.

And often did.

Like crashing Henry Kissinger's fiftieth birthday party.

In honor of the occasion, Guido Goldman, a Harvard crony, was giving a dinner at New York's Colony Club for seventy of Henry's friends: Happy and Nelson Rockefeller, Katharine Graham, Jacob and Marion Javits, Winston and Betty Bao Lord, Rosalind Russell, Walter

and Betsy Cronkite, Mike Wallace, Barbara Walters, movie producer
Bob Evans, and Nancy Maginnes, who, five years later, married the
Secretary of State.

As usual, the press wasn't invited—at least inside. But outside the
Colony, the zone was duty-free as photographers and reporters snapped
pictures and grabbed one-liners from arriving guests. I'd dressed in a
strapless black evening gown, just in case. That is, just in case I could
talk some single man into taking me in as his date (tricks of a society
reporter's trade—useless, alas, when I discovered the dinner was a
sit-down . . . with place cards).

Around eight, the door finally slammed on the media. Everyone left,
except me and another woman, an attractive photographer with two
Nikons dangling from her neck. Her name was Sahm Doherty and she
worked for *Time*. We both knew the story was inside the club and,
within thirty minutes, we'd joined forces to try to sweet-talk the guard.
But our combined charms evaded him. Feigning defeat, we drifted
away. A few minutes later he stepped inside the building. Seizing the
moment, we slipped in the door. No one was in sight .

Suddenly, echoing in the empty foyer, we heard a distinctively
Teutonic accent rapidly approaching. As we dove into the nearest
alcove, Kissinger, escorted by a butler, rounded the corner and
headed directly toward us. Just short of our hiding place, he stopped.
"Where the hell are you?" he boomed. Sahm and I exchanged terrified glances. Jesus. Caught. By no less than the secretary of state.
This could be trouble. Federal offense–type trouble. We were on the
verge of surrender when we realized Kissinger was still talking—but
not to us, to someone on a *phone*. Nixon? Ehrlichman? Brezhnev?
No. Danny Kaye.

When Dr. K. finally hung up and returned to the party, Sahm and
I raced up the stairs. Obviously, we couldn't walk into the middle of
a seated dinner, but there had to be another way to get a look—an attic,
balcony, window. We cased the place. If there was a party going on,
we couldn't find it. Suddenly the butler reappeared on the stairs.
Startled, I saw a door and pushed it. With an ear-splitting screech, it
opened, and I tripped over my dress onto a mezzanine overlooking the

dining room, trailed by Sahm, whose Nikons, as we hit the floor, echoed like Ming Dynasty gongs. Horrified, we crouched on the floor and waited for the storm troopers to come haul us off.

But instead we heard Nelson Rockefeller:

"There's always the question of whether the man makes history or history makes the man," he was saying as I grappled for my notebook. "Henry settled that question. The man has made history."

We peeked over the edge of the banister. Below us several tables of ten were being served coffee and dessert. The toasts had started.

"Winston Lord, Kissinger's assistant at State," Sahm hissed, as the boyish Lord likened working for his boss to childbirth. "It's uncomfortable, painful, sometimes bloody, but it always reflects you're being stretched." (Ah, poetry.)

Now Barbara Walters, a frequent Kissinger date: "I hadn't planned to speak, but Gloria Steinem and Barbara Howar [other Kissinger escorts] couldn't be here tonight," she began, amid laughter, before praising Kissinger for "having made careers for the countless women who've sat next to him at dinner. He had the capacity to make us all feel special and feminine, no matter what age. Of course, that was before people knew about Nancy. Henry has friends and he has women. We know we're friends, which is lovely and outlasts other relationships."

(Did Nancy Maginnes know this?)

Finally, Kissinger took the floor. "The warmth of my friends' speeches reminds me of the warmth and closeness of the White House staff," he wryly noted, to laughter—a reference to the back-stabbing daily fare at 1600 Pennsylvania Avenue.

By now totally brazen, we were draped over the balcony. "Interesting how nobody ever looks up at these things," I whispered to Sahm just as I locked eyeballs with Walter Cronkite. As America's most trusted face peered into mine, America's most frightened, I put my finger to my lips, begging for his silence. For thirty interminable seconds his face remained inscrutable. Finally, he winked and nodded his collusion as we ducked out of sight.

After the last speaker, jubilant at having gotten the only eyewitness account of this monumental event, we joined the regrouped paparazzi outside. Sahm started shooting. As Kissinger's limo pulled away, she headed for *Time* to drop off the film, while I followed Henry and Nancy to her East Sixty-eighth Street apartment. After the couple dashed into the building I ferreted out the doorman.

"How long does Dr. Kissinger usually stay when he brings Miss Maginnes home?" I inquired.

"He's never stayed more than twenty minutes."

Interpretation of this information I leave to you. Suffice to say that exactly twenty minutes later Kissinger emerged.

"Glad I didn't stay longer," laughed the Secretary of State when he saw me. Then he sped off.

I could go home. The party was finally over.

—

Women's Wear and its cast of fabulous characters became home. The thought of leaving was scary. Where else would I sit around the newsroom with colleagues serendipitously devising an annual In and Out list that made grown men weep?

"Spinach?"

"In."

"Broccoli?"

"Out. Of the ballpark."

"Oregon? What do we think about Oregon?"

"In," somebody from the fashion section would volunteer.

"Okay, in."

Marella Agnelli?

"She's *always* in," Fairchild would impatiently insist before wafting off to point the fickle finger of social fate at some unsuspecting designer or Lady Who Lunched who, dropped onto the Out list, faced a future of true grimness: the back table in the back room at La Grenouille.

And then, of course, there was the controversial Coady. The man who captained the chicest newspaper in the world looked and talked like a Boston pol (in fact, started his journalism career writing for the *Boston Herald*). Thin and wiry, with glasses that traveled relentlessly up and down his nose, Michael was the protypical black Irishman: equal parts brilliant and crazy. His moxie created *W* and took it into immediate profit. His outrageousness saw him whipping out his dental bridge and shocking aristocratic doyennes with a gap-toothed smile. He could be cuttingly ruthless—or stunningly romantic, as I discovered first-hand.

A year into my tenure at *WWD* I fell desperately in love with a man whom I found enormously difficult to leave in the mornings. Three weeks into the romance, I'd been late to work nearly every day (highly unusual behavior, might I add). One day around noon, I crept into the Fairchild building on Twelfth Street and sneaked up the back stairs, ready to claim I'd spent the morning "in the market" (on Seventh Avenue). Bursting in the exit door, I collided with Coady, who, as it turned out, had been frantically asking for me in order to assign a party.

"Well, Miss Collins, and how are you this *afternoon?*" he saluted with undisguised sarcasm.

"In love," I blurted out with the unbridled candor of the irrationally smitten.

When Coady didn't respond, I instantly regretted my truthfulness. "Baby, you just walked into your walking papers," I thought as the silence hung heavy.

Finally, he spoke. "Is it serious?"

"Yes . . . I think so."

"Well, then enjoy it. If you're lucky it'll happen maybe three times in your life." Whereupon he walked off.

Yet, by 1976 I was desperate to leave, even though it meant giving up my seat on Killer Row, the chorus line of smart, talented, competitive female reporters hired by Coady whose desks threaded across the newsroom in a column as eccentric as its occupants. Bobbie, Keitha, Katherine, Barbara, Marian, Francesca, Joan . . . all in our twenties, Coady corralled us to pump energy into *WWD* and breathe life into *W*—for it was with us he started the full-color biweekly supplement. Delighted to have another place for our bylines, we barely noticed we were doing two jobs for one salary. How could I care about something as mundane as money when I was allowed to fill practically an entire issue of *W* with my coverage of the Tall Ships arriving in Bermuda?

Or spend hours sitting on the floor of Lena Horne's dressing room, absorbed in the stories of her early days at the Cotton Club?

Still, the girls in Killer Row were destined to move on to bigger jobs and more money, and Coady knew it. *Women's Wear* was the beginning, not the end, and when I told him my chance had come he was genuinely pleased that one of his own was moving up to the Show.

In the years post–*Women's Wear,* the majors came in many different forms, from *The Washington Post* (more on this later) to free-lance writing to television. When opportunity didn't present itself, I created it. When it did, I capitalized on it like mad.

In 1980 I decided to break into television. For years TV people had been telling me I ought to be on-air. But nobody was putting me there. Endless interviews produced endless rejection. Fortunately, I didn't take it personally. After all, I knew I had the two most important prerequisites for a career in broadcasting: I was a blonde and a journalist. What I lacked was time spent in Des Moines anchoring the evening news. But then I didn't want to be an anchor; I simply wanted to do interviews (I *still* wanted Barbara Walters's job). This made it difficult, since nobody much was hiring "just interviewers," especially one with practically no on-air experience.

On top of that I was getting into the game a little late. I wasn't forty, but I wasn't twenty, and I couldn't forget what Dan Rather once told me:

"Broadcast journalism remains a man's domain," he'd declared when I interviewed him in 1979 for *Playboy*'s "Twenty Questions." "There's no joy in my saying that, but that's the reality. It takes such a long time for women to work up. Let's say a woman gets into journalism and says to herself, 'I've got to prove myself as a reporter.' So she does those things that it takes to prove oneself as a reporter—such as standing in the rain outside the police station for ten or fifteen years. After ten or fifteen years of that, it's pretty hard to hold your complexion together, honey, and pretty hard to keep your figure. And by the time she's forty, they begin to say in the business, 'Well, old Jill is one hell of a reporter, but she looks hard around the edges.' When they say that about a man, it's a compliment."

Ruthless stuff. But, so what? If Arnold Schwarzenegger could do talkies, I could do television. All I needed was a shot. I got it in 1980, when a small TV production company with the oxymoronic name the Personality News Network asked if I was interested in being the host of a daily, two-minute celebrity-oriented news strip to be syndicated to eighty markets. It meant moving to Los Angeles, but it also meant television.

Two months later I was living in West Hollywood. PNN turned out to be guerrilla TV: fast, cheap, and plenty of it. We operated on a shoestring. A very short one. There was a cameraman, a producer, and an assistant producer who doubled as my makeup man and wardrobe consultant. The four of us did everything: booking, editing, research. In a normal day, it wasn't unusual for me to do three or four one-hour interviews.

Thanks to all those years pouring over *Photoplay,* I carried movie-star bios around in my head as a matter of course. So when Ginger Rogers unexpectedly said yes to an interview, I showed up already armed with the knowledge that she had had five husbands, was a Christian Scientist, once had a soda fountain in her living room, and broke in *new* tap shoes every time she danced with Fred.

"Miss Rogers, I'd like to talk about the Fred Astaire movies—"

"The *Fred Astaire* movies?" she testily snapped. "Wasn't there a *girl* in those movies, too?"

At parties, I learned to be as fast on my feet with a TV crew as I'd been with a notebook. A roomful of celebrities meant a week's worth of shows. It was a tough, tight ten months, but I got what I needed: experience and an audition reel.

Before beginning my assault on national television, I devoted a couple of years to forging a free-lance magazine career, specializing in interviews. To compensate for the time I hadn't spent in Cleveland reading wire copy, I knew I had to march into the networks forcefully armed. If I got enough important interviews published in enough important places, I figured even the most unimaginative TV executive might conclude I could deliver the same for him. Besides, television, as I'd discovered during my brief foray into it, was not a business you *ever* wanted to be dependent upon—especially as a woman. Always have a marketable skill that doesn't depend on your looks. In practical TV terms, a successful writing career was Crow's-feet Insurance.

When I finally focused on the networks, I decided to start at the top and work my way down. I began a calling crusade to Steve Friedman, the brilliant producer of the *Today* show. If anyone might appreciate my wild-card credentials, it would be the iconoclastic Friedman, who'd snatched Bryant Gumbel out of sports, championed Jane Pauley's career, "discovered" Willard Scott in Washington, and was piecing together the "family" of correspondents and contributors who eventually catapulted *Today* into first place in the early-morning sweepstakes. Determined to be on the Friedman team, I called and called and called and called and called. Finally, in self-defense, he agreed to see me. Once I got my foot in the *Today* door around 1983, instead of slamming it, Friedman gave me a break. If I could deliver hard-to-get interviews, he'd deliver airtime.

I owe my network television career to Shirley MacLaine. We first met when I profiled her in *The Washington Post* in conjunction with the capital premiere of *The Turning Point.* We hit it off, and when MacLaine took a small group to Cuba the next year to show the movie at a Cuban film festival, I went along. In Havana we drank rum at Hemingway's favorite haunts and had an audience with Fidel Castro.

Since neither Fidel nor Ernest was available for my NBC audition, I called Shirley's press agent. I told him the *Today* show was interested in my interviewing his client. I didn't say it was a try-out; I didn't know her *that* well. Since I was selling access, it was imperative to establish I had it. Mercifully, she came through, and a month later I began my NBC career with a two-part MacLaine interview.

A chubby kid from Chicago, who lived and died for the Cubs and spent half the year downing pastries and the other half sweating out the Stillman diet, Friedman had created his own predawn principality of which he was the undisputed and unrestricted king. Within NBC, the enormously profitable *Today* show was a castle surrounded by a moat. If he trusted you, Friedman lowered the bridge and pulled you into his creative insanity; if he didn't, NBC brass notwithstanding, you couldn't buy your way across the water. He was a showman, a newsman, and a television baby, the first *Today* chief raised on the medium. Though five days a week, from seven to nine, his screaming kept the control room on tilt, he was our dragon slayer when it came to the world outside. It was Us against Them—whether "Them" was the president of NBC or a megastar playing hard-to-get ("Fuck 'em—tell to go on *Good Morning America.* We don't need them"). Early-morning television was war, and Steve was determined to win it. Any doubters had only to check the giant blowup of the forty-year-old Friedman, decked out in an army helmet, that covered his office wall.

Friedman ran *Today* like America watched television—with distractions. In a corner of his office-cum-bunker, four television sets, stacked one on top of the other, kept track of the networks and CNN, to the accompaniment of rock and roll blaring from overhead speakers. Though he prided himself on not reading, he was incessantly flipping through newspapers, perusing headlines, as, outside his door, in a stack-up resembling O'Hare on Christmas Eve, people waited to air grievances, ask for a raise, okay a story, or simply hang out. At four every day, business ground to a halt for *Jeopardy,* Friedman's favorite game show—next to the *Nightly News.* If you knew that *Catch-22* was originally called *Catch-18,* your stock as an NBC correspondent could soar. Anyone clever enough to answer Final Jeopardy would be ringingly rewarded by *Today*'s fearless leader hoisting a baseball bat and banging it against the overhead neon light. The Friedman shop was a happy shop, largely because, beneath the hoopla, Steve was a soft touch. He had heart, and his show reflected it. Creativity overshadowed intrigue, nobody counted pennies, and management kept its distance. We were number one. Little did we know it was the last days of Pompeii. (In 1987 Friedman left *Today* to produce the ill-fated *USA Today* TV show. When he returned to NBC in 1990 as executive producer of the *Nightly News,* Jane Pauley had left *Today* and viewers had left as well, making *Good Morning America* number one.)

Over my first four years I delivered, among others, Bette Midler, Jacqueline Bisset, Ann-Margret, Cosima von Bülow, Elizabeth Taylor, David Puttnam, and Adnan Khashogghi just as the Iran-contra scandal broke. (During the taping at his multimillion-dollar Olympic Tower duplex—complete with swimming pool—Taylor and her entourage unexpectedly dropped in and plopped themselves on the floor to watch.)

Right away I loved television. Compared to the isolation of writing, it was a well-paid picnic in the park. Yet even when I got a contributing correspondent's contract with *Today,* I kept on writing. In the space of two years I had eight *Rolling Stone* covers, three covers for *Interview,* and a handful of conversations that ran in *Playboy* and *New York.*

Keeping a television and print career going simultaneously racked up my frequent-flier miles between Los Angeles and New York. It also taught me to expect anything, particularly when it came to movie stars, Jamie Lee Curtis being a case in point. The daughter of Janet Leigh and Tony Curtis was hyping *Love Letters,* a film in which she spent a lot of time undressed. As well she might. Her topless outing with Eddie Murphy and Dan Aykroyd in *Trading Places* had proven she had a body of which she could be justifiably proud.

It was August, and the 1984 Summer Olympics had taken over Los Angeles. With camera crews and producers at a premium, I got assigned not an entertainment but a news producer, Philip Wasserman, new to the West Coast from covering politics in Washington and New York. Smart, funny, and verbal, Phil was thrilled with the job—his first movie star!—since he thought Curtis was a knockout.

Wasserman and the crew preceded me to the actress's West Hollywood condominium by thirty minutes. When they arrived, the overworked cameramen stayed in the car while Phil went upstairs to lay the groundwork. Upon arrival, he found Curtis's penthouse door ajar. When he knocked and announced his presence in a decidedly male voice, the door was immediately opened by Jamie Lee, dressed only in bikini underpants and a filmy see-through bra that left nothing to the imagination.

As Wasserman's jaw dropped, Curtis motioned him in, fixed a drink, and suggested he follow her into the bedroom while she dressed.

Ever the hands-on producer, Phil obeyed. As he shifted uncomfortably from foot to foot, Curtis finally noticed his embarrassment. Coyly motioning to her scantily clad bosom, she purred: "I guess you've seen these before, haven't you?"

"Well, actually, I haven't," replied Phil, who had yet to see Curtis, much less her anatomy, onscreen. Unperturbed, Jamie Lee turned around and slipped into her clothes.

By the time I arrived, Phil was catatonic. He sat in a corner, a dazed expression on his face. Since he was more accustomed to talking to sweaty pols than attractive actresses, I chalked his reticence up to a crush.

The next afternoon I ran into Wasserman at the Burbank bureau. Why, I asked, had he been so reserved the day before? He blushed, a look of incredulity crossing his face. Explaining what had happened, Phil admitted he was still reeling. "I'm used to covering guys who wear suits and ties . . . actually, I'm used to covering *women* who wear suits and ties."

In December 1984 I went home to Montana to visit my mother for the holidays. On the day after Christmas, she was diagnosed with pancreatic cancer. My brother and I took her to doctors at Minnesota's Mayo Clinic and Memorial Sloan-Kettering in New York before she decided to check into the National Institutes of Health in Bethesda, Maryland, our base of operations for the next eight months.

Upon hearing the diagnosis, almost certainly fatal, I dropped everything. I informed my employers I'd be out of commission indefinitely. It was frightening. After finally negotiating myself onto network television, I was now telling Friedman I couldn't show up. He easily could've said, "Thanks, but no thanks," but he didn't. He said to keep in touch.

The only television interview I did during that period was with Senator Joseph Biden, Democrat from Delaware. Young, attractive, and dynamic, Biden was expected to make a run for the 1988 Democratic presidential nomination, which alone made him newsworthy. And then there was his compelling personal story.

In 1972, at twenty-nine, Biden, in an uproarious political upset, had beaten Delaware stalwart J. Caleb Boggs for the U.S. Senate seat, making him the second youngest man to ever serve in the Senate. It had been a personal as well as professional victory, since Biden's bid had been strictly Mom-and-Pop. His sister, Valerie, managed the campaign, while his staff was manned by his brother, his parents, and his wife, Neilia, also twenty-nine, and mother of his three small children.

Biden's life seemed blessed—until December 18, 1972. With the senator-elect in Washington putting together his office, Neilia and the children drove to buy a Christmas tree. Returning home, their car was blindsided by a truck. Neilia and baby daughter Naomi were instantly killed, two-year-old Hunt and three-year-old Bo seriously injured.

Shattered, Biden nearly pulled out of politics, until colleagues like Mike Mansfield, Hubert Humphrey, and Ted Kennedy convinced him otherwise. Vowing to give it six months depending on the health of his children, Biden was sworn into office during an emotional ceremony next to Bo's and Hunt's hospital beds.

Promising his sons he would always be with them for breakfast, Biden didn't move to Washington. Instead, he commuted, a ninety-minute train ride each way, between Capitol Hill and Wilmington. Although he rebuilt his life in the ensuing thirteen years, remarrying and fathering another daughter, Biden had never discussed the tragedy on television. If he were to seek the presidential nomination, he knew it would come up. He wanted to get the story on the record, right, in one shot.

Since I was stationed in nearby Bethesda, I began campaigning for the interview. Biden was interested, but wary. The only time he had talked about Neilia's death, to *Washingtonian* magazine in 1972, he felt he'd been burned. Biden had to be convinced. I took his wife, Jill, to lunch, and subsequently spent two hours in the Senate Dining Room trying to persuade the senator. Finally, the Bidens decided to trust me. I'd come to their home to film Jill and the family. The senator and I would talk in his Capitol Hill office.

In the midst of this negotiation, Mama took a sudden and radical turn for the worse. The night before the interview, her doctor said he felt she'd be gone within six weeks. It was a devastating deadline. When I walked into Biden's office the next morning, I felt like a displaced person, so immeasurable was my despair. Of course, I said nothing. Work had always galvanized me. I was counting on it to do so again.

Biden, meanwhile, was understandably uncomfortable at the prospect of discussing the deaths of his wife and daughter. Our mutual sadness, though unacknowledged, was palpable, even on tape:

"Senator," I quietly began an hour into the taping, "could you describe your first wife, Neilia, for me?"

"Neilia was pixilated," he said haltingly. "She was extremely bright, extremely beautiful, and very, very beguiling. And she was very strong, very much like Jill, my present wife. She had a backbone like a ramrod." Recalling the excitement they had felt upon his election, Biden was eloquent:

"Campaigns where families are in love—and I say *in love*—are wonderful experiences."

I leaned toward the senator, who was sitting opposite me at the end of a leather couch. "I'd like to talk about a day I'm sure is one of the most tragic, if not *the* most tragic, days of your life. December 18, 1972. . . ."

As my sentence finished, Biden's hands, clasped over his knee, tightened. He hesitated and his voice trembled. "I don't mean to be disrespectful, Nancy, but there's not much to say." He paused, his eyes searching the air for words. "I think it was, unfortunately, the most graphic demonstration in the world for me as to how little control one has over [one's life] and [one's] destiny, how much a role fate plays and how vulnerable we all are.

"But at the time I didn't think of any of that—I just felt rage, absolute rage. Anger. I mean, it just didn't make any sense. And I could not understand that. And when I dwell on it, I still don't understand it."

"But, Senator, there must have been so much pain," I urged, addressing myself as much as my subject. "I mean, didn't you feel at times that you were going to literally break in half?"

"Yeah, but you know, Nancy, I'm not sure . . . You're getting me to talk about things I never talked about before . . . publicly. I believe that the legacy that Neilia left me personally, and left the boys, was the ability to draw strength from what she was and not weakness from her no longer being."

It was a beautiful eulogy. Two weeks later Mama died in my arms. She had just turned seventy-two. In the lonely months to come, as I learned to breathe without my prime source of emotional oxygen, I would return repeatedly to Senator Biden's words.

—

In the three weeks following the funeral Pat and I struck the set of our childhood. With Mama's house going on the market, we divided up furniture and sorted out closets, deciding what to give away and what to store, packing up tutus and tennis trophies, cheerleading uniforms and Bobbsey Twins books, a favorite rosary, the beautiful old cherrywood bedroom set Daddy bought for Mama when Pat was born. All too soon, the rooms in which we'd grown up were empty; 704 Desta Street was now a memory. Early one September morning we drove across the Silver Bridge outside Hamilton toward Missoula and the airport, forty miles away, knowing that a seminal part of our lives was forever finished. Pat returned to Washington, D.C., and in October 1985, I moved back to New York. I had a thousand bucks to my name. I had to hit it running. Hard.

In November, when the Biden interview aired, it opened the door to political interviewing, and I sprinted in. The room, alas, was crowded, mostly with male reporters. This was coveted terrain, staked out by political aficionados none too happy to see more competition for the same handful of interviews. But Friedman was always fair. First come, first served, he said. You got the interview, you did it.

The more complicated problem lay in having politicians understand that just because you talked to movie stars didn't mean you couldn't talk to them too. (Can Linda Ronstadt sing opera?) I had no intention of giving up one for the other. But how to let people know you're serious while remaining glamorous?

Astrologer Michael Lutin floated an engaging suggestion in *Vanity Fair:* "Try pinning a grenade to your evening gown."

So, with an Uzi under my Ungaro, I trekked to Maryland to interview Jack Kemp, to Lake Tahoe to ask Senator Paul Laxalt about his alleged ties to the Mafia, and to San Antonio, where Hispanic mayor Henry Cisneros, a Catholic, made headlines when he admitted to doubts about making abortion illegal.

When another Texan, former governor John Connally, declared Chapter 11 in August 1987, I flew to Houston the next day and prepared to interview him in the multimillion-dollar home that would go on the auction block two months later. At seventy, this proud man was about to lose a lifetime of acquisitions—legally keeping only $30,000 worth of personal belongings and his ranch, plus two hundred acres. Would having survived the Kennedy assassination be enough to provide perspective on such traumatic loss? At midnight on the night before the interview, a telling clue presented itself in my final research article. The Connallys had had four children. Only three were living. Their daughter's death, it was rumored, had been a suicide. This was certainly the first time I'd heard about that tragedy.

"You have three children living, one child who died," I said, easing carefully into the topic with the governor the following afternoon, two hours into our conversation.

"Yes, we lost a daughter."

"What happened?"

"She was killed in Florida. This was in 1959."

"Do you mind if I ask how she was killed?"

"By a gunshot."

"How did that happen?"

"I don't know. I never have fully known. I think the coroner's verdict was that it was self-inflicted. But I never believed it."

"How old was she?"

He paused. "I guess she was seventeen."

Big John Connally had tears in his eyes.

"You've had such strong brushes with death . . . moments most people haven't. Your daughter's tragedy must help you put this current situation in perspective. . . ."

He nodded. "It was by far the worst thing we've ever suffered . . . which is why Nellie and I can, with considerable equanimity, bear this bankruptcy because, in the final analysis, we've given up things

. . . but you always reacquire things. You can't reacquire family, friends. You can't necessarily reacquire health. We have those. . . ." (When the interview ran, Nellie Connally called to thank me and report that her husband, upon seeing himself on air, announced he needed a face-lift.)

Equally surprising, in quite another way, was Robert Kerrey, Nebraska's attractive forty-one-year-old governor—divorced, and the boyfriend of actress Debra Winger—who had decided in 1985 not to seek reelection. (Today Kerrey is a senator, elected in 1988.) A genuine war hero, he was the recipient of a Purple Heart, having lost part of a leg in Vietnam. When asked why he had chosen not to run again, a decision that stunned the public, he defended his action as one from the heart.

"I'm looking for a little danger," Kerrey said, explaining the unexpected political pullout. "I don't have physical danger in mind but I do have emotional and intellectual danger in mind."

A politician yearning for emotional danger? What might that constitute?

Kerrey shot me a bemused, skeptical look. "You know what that is, Nancy. You're alive. That means trusting . . . that means surrender . . . that means love."

Whoa! Bob Kerrey for president!

"Well, if you *were* looking for a mate," I probed, "what qualities would you look for?"

The governor hesitated, a provocative smile slowly crossing his face. "Passion. That's it."

When the interview ran I was inundated with phone calls from women saying they wanted to (a) vote for Kerrey and (b) have an affair with him—though not necessarily in that order.

In the mid-eighties, when I found myself turning to the business pages of The New York Times first, I knew something was afoot. If a woman who had trouble quoting her bank balance was suddenly intrigued by leveraged buyouts, then clearly the new media stars were on Wall Street. "The curiosity other women have about Baryshnikov," I mused in Vogue in 1987, "I feel about Ivan Boesky."

But before I could say "junk bond," Boesky was in the slammer. So I talked to takeover specialist Carl Icahn, British media magnate Robert Maxwell, LBO king Henry Kravis, and Texas billionaire and political conservative H. Ross Perot. I loved Perot; so did most everybody who saw the interview. Even liberals called to proclaim they wanted to vote for him. It took ten months to get him to sit down with me in Dallas, but when he finally did, we spent over three hours talking: Perot, the *Today* crew, me—no press secretaries, no spin doctors. At the end of our conversation, I asked this man, whose airlifts to American POWs during the Vietnam War had turned him into a folk hero, whom he admired:

"Churchill was a very, very interesting man. He was asked to speak at the school he attended as a boy. He was an old man and they were afraid he might not be able to deliver his speech. They had to help him stand, and when he stood, they had to help him stand there for a minute. And then his eyes glistened and he leaned forward and said, 'Never give up, never give up, never, never, never give up. And I think that's the key. *If you haven't got the stomach for it, don't get into it.*' "

H. Ross Perot, billionaire, was, as it were, right on the money again.

Once, in the autumn of 1985, at a party swarming with New York's haute literati in Norman Mailer's Brooklyn Heights home, *60 Minutes* reporter Morley Safer, one of my favorite men on earth, beckoned me to where he was standing with author and humorist Calvin Trillin and his wife, Alice, neither of whom I knew.

"Nancy," said the mischievous, witty Safer by way of introduction, "has the amazing ability to make the most boring people in the world sound interesting."

"Really?" said Trillin in utter seriousness. "How did you learn to do that?"

"Oh . . . just all these years of dating."

"Only now," guffawed Safer, choking on cigarette smoke, "only now you get paid for it, right?"

Right. But interviewing isn't a job, it's a passion. And, even if I didn't marry them, all those interesting people and all those dinner conversations were exquisite training. Men don't lead lives of quiet desperation; they lead lives wanting, desperately, to be heard. So I learned how to listen.

After all, like a good man, a good interview is hard to get.

ROLLING STONE

March 1984

"I'm buzzed by the female mystique.
I always tell young men there are three rules:
They hate us, we hate them; they're stronger,
they're smarter; and, most important,
they don't play fair."

In January 1984 I spent eight hours, over two days, with Jack Nicholson at the Hotel Carlyle, New York's elegant but discreet hostel to the celebrated. Like the consummate pro that he is, Nicholson was still working on his latest movie, *Terms of Endearment.* The filming was long over, but from Nicholson's point of view, he was still on the payroll—and always is—until he promoted his product. And in this case the product was particularly important. *Terms of Endearment* was a pivotal, transitional role for Nicholson. It moved the forty-seven-year-old superstar gracefully and wittily into middle age; it took a guy with a hairline receding north and a stomach heading south and reestablished him as a sex symbol. Garrett Breedlove, the lascivious former astronaut of the untended physique, proved to be the perfect antidote to the overjogged, over–bench-pressed, overanalyzed eighties American male. Breedlove was a seminal role for Nicholson, and he knew it.

Which is why editor Jann Wenner had sent me to talk to him for
Rolling Stone. (Nicholson, wisely, never does television. He doesn't
need to.) The interview took place in the actor's lavish suite, where
Nicholson, wearing blue jeans and a patterned ski sweater, sprawled
on a large cushy sofa. Sometimes he got up and paced around the
room, took a phone call, or scrounged around for a Marlboro, but
mostly he sat.

The first day I arrived just as Nicholson returned from a photo
session with Richard Avedon. I thought I looked pretty spiffy myself,
since I'd plunked down fifty bucks to a professional makeup artist to
have my paint done. I was that nervous.

For our second session I shelled out another fifty and piled on the
maquillage again. This time I arrived at two and left around five.
Occasionally, Annie Marshall (Herbert's daughter and Nicholson's
longtime assistant) wandered in and out, but other than that we were
left alone. The phone rang a lot. He took a call from *Terms* director
Jim Brooks, but told Annie to tell Warren he'd call him back.

In the two days I spent with Nicholson I learned five important
things:

1. He loves being a movie star.
2. He's convinced he has the best job in the world.
3. He's likely one of the most intelligent actors I've interviewed.
4. He's also one of the most complicated.
5. Most important, Nicholson is fun. Hang out for eight hours with
   him and you say, "This is work?"

It's interesting to note that the title of this piece was "The Great
Seducer." It is, I think, one of Jack's strongest interviews to date,
precisely because we both understood this dynamic. Jack, you see, was
supposed to seduce me—that's his job as a movie star. My job as an
interviewer was to figure out how to seduce the seducer.

In this case we both played our parts well, as Nicholson noted when
he called me at home in Los Angeles to tell me he liked the piece.

"Well, Nance," he hummed into the receiver, "looks like we did some good work, huh?"

"Looks like we did."

"Well, I enjoyed it."

"So did I."

"Thanks, kid."

"Pleasure was all mine."

"But, Nance . . . one thing?"

"Yeah, Jack?"

"Don't wear so much makeup. It's bad for your skin."

I hung up the phone, walked into the bathroom, wiped off my mascara, and never looked back.

—

What are the similarities between you and Garrett Breedlove, the astronaut you played in Terms of Endearment?

He's very nonjudgmental, he has a fatalistic sense of humor about other people, and doesn't try to change them very much. I don't think he was always that way. He's changed, grown.

With the exception of Warren Beatty, you've never—since 1971— worked with a first-time director, yet you apparently didn't hesitate to work with James Brooks.

I didn't know Jim at all. I made the deal with him based on the fact that he wrote a brilliant script and the way he talked to me on the telephone. I didn't even ask him if he had directed other movies. . . . By now I can tell if someone is talented, and he's an easy call. I'm not obviously talented. The work looks talented, but if you just met me—well, I have to do something to get you interested. I felt like they liked me on this movie, and even though I work with friends a lot, this is a feeling I don't always have. I'm successful because I only work with great people.

Garrett Breedlove is hardly a matinee idol. Any qualms about playing a clearly middle-aged, out-of-shape guy?

No, because I've always wanted to play older. Some of my early heroes [were] Walter Huston, Edward Arnold, Charles Bickford. And they didn't have any problems with it. This middle-life thing has become a phobia; people think it's *got* to be a big problem, when it's simply not. I know from real life that middle-aged people are very attractive. I feel I'm beating out all those guys who stay on rigid diets. They run; they go crazy; their skin is always in fabulous shape. I feel like I'm going to scoop the pot going the other way. Besides, I've been physically dissected more than any frog in a biology class—it's my eyebrows, my eyes, my teeth. And now it's my stomach. For twenty-five years, they've been writing that I'm totally bald, and now *they're* all bald and—have a look [*points to his head*].

I've been overweight since I was four years old. Of course, I have all the normal defenses against it. But it's always bugged me. I don't want to overinflate my role and my job, but isn't there more to me than what I weigh?

One of the themes of Terms *is middle-aged sexuality and crisis. You're forty-six. Have you suffered any form of midlife crisis?*

Oh, sure. You're aware of the rings in your tree. It's like when Mick Jagger [said] it would be terrible to be singing rock and roll at forty. Well, it's not so terrible, as he now appreciates. I'm aware that in the job I do, age is a big factor, so it's the first time in a professional way that I've accepted any limitations. I don't want to be a man who, just past a certain point of physicality, believes it when young women . . . say they actually prefer you this way. It's an image I've always feared. I hope I'm not that vulnerable, but I could be. It's a goofy, clownish part; I don't mind acting it, but I don't want to be it.

In Terms *you have an affair with Shirley MacLaine, who plays a fifty-two-year-old woman. You've basically been involved with younger women in your own life; could you see yourself ever having a relationship with a lady that age?*

Could I see myself? [*Laughs.*] It shouldn't even be a question in my case. I've been with Anjelica Huston for eleven years—and she does happen to be younger than me. I'm not always sure if I'm physically attracted to a woman who is seventy years old, but when I saw [author] Han Suyin on a television interview—and this makes Anjelica mad—

she got me excited. However, if I tried to seduce her, I don't know how much *she'd* like it.

I gather you know you have a reputation as a womanizer. Is that guilt by association, because of your friendship with Warren Beatty?

That's right, guilty by association. I mean, what night is this? Do you hear women calling me on the phone? They know I'm here, don't they? Look, that's just bullshit. I can't go around saying I'm not a womanizer, because that's silly. First of all, it's good for business if people think I'm a womanizer. Beyond that, I've no motivation to deny it, unless it begins to dominate . . . my situation.

As a child, I had one of those scaldingly embarrassing experiences when I realized that all these other boys were lying about their sexual prowess. I always assumed they were telling the truth. I believed them when I was six through ten, and at eleven, I said, "Those guys are lying." The result of that lag is that it's very hard for me to lie about my prowess or my experience. It's apropos of my reputation that I'm a little embarrassed that people look at me that way, because they're giving me too much credit.

But your audience wants to give you that credit. Men, in particular, like living vicariously. They want to think that being a big-time movie star means having lots of women.

That I like. That part I don't mind. That's getting even [*flashes the smile*].

Are you monogamous? Could you stay faithful in order to maintain an important relationship like, for instance, yours with Anjelica?

By nature, I am not monogamous. But I have been monogamous, which is the only reason I'm comfortable saying this out loud. It doesn't make any difference, except in a positive way, [and that's] primarily for appearances. I only believe this because of experience. Once I've had enough experience [with] something, I don't give a fuck about anybody else's theory. I say monogamy doesn't make any difference; women suspect you whether it's true or not.

You were raised by women: Ethel May, whom you believed to be your mother, and her two daughters, Lorraine and June, who was seventeen years your senior. Ethel May's husband, a drinker, wasn't around much, and she supported everybody by opening a beauty shop in your house in Neptune City, New Jersey. When June died in 1975, the real truth emerged: You were illegitimate. Ethel May was actually your grand-mother, posing as your mother, while June, whom you thought to be your sister, was your natural mother. How did you feel about this?

I was making *The Fortune,* and someone called me on the phone—I think it was turned over by the investigative reporting for the *Time* cover story they did on me. Ultimately, I got official verification from Lorraine. I was stunned. Since I was at work, I went to Mike Nichols, the director, and said, "Now, Mike, you know I'm a big-time method actor. I just found out something—something just came through—so keep an extra eye on me. Don't let me get away with anything."

Do you know who your father was?

Only June and Ethel knew, and they never told anybody.

Who was this woman June?

Fast-cutting? A talented seventeen-year-old child who goes to New York and Miami as an Earl Carroll dancer and progresses through the gypsy line. . . . [Entertainer] Pinky Lee's straight lady for a while. . . . And when the war comes, she's the Irish-American patriot, the girl in the control tower at Willow Run, the central domestic-sending center for the military in World War Two. She marries the son of a wealthy eastern brain surgeon, one of America's most glamorous test pilots. . . . And they live a very country-club life in Stony Brook, Long Island, where I [spend] my summers in this very upper-class atmo-sphere.

All the time thinking June was your sister?

Right. The marriage [breaks] up over a drinking problem and, like all great chicks, she comes home. She commutes to New York, teaches dancing at Arthur Murray's, and, taking a shot on her own, drives to California with her kids . . . where she works in an aircraft factory, teaching herself to be a secretary. I come out to California and veer out on my own. She becomes an assistant buyer at J. C. Penney's, gets cancer, and passes on.

June and I had so much in common. We both fight hard. It didn't do her any good not to tell me, but she didn't because you never know how I would've reacted when I was younger. I got a job in Mexico when June was dying. First time with a studio, a lot of weeks. Sandra [Nichol-son's first wife] was pregnant with Jennifer, and June was in a terminal state. She looked me right in the eye and said, "Shall I wait?" In other words, "Shall I try and fight this through?" And I said no.

I'm very contra my constituency in terms of abortion because I'm positively against it. I don't have the right to any other view. My only emotion is gratitude, literally, for my life. [If June and Ethel had been] of less character, I would never have gotten to live. These women gave me the gift of life. It's a feminist narrative in the very pure form. They trained me great, those ladies. I still, to this day, have never borrowed a nickel from anybody and never felt like I couldn't take care of myself. They made the imperative of my self-sufficiency obvious.

You genuinely like women, don't you?

Yeah, I genuinely do. I prefer the company of women, and I have deep respect for them. I'm buzzed by the female mystique. I always tell young men there are three rules: They hate us, we hate them; they're stronger, they're smarter; and, most important, they don't play fair.

What attracts you to a woman? You once said you like women who are alluring but unobtainable.

It's not categorizable. The heaviest prejudice to deal with is the beautiful woman. I'd like to say, "No, it doesn't matter whether some-body's beautiful or not," but whatever I find beautiful is what I'm attracted to. As for the other, I'd like to have all the women I'm attracted to *still* with me. I don't want them unattainable. I don't even want them unavailable!

Do you think you're sexy?

I know I'm sexy to some people. In the moment-to-moment thing. I always assume that my superstructural identity is working against me with women. It helps you because they know about you, and women like to be involved with known people. But in the case of my specific fantasy, it works against me. I find myself apologizing for being a film star if I'm interested in a person socially.

You've said that in all your major relationships, you were the one who got left.

In all cases but one in my life, that's true. But, again, it's like every male: You're not sure that you're not driving them away because you don't know how to leave them.

Speaking of former lady friends, actress Susan Anspach has a thirteen-year-old son she claims you fathered during the filming of Five Easy Pieces. *Is he your child?*

She says that all the time. But because of the way she's been toward me, I've never been allowed a real avenue to find out about it. That's her privacy. She's an avant-garde feminist who, when I met her, was proud of the fact that she already had a child whose father no one knew. She didn't mention her second child to me until six or seven years later.

You've never spoken with her about it? Have you ever met the boy?

No.

Do you ever call and say, "Susan, can I see this kid? Can I talk to you about this?"

I actually made a call a couple of times, but I've never reached her.

So you're not convinced that this is your son?

No, I'm not. But I haven't had the opportunity to look into it. I know Susan slightly and feel she's an extremely respectable person who is powerful, smart, and, I'm sure, in very good control of what she does. And I guess I like the idea in a certain way.

The idea of her son being your child?

Yeah, if it were true. Hey, I'm ready to meet anybody. Do you know what I mean? And that's all I can say about it.

Incidentally, have you ever been in therapy?

My therapy was Reichian, which is all sexual.

Did you do the whole Reichian shot, taking off your clothes and getting analyzed in the nude?

Um-hum. It didn't take any rationalization. It worked with me like this [*snaps fingers*].

In 1976 you won an Academy Award for One Flew Over the Cuckoo's Nest. *How would you describe the period of your career from* Cuckoo's Nest *to* Terms?

I look at it as extremely productive, creatively adventurous, aesthetically rewarding, exciting, and vital. I'm very proud of that body of work, even though it's consistently been written about in a light-that-failed metaphor. I see it as quite the opposite. I was nominated for an Academy Award for *Reds.* The best reviews I've gotten since *Cuckoo's Nest* were for *The Border,* one of the very few commercially unsuccessful movies I've worked on. *The Shining* will be there when all the rest of the horror films have receded. I understand my weaknesses as a director, but I liked the movie I directed, *Goin' South.* I got some very good notices for *The Missouri Breaks* and, of course, *The Postman Always Rings Twice* was a respectable piece of work.

You once said about acting, "You have to determine, What is your sexuality in this scene? Everything else comes from that." The sexual part of acting is very important to you, isn't it?

It's the key. The total key. Actually, sex is my favorite subject. But it's scary for me to talk about because of Anjelica. It's like she says: "How would you feel if I were sitting down with some interviewer, telling him all I felt about sex and fucking. You know you'd flip out." And a certain part of me says, "You're absolutely right, I would." But that's the dichotomy. I yearn for honesty in life. As an artist, I yearn for the clear moment. I would tell anybody any living thing about me, and there's a lot of stuff that ain't great.

Given your sexual theory of acting, what did Postman *mean to you?*

I did *Postman* because I hadn't come down the middle with the fastball about sex in a movie. The whole reason for that movie is sex, and that's why I wanted to do it. See, Americans don't like sexual movies, they like sexy movies. If you actually start feeling warm in your groin in a movie, it becomes like a dream . . . a little too real.

The obligatory scene in *Postman* happens when the two kill her husband and she gets so hot she has to fuck right then. Now, that's those two people, not everyone. But the fact that no one who'd ever made that material had ever even attempted to do that scene was amazing, because that's what James Cain's entire book is about.

I kept saying, "Don't try to make me be the boy next door in this movie." This guy has solved every problem in his life with violence, which is why I was heavy in the movie—not as heavy as I am now, but I didn't go for the Henry Fonda look, like every other Depression picture, because a guy who's solved every problem in his life with violence doesn't go hungry.

But then, what is erotic acting, anyway? For instance, I like the idea there is not a speck of nudity in *Postman*—another stylistic thing we did. I also liked the idea of an obvious, fresher image. There was a shot I wanted to do when he first makes love to her, when he backs her off the chopping block—a reverse angle with my clothes on, but I wanted to have a full stinger, because they'd never seen that in movies. I just knew this odd image would be a stunner. Well, I went upstairs and worked on it for forty-five minutes, but I couldn't get anything going because I knew everyone was waiting down there to see this thing. Somebody else might have said I was a pervert, but in my terms, this would've been extremely artful. Do you get turned on doing a scene like that? I don't go through many hours of the day that I *don't* get turned on, although it doesn't mean I'm going to wind up in some sexual expression of it. I particularly make a point not to be actual with actresses with whom I work.

You've said that all of your work is in some way autobiographical. What did you learn about yourself from Postman?

I'm very clear about what I accomplished in this movie. This movie got rolling during the period of time when they were banning the Rolling Stones billboard [for the LP *Black and Blue*] because the woman had bruises on her. It wasn't nice to think that maybe women like to get pinched. But if someone contracts when you squeeze her, I don't care what they say, I know what she feels like. Now don't throw me in with Larry Flynt—that all women are looking to get raped—but in this area, *Postman* did clarify this for me. I'm not talking about everybody, but those two people in that movie liked it. I'm not looking to beat up the next woman tomorrow morning. In fact, if anything, I suppose I'm overly gentle with women. In some ways, I'm a physical coward, so I don't like to give or take pain, but as far as the *idea* of violence, yes, it can be erotic.

You realize you have a reputation as a man who indulges in a slew of drugs. Is that true?

A slew of drugs? No. And never have. Do I relate to drugs? Yes, I do. But, for instance, though I've said—forever—that I smoke marijuana, I've never told anyone that I actually do cocaine. I've never said that to anyone.

Then why do you think people believe you do cocaine?

I think it's the normal assumption to make, particularly about someone who's been candid about his privacy. I can only blame myself. I'm not so sure I should've been this candid. I thought it was a very good thing to do because, first of all, I'm for legalization, and because I know what the costs are. The costs are lying.

How would you describe your drug use?

Convivial.

What does that mean?

It means I have a good time. I don't drink, although the last couple years, I've started to drink a little alcohol—a glass of wine, maybe two brandies at night after coffee.

Do you still smoke marijuana?

Why talk about it? I'm not helping anybody. I've no desire to conceal what I do, but I've tried not concealing it, and it has the opposite effect. People love to have a reason to level you. They don't have to deal with me as directly because they have this disqualifying clause in their perception of me. It's hard for me to think I live in a world where it's not good for you to be candid about something that, in your heart, there's nothing wrong with.

Would you be willing to say you don't use cocaine?

Would I say it? I really have decided I have nothing further to say about this that's of any use to me or anyone else.

Some people seem to be more worried about your health than your morals, in terms of your alleged drug use.

Doctor, cure yourself. I feel that most of the time I know what I'm doing. I missed no acting classes during the twelve years I was in class, and I haven't missed a day's work from illness in thirty years. I'll put

my medical charts, my sanity charts, up against anybody's. I'm not
doing anything wrong. I'm not doing anything but trying to do everything right. I know what's true, who I am. I would like to say I don't
care what people think, but I do. Everyone who knows me may think
I'm . . . a tad boyishly fun-loving, but I don't think anybody thinks I
have any negative momentum, corrupting philosophies, or overly radical moral opinions. As a workman, I'm known as a model of professionalism. I have to put up with being falsely described because it's unhip
to bridle at it. Besides, it's just like womanizing. I'm not so sure it ain't
good for business.

*You were close with Roman Polanski, whose autobiography mentions
you and details his arrest for allegedly raping a thirteen-year-old girl at
your home in Los Angeles. He, of course, fled the country before his trial.
Do you think he'll ever return?*

It's hard to say. Roman's been the recipient of Western justice—
that is, "Here's a very complicated moral issue, so we heat you up until
you get out of town," which he did. Having been the object of that
and being strongly self-sufficient, I imagine Roman's point of view is,
"Hey, I left. My life didn't miss a stroke. I'm not an American. I'm
living in Paris, the culture capital of Europe. I've won the acting prize;
my book is out; I directed a movie. I haven't missed a day's work. I
don't need America." The tragedy is that I was watching Roman fall
in love with America after some difficult times here. His situation is a
very interesting case of what notoriety can do to you. I always felt
Roman was exiled because his wife had the bad taste to be murdered
in the papers.

*When the police searched your house for evidence against Roman,
they wound up arresting Anjelica after finding some cocaine in her purse.
[It was reported at the time that the cocaine charges against Anjelica
Huston would be dropped in exchange for her testimony against Roman
Polanski. The charges eventually were dropped.] What really happened?*

I was in Aspen. And when I heard about [Polanski's arrest], I was
told, "Don't talk about it. Don't find out anything, don't become
involved, since you aren't at all." And since I never knew what might
happen as a result of its being my residence, I was advised to not

communicate for the good of all concerned. So I know very little about it. Anjelica was actually moving out of my house at that moment.

You were splitting up?

Yeah. And to this day, I don't really know much about this particular thing. . . .

Surely you talked to Anjelica about it?

I spoke with her about it. She's been very wronged. The district attorney sent Anjelica a letter saying they'd been unethical, because in reality, Anjelica could not say anything because she simply didn't know that much about it. But it was implied in the papers that she had said something and was building a case. She reacted strongly to being mislabeled, and the DA's office wrote her a letter of apology.

Jack Nicholson and Warren Beatty. What attracts you to him as a friend?

The noncommunicable things about an unusual circumstance in life that we have in common. He's very smart, very free of bullshit, and emotionally undemanding. I haven't seen him in months, but Warren is the type of person that, if you don't hear from him in a year, it doesn't shake anything. He can say no simply, and I can't, while I can say yes simply, and he can't. He can presume he knows better for you than you do, and he's right; I can never presume I know better for anybody, and I'm wrong. I tease him about being a pro. Warren will never relate to this, but he could be a friar. For instance, I take a reverse narcissistic pride in not overtarting it up as an actor. He knows this is my narcissism, and I'm comfortable when he says it. I always tell people a little too much that I don't wear makeup. But I don't, because I look bad. Right now I've got makeup on because I just came from Avedon's. It's not really makeup, it's something I got from Warren, a trick he learned in English theater. If you're going to be lit for a photograph, you put dark powder here [*points to hairline*] because it keeps the light from making the hair you do have disappear. There are certain things Warren is just not ashamed about, but I am. Other than that, if I don't know what I'm thinking and I've got to talk sense, I talk to Warren. He can also, however, bore the shit out of me.

How?

If you're supposed to leave at two, he can't get out of the room until six. I've told him that's why he has problems with women: They can only give so much time to one man's life. We also rarely like the same girls, which is one of the reasons we get along.

Really? You both, at different times—you first, and he second—lived with Michelle Phillips. And rumor has it that during the filming of Reds, *you developed, shall we say, a mighty crush on Diane Keaton.*

Michelle and Warren's relationship had nothing to do with me. I was going with Anjelica Huston when they got together. It's just an attractive story for the press. Warren's high-school-principal parents would've been proud of the way it was handled. Michelle, being the lady she is, took the trouble to call and ask if I had any feelings about [her and Warren], which I did: I thought it was fabulous, because I like them both very much. Michelle's a real stand-up woman. You can't *get* her to do a dishonorable thing. And . . . can she move it!

As for Miss Keaton, I don't want to hide behind this, but during the production [of *Reds*], that's the way it began to feel. . . . Nothing happened as a result, but there is something actorish about thinking, "My God, I've got a real crush and, holy fuck, this is my best friend and his girlfriend." But that's also what the movie was about—my character was attracted to Keaton's character. And I'm focused on my job all the time. In fact, during the work, I would allow myself to get overinflamed about it with Warren right there—just to see what would happen. Absolutely nothing happened between Diane and me. They're still going around. I'm not an asshole.

Warren himself seems to be in transition. For once, he doesn't even appear to be seriously involved with anyone.

Since he doesn't do interviews on himself, I don't want to say, "Wait a minute, what do you mean he doesn't have a relationship?" But I certainly know that he loves Diane Keaton. Maybe I shouldn't say that, because he doesn't want to have his personal life discussed, but in this case [*laughs*]—fuck him.

Do you see you and Anjelica staying together indefinitely? Is this a marital situation?

I've always viewed it that way. For lack of a better cliché—Jean-Paul

Sartre and Simone de Beauvoir. I'm iconoclastic about marriage. I got married one time, not thinking one way or the other about it; I just did it. I didn't feel threatened. I loved the girl, but it wasn't a big-time act to me. Just like not being married now isn't. The fact is, a lot of people have been married two or three times in the period that I've had this allegedly impossible-to-maintain relationship, which, quite frankly, I've been very happy with, for the most part.

Does Anjelica want to get married?

Hard to say. There's a lot of things Anjelica expresses desire about, but if you begin to produce them, the desire disappears. Children are the primary reason for marriage.

Does she want to have children?

I'm sure she does. But this is her privacy I'm talking about. I've always wanted a lot of children. I'm vitally moved by family. This would be an area where I'd say I haven't done quite what I would like to have done.

What has kept you fascinated with Anjelica for eleven years? Why have you been able to maintain this relationship?

Love! I don't know. Because we want to. I don't think fascination is the right word. I respect her more than I do other women. And there's something about the way she is that I just adore. I also get furious with her because she makes me feel weak. I let her limit me in ways where I know I'm right. But I've learned as much from her as from anyone in my life.

But obviously your relationship has meant enough that you've been willing to change to accommodate it.

Oh, yeah, I've changed a lot. If you told me twenty years ago that some woman could go off and fuck one of my best friends [Huston briefly left Nicholson for Ryan O'Neal], and I'd end up reading about it in the newspapers, and that four years later I wouldn't even give a shit, I'd say, "You're talking to the wrong guy here. That's not the way I am. I might want to be that guy, but I'm not." [*Claps hands.*] Now I am.

Why were you able to understand Anjelica's actions?

I didn't blame her in the beginning. I didn't like it, but I think being my girlfriend has so many things even I couldn't deal with that I can honestly say I don't blame her, although I was hurt. But—it doesn't make you feel better.

You started out in Hollywood writing and producing as well as acting, mostly as part of the Roger Corman B-movie stable. You also directed two films, Drive, He Said *and* Goin' South—*neither of which was a big hit but both of which got some decent reviews. Yet directing doesn't seem to be a burning ambition of yours.*

It comes and goes. It's not burning because I don't like criticism. I'm not that good at it yet. If I didn't have another career, I'd be getting more encouragement to do it. I like the action. Directing is a pleasant job to me. I don't have to go through the self-doubt. So what if I showed my stomach? As a director, I'm just there to help people, and I like that. I don't have to question my own greed. I also haven't been writing much, which is one of the banes and torments of my life.

Why aren't you writing?

Can't sit down. Life is not going that way—one of the problems about having a lot of possibilities. In the early days, I was writing for my life. That was big money to get Screen Actors Guild minimum of any kind. I wrote quite a few things during that period. It was improving me as an actor. I started producing, which, again, broadened me as a filmmaker. About that time, I adopted my work credo: You're a tool in the hands of a filmmaker, and you serve the film. If I had no conventional work, I believe I could start from here and have a movie in theaters by the end of the year, doing whatever I had to do. I was the first person of my own generation to be one of these hyphenated people. It wasn't the big leagues, but the action of making a movie is the same. I try to collaborate with everyone on all aspects, but I long ago stopped worrying about who got the credit for the writing.

Are you a self-confident man? What things don't you like about yourself?

Basically, I am self-confident. I don't like it if I'm not creatively free-flowing—it worries me and I wonder, Is this the end? Is the well empty now? I worry about the lack of self-confidence of someone who, at times, has to get himself up or hype himself. I wonder why I think

I have to do it. Sometimes I'm not able to take in the positive communication that's directed at me because I'm not sure I deserve it. The difference now is, I let all these symptoms of lack of self-confidence just be. I don't let them define me. In other words, I'm more comfortable with my lack of self-confidence, so in a way, it's more self-confidence.

Were you always sure of your talent?

I was at times surer than I am now. Nobody was ever bored with my work, even when I didn't know what I was doing. But I worried about the other side of it. I thought, "Well, anybody can fool these idiots. So where's the million dollars? Why doesn't everybody love me? Where's the ego gratification?" I talk to most good actors, and none of them know they're any good. Last night [at the New York Film Critics Circle Awards] I saw Bobby Duvall, who is obviously a brilliant actor. He's one of the guys around my age who was brilliant long before I ever got rolling. Just his work on *Naked City* will bury you. Anyway, he got the award for leading actor in *Tender Mercies,* and I told him how much I [liked] him in *The Betsy.* After I came home, I thought, "I wonder if Bobby took it weird that I told him on this particular night how much I [liked] him in some movie everybody hated five years ago?"

Do you have another movie lined up right away?

No, but I've got work. I'm going to promote *Terms of Endearment* overseas. That's as much a part of it as anything else. I always have something germinating. I bought Saul Bellow's book *Henderson the Rain King,* and I'm going to try to get that made. Robert Towne and I have been working on a script based on the murder of Napoleon. After *Reds,* I took two years off because I had worked every day for three years prior to that. Even the president of the United States doesn't do that. And I mean I *really* took off. I didn't even talk about movies for a couple of years. Those two years proved to me that I don't have to act. I'm now confident that I'm not an applause junkie. I loved being out of the movie business. I like almost ninety-five percent of the people in the movie business, and I don't like what they're doing an equal portion of that time. I call it the Hollywood Virus.

What's the Hollywood Virus?

You can't get out of town, can't stop making calls, and can't really focus on what it is you want to do. You can't get out of your ritual. If Mom dies, sometimes you don't even get the day off—and you'd better be happy [if it's supposed to be a funny scene], because if you're not really happy, you're not really good.

There's no point in lying to yourself about what it is you do. If your mother does die and you have to express a volume of emotion . . . and you mean it . . . to the point where you have suppressed it about your mother, then it's not sick, it's integrated. That's who you are now.

Does it matter to you if you win the Best Supporting Actor Oscar for Terms of Endearment?

I told my betting friends before I ever met any of the people involved and read all of the script that they should bet in Las Vegas if they could get a price. That's how much I liked this part. I'll tell you another childish reason why I'd like to win. I think you gotta have nutty goals in life. I'd like to win more Oscars than Walt Disney, and I'd like to win them in every category. And I've been after this category for a while. Unstylistically, I love the Academy Awards. And I'm very fifties Zen—all tributes are false, all is vanity—but I like seeing a Mount Rushmore of 1984 movie stars in a row for the one night, no matter what nutty ideas they've got. It's fun. Nobody gets hurt. With a couple of exceptions, I've known whether I was going to win or not because I've been following these things since I was a kid. And I've always had a better time when I know I'm not going to win, because then I'm just into the evening. I'm Mr. Hollywood. I love everybody. Of course, I've also done the opposite, gone deciding I'm going to be the worst loser in history and just said outrageous things. Even when I don't go, I love the Oscars. I sit at home and talk about the slime-green dress and say, "God, if I ever had this kind of breakdown on television, I'd shoot myself."

How do you spend your money?

I run a few houses [in Aspen and Los Angeles] that are going all the time, so I piss away a lot of money on that. Paintings—but I hate to call them an investment; it's banking rather than investment. I'm not a trader or collector, but I'm aware that I don't throw ten thousand dollars out the window. I own two tickets to the Lakers game that cost about a hundred and sixty bucks a night, even though I'm not there half the year. I follow the theatrical tradition [that] whoever's making the most money picks up the check. And I like buying presents for people.

Are you happy nowadays?

Extremely. I would love to see a big wide avenue of tremendous productivity inevitably spread before me, but that's not the nature of the thing. Other than that, nobody's mad at me right now. I'm in shape. Things are going well for my friends. But then, I've been on bonus time since I was twenty-eight. I had a great enough life for anybody who ever lived up until then, so past that, it's been a *big* bonus.

What's the secret of your appeal?

I don't know. As a teenager and in my early twenties, my friends used to call me the Great Seducer—even though they definitely were not sure I was attractive—because I seemed to have something invisible but unfailing.

And now, as an actor, you get paid for it. Seduction is your business.

[*Laughs.*] Right. But I don't want it to be. I don't want to enforce my will on anybody. I want it to be willing. I want it the way it is, and believe me, the way it is [*flashes the killer smile*] is pretty damn good.

PLAYBOY

November 1986

**"Men have taken my self-esteem
and flushed it away; it's somewhere
in the mid-Atlantic right now."**

If Joan Rivers had her way, I'd be married to a Jewish doctor today.
God knows, she tried.

I first met Rivers in 1981 at Harrah's, in Reno, Nevada. *People*
magazine had dispatched me to speak to her for a possible cover story.
The interview went beautifully. She liked me; I liked her. Far removed
from the hard-edged harridan she portrays onstage, Rivers was eager
and emotionally open. She was also funny. In fact, I found her natural
perceptions far wittier than the "jokes" she labored over for her act.

We laughed a lot during that first day, a long one that included two
performances and dinner. After her last show, we boarded the Harrah's
private jet for the trip back to Los Angeles, where a limo met us
planeside. When we reached Rivers's exclusive Bel Air home, a tasteful,
pillared structure that came complete, as I later discovered, with an-

tiques, butlers, and finger bowls after dinner, she leaned toward me conspiratorially.

"Are you married?" she asked.

"No."

"In love?"

"Not at the moment."

"Great. I have some men for you to meet. Do you mind?"

"Of course not," I said and instantly forgot about it. A week later I called Joan at home to check facts. "Hello" had barely escaped my lips when she blurted out:

"Have I got a man for you."

"Already? Who?"

"My gynecologist."

"Your gynecologist?" This had to be a joke. "What are we going to talk about—his work?"

"I don't know," she bubbled, "but when I found out he was available, I sat up in the stirrups."

A week later, Joan Rivers's gynecologist telephoned, asking for a date. It was the beginning of what would be a string of doctors whom Joan ran through my life. They were all attractive, they were all nice, they were all successful, but none was Dr. Right.

Still, I found Joan's dedication to finding a husband for me, and her horror, I might add, at my own nonchalance in pursuing one ("You've got to get more Jewish about this"), quite touching. She was positively selfless in her quest. Entire lunches were spent discussing the pros and cons of various available swains. When playwright Neil Simon got separated, Joan was ecstatic, even when I indicated he wasn't my type.

"You'd be surprised how much better-looking a man gets when you know he's worth a hundred and fifty million dollars," she declared.

Although the odd actor or businessman appeared, doctors remained Joan's specialty. From her gynecologist we moved, as it were, upward; I was told to expect a call from the plastic surgeon who "did Michael Jackson's second nose" (the one, the doctor himself assured me, on the cover of *Rolling Stone*). When sparks failed to fly, Joan's ear-nose-and-throat man gave a jingle. Two years and another operation later, she suggested her liposuction surgeon, who was not only single and attractive but could guarantee a lifetime free of cellulite. Though the thought of being swept off my feet by the trendiest of medical specialties had its appeal, I'd had it with the AMA.

"Joan," I finally said, "let's face it. I've dated every part of your body. Unless you have a heart attack, we've run out of organs."

As you can see, it's very difficult for me to write objectively about Joan Rivers because I really like her. I liked her when we did *People;* I liked her more in 1984, when I interviewed her for the cover of *Interview;* and I even liked her after she stopped talking to me in 1986, claiming I'd misquoted her in *Playboy.* Misquoted? Could I make this stuff up?

Cybill Shepherd?

"Not a major talent, just lucky, lucky, lucky, lucky."

Johnny Carson?

A "very cool" customer . . . "wrapped in cotton by everyone around him."

Burt Reynolds?

Said "vicious things about me because he had a bad day. His toupee was twisted or his caps might have fallen out or the heels of his boots could've been broken or his dildo was pinching."

But wait, I'm getting ahead of myself. In the autumn of 1981 Rivers began a five-year publicity assault that ultimately turned her into a supermarket and household name. She was, of course, already a star, a woman whose comedy career began in Greenwich Village clubs like Upstairs at the Downstairs, where, invariably, she was the only female in a crowd of male upstarts like Dick Cavett, Bill Cosby, and Richard Pryor.

Over the years she'd written books (*Having a Baby Can Be a Scream; Enter Talking,* her best-selling 1986 autobiography); directed, financed, and starred in a film (*Rabbit Test,* the 1978 saga of the first pregnant man); and, most important, developed a key relationship with Johnny Carson.

In 1965, unknown and despondent, Rivers finally wangled an appearance on *The Tonight Show,* having already been turned down seven times. Perched next to Johnny, Joan prattled on about her ordinary looks, her inability to get dates, her hairdresser, Mr. Bruce. Carson was beguiled. Wiping tears of laughter from his eyes, he proclaimed, "God, you're funny. You're going to be a star." In 1971 Carson asked her to guest-host, a job that, by the 1980s, had expanded into a role as permanent guest host, several weeks' duty a year. But the Carson love fest ended abruptly and publicly in 1986, when she deserted *The Tonight Show* for her own talk slot, *The Late Show Starring Joan Rivers,* on the new Fox television network. But when Joan failed to pull in big numbers, the new arrangement soured. (In addition, her contract, three years at a reported $10 million, also guaranteed that her husband, Edgar Rosenberg, would serve as the show's producer, a condition that proved acrimonious when Fox fired him.)

When we met at Harrah's in 1981, however, Joan still whispered Carson's name in worshipful tones.

"Are you hungry?" she asked as I walked through the door to meet a woman who, with reading glasses perched atop her head and dressed in cashmere sweater and pants, looked like a well-to-do suburban matron. "What would you like? Let's order something." She was already on the phone to room service. "Tuna salad. With French fries?"

When I said no, she looked crestfallen.

"No? Listen, you get them and I'll just have one," she renegotiated, beginning a friendship often based on our mutual desire for, and reluctant rejection of, food. Within minutes a room-service cart appeared, pushed by an expectant waiter. (To her credit, Joan was always generous to those who made her road life easy. At the end of an engagement she'd dispatch Edgar or her manager, Bill Sammeth, with envelopes of gratuities for the dressers, manicurists, and hairdressers who comprised that week's entourage.)

Although she pitched comic hardballs at the rich, famous, and powerful, she truly believed they were fair game. "If I thought I hurt anybody, I'd go crazy. That's why I pick on the biggies. They can take it." (Not always. Elizabeth Taylor later told me she'd been deeply wounded by the comedienne's remarks.) Joan, meanwhile, claimed that "everything" hurt her. "I'm terribly sensitive."

During that first interview we covered everything from plastic surgery (she'd had her eyes done and nose "thinned") to husbands (her first had been "a prince with a big ring, an apartment on the East Side, and a maid; it lasted six months").

Husband number two was faring better. She and Rosenberg, a Cambridge-educated, English press agent/producer, had been together for over twenty years—a union cemented four days after they met. From then until Edgar's suicide in 1987, the two were joined at the hip. Joan never made a move without Edgar. He simply became part of the Rivers package; if you hired Joan, you hired Edgar. He was Joan's producer, manager, adviser, and hand-holder. He was also, many thought, her spoiler. Yet, for better or worse, their lives were inextricably intertwined, for Edgar, as Joan said repeatedly, was the only person she truly trusted.

"People think he's the son of a bitch, but I'm the one who says, 'You tell them to go to hell.' Edgar just makes the call."

Joan could be a tough cookie, all right, a general capable of leading the troops onto the beaches at Dunkirk without breaking an acrylic nail. Yet she could also disarm with tenderness, as she did during that first interview with me, when I asked what was the saddest moment in her life.

"My mother's death six years ago," she instantly replied. "I still can't talk about it. She was my best friend. Here she was, my mother, who looked like a dowager with pearls, and we'd go to the movies and throw spitballs. It was so sudden. I spoke to her Wednesday afternoon. She died that night of a heart attack. I was so angry I started throwing out her clothes. I said, 'Just give me one hour back.' When was the last time I'd said, 'I love you'? You know what saved me? She ordered clothes that kept coming after she died. And she had two chairs reupholstered—they came the day of the funeral. Until the day she died, she kept going."

Rivers stopped. "Is your mother alive?"

"Yes," I replied.

"Are you close?"

"Very. The thought of anything happening to her is unbearable. . . ."

"Oh, God, I know exactly what you mean," she said, tears trembling on the tips of her faux lashes. She grabbed my hand. "Promise me that if anything ever happens to your mother, you'll call me. You've no idea how terrible it is. I'll help you get through it."

It took five months for *People* to finally run Joan Rivers on its cover. Week after week precocious princesses and notable deaths took precedence as Joan agonized. "When I read the obituaries today and saw that Meyer Lansky kicked the bucket, I knew I was in trouble," she cracked sometime in February as she, Edgar, and I sat under the plastic umbrellas at Ma Maison, then Hollywood's chicest boîte. Joan wasn't eating. Obsessed with weight ("the best compliment I can get is 'God, you look thin' "), Joan's dietary peculiarities extended to her own dinner parties, where guests would gorge themselves on delectable food while the hostess sat in front of an empty plate.

The April *People* cover kicked off a veritable Joan Rivers festival, culminating when Carson named her his permanent guest host. Our friendship also grew. Getting chummy with celebrities was something I assiduously avoided, but with Joan I broke my cardinal rule, even before I noticed what I was doing, because she made it so easy.

Joan loved being famous and sharing the perks with her pals. To friends, she was a hip Jewish mother, dispensing advice on everything from condoms to collagen, hair to husbands—she found the first-class section of airplanes particularly fertile hunting ground. It was there, for instance, she met Chuck Connors.

"You mean *The Rifleman?*" I asked in disbelief.

"Well, when he told me about all the jewelry he buys for his secretary, I figured he might as well be buying it for you."

Although our socializing was relegated to the occasional lunch in Los Angeles or outing in New York (where her entourage ranged from hairdressers to Elijah Blue Allman, Cher's son), we always had a good time. One thing about Joan Rivers, she's plenty of fun.

When Edgar was around, and he usually was, things got stickier. He could be imperious and arrogant one moment, funny and warm the next. You just never knew. Though he'd built a role as Tonto to Joan's Lone Ranger, this was a man with a desperate need to be humored and recognized in his own right.

He was short, with a slightly crooked carriage, the result of a war wound, I believe, even though probably the larger, and ultimately lethal, injury was to his ego. For no matter how you sliced it, Joan was the breadwinner—despite her frequent proclamations that she "couldn't have done it without Edgar."

Their lives, destinies, bank accounts were intrinsically linked. They'd created something they called the Career, which was planned, fought for, nurtured, and addressed almost as if a member of the family. Its care and feeding involved their every waking hour. Decisions concerning it were hammered out in excruciating detail with the revolving battalion of lawyers, agents, press agents, and managers who passed through their lives.

It was often difficult to know where Joan's thinking ended and Edgar's began. In interviews, Edgar customarily sat in, often interrupting questions addressed to his wife to say, "Joan thinks . . ." or "Joan feels . . ." and she would nod in agreement. Her acquiescence always surprised me. Why did this articulate Phi Beta Kappa from Barnard let her husband speak for her? Alone, Joan had no trouble.

In August 1983 I wasn't surprised to get a call from Barry Golson, editor of the *Playboy* interview. Did I think Joan would be interested in doing the interview for December, their biggest issue?

"Yes. Absolutely. Great," Rivers replied.

And then the trouble started. Naturally, it was Edgar who made the call. He informed me that although *they* would do the interview, there had to be "ground rules." They had to see the transcript before it was published. They couldn't, I explained; it wasn't kosher. "That's not so," Edgar said. "Barbra Streisand saw her *Playboy* interview before it ran." This information left me dumbfounded but dubious. I'd call *Playboy*, but even if they agreed, I wouldn't. No one was allowed to see my questions or read my copy. Backtracking, Edgar assured me they trusted me. The problem, he said, was *Playboy* and their editing—even though I assured him I did my own.

At *Playboy*, Golson supported me. Edgar's response was to again cite Streisand (tantamount in Hollywood to "The Word was made flesh . . ."). I reiterated that our position was nonnegotiable. Finally, they capitulated. A week in early August was slotted into both our schedules. I declined all assignments for the month while the magazine set aside a healthy chunk of blank December pages marked "Joan Rivers."

Three days before I was to sit down with Joan, I got a frantic call from Golson. "Rivers just backed out. What happened?"

"What are you talking about?"

"She says she's not doing the interview."

"Why?"

"I thought you knew."

I knew nothing. I tracked Joan to Caesar's Palace in Las Vegas. When I got her on the line, I heard a telltale click as Edgar picked up an extension. "What's going on?" I asked, thinking there was a misunderstanding. Edgar said that they weren't going to do the interview. Joan was overwrought; the press, including *Playboy*, was out to get her. They trusted me, but they didn't trust *Playboy*. Of course, if they could see the transcript before publication . . .

They couldn't. For the next three days, I tried to reach Joan alone. The Rosenbergs weren't taking calls. Finally, Bill Sammeth phoned: "Joan says to tell you she loves you but she just can't trust *Playboy*." Our communication ceased.

The following summer, just as quickly as they'd departed, Edgar and Joan came back into my life. *Interview* asked if I'd be interested in talking to Joan for their December cover.

No, I didn't think so.

But Joan wanted me, the editor insisted.

Now, why, you may ask, did I say yes? Primarily because I needed the work. I was also curious. What would Joan and Edgar say when I marched in, tape recorder in tow? An interesting scenario, to say the least. Besides, all our last encounter had proven was what I instinctively knew: Never trust a star.

The day after the Los Angeles Olympics opened, my VW Rabbit, replete with dents celebrating my first year of California driving, wound its way into Bel Air. I was game but exhausted, having flown in the night before on the red-eye from New York. As I pulled into the carport, I saw Joan, dressed in a caftan, anxiously awaiting me at the edge of the sidewalk. She looked unusually subdued. Stepping out of the car, I smiled.

"I like your hat," she said, referring to the red straw fedora I'd plunked on my head to cover hair suffering from a night flight across America.

"Thanks," I replied as I noticed Edgar standing behind the screen door and looking equally uneasy.

Joan began stammering an explanation of the *Playboy* fiasco as we walked toward the house. "The last year was so tense . . . the press so tough on me . . . it was all too much." When we reached Edgar, he picked up the chant.

Finally, I asked for some cranberry juice. Edgar darted toward the kitchen and Joan called out, "The tuna dip, Edgar. Bring the tuna dip." He returned to the patio with a tray, placing it on the table before settling into a nearby chair. So I was interviewing Joan *with* Edgar. Business as usual.

Three hours later we'd pulled off another good conversation. Joan and I were born to talk to each other. She made me laugh; I made her think. Joan was one of the few people I could repeatedly interview and come away each time with fresh material.

When the session was over, Edgar and Joan's relief was perceptible. I'd been forgiving; they'd been on their best behavior; we'd had fun. In many ways Joan and Edgar were like the little girl with the curl: When they were good, they were very, very good—warm, considerate, protective, witty, familial. But when they were bad, it was the world versus them, ever the underdog, ever the victim. And even though I knew that, I still liked them.   .

As I was climbing back into my Rabbit, Joan inspected my body. "God, you look thin." I smiled. She'd apologized after all.

When our *Interview* cover ran in December, the Rosenbergs loved it. Shortly thereafter, my mother was diagnosed. Somewhere in the ensuing months, I recalled Joan's invitation to call if anything happened to Mama. I did, and she was there for me.

Playboy Redux

Don't ask how it happened—if you're a reporter your job is to make it happen—but in August 1986 I finally sat down with Joan to do our long-delayed *Playboy* interview. Joan was America's tabloid queen, having just abruptly and controversially left Johnny Carson for Fox. Under these circumstances, *Playboy* was willing to forgive all for the promise of getting Joan's side of the story in their November issue.

This time around the mood in the Rosenberg household was changed. When I told Joan that Edgar would not be allowed to sit in, there was no problem. Though he brought up the notion of their lawyer checking the transcript before publication, Joan dismissed it even before I could. I sensed a new liberation on her part. Edgar's heart attack the previous February had changed the dynamic between them. During his illness, Joan had assumed total responsibility for her career—and discovered she liked it. Edgar, meanwhile, was already exhibiting the detachment and depression that, sadly, led to his suicide a little over a year later.

When the interview ran in November, Fox, reportedly, was unhappy. How could Joan have publicly skewered so many stars when she needed them as guests on her show? Her response, via her press agent and reported in the *Los Angeles Times,* was to indicate that I'd misconstrued what she said.

That, of course, simply wasn't true—as I informed Barry Diller, head of the Fox network, a man familiar with my work and for whom I had great professional respect.

Less than a year later, Fox and Rivers called it quits.

—

We've seen a lot of Joan Rivers this past year—the huge controversy over your leaving the Carson show, a best-selling book, Enter Talking, *your new show. Aren't you flirting with overexposure?*

We didn't mean this *Tonight* thing to blow up the way it did. It happened during a slow media week, so I became a media star for a second. I felt like Madonna. I don't feel overexposed, but certainly, the public has had enough of me—*I*'ve had enough of me.

The way you left The Tonight Show *has become one of the most celebrated departures in show business. Clear it up for us. Why didn't you talk with Carson before you signed with the new Fox network? Why didn't you postpone the press conference for a day until you had time to reach him and tell him the news?*

In our business, until a contract is signed, there is no contract. I defy anybody in any job who's making more than thirty dollars a week to jeopardize that job by walking away from it until the next job is secure. We couldn't tell anybody about the deal until all the *i*'s were dotted and the *t*'s crossed, which happened on Monday, the day before the press conference. As soon as that happened, I called Johnny—I went through my hotel switchboard in Las Vegas, so I have my bill—and reached his secretary, who said, "Hold on. I'll put him on." And then the phone went, "Click." Tuesday morning, I called him from the makeup room at Fox, through the Fox switchboard. I got him on the line and then he hung up on me.

As for the press conference, it was Fox that wanted to have it right away. There were so many rumors on the street, not just about me but about who was going to be president of Fox, and so forth, that Fox wanted to make the announcements as soon as possible so the news wouldn't dribble out. In fact, no formal announcement had even been made saying there would be a network, so it was to be a two-pronged press conference, like Hungary and Austria, a two-headed empire—me and Fox.

But I had no idea there would be the hysteria. I don't know why NBC is so angry with me. I have done nothing. I was Johnny's guest host; they didn't renew my contract; I went someplace else. I didn't owe him. I didn't ask him for money when I left him. I didn't do anything.

When Fox offered you the deal, why didn't you go to NBC or to Carson and say, "Look, I've been offered this deal; do you want to meet or better it?"?

That's tacky. That's groveling, coming hat in hand. I would never have done that. I have too much pride. If they wanted me, they should have sent me a Christmas card last year.

Freddie De Cordova, the executive producer of The Tonight Show, *said that during the previous week, while you were hosting* The Tonight Show, *he had chatted with you frequently and you never mentioned a thing about your plans.*

Nor had Freddie told me *his* secrets. We sat for a week in the dressing room talking, true, but the deal hadn't been completed. I wasn't going to tell Johnny's producer, "Hey, I'm thinking of leaving and going to another network and doing my own talk show." Did Freddie confide to me whether or not Johnny was renewing his contract? We never knew that Johnny renewed his contract with NBC until the day it was signed. We were never told. These are *not* my buddies. They're all frightened over at Carson. They all think they have to prove their loyalty to the king.

Do you think Carson expects toadyism from all his employees?

Johnny expects nothing, but he's had nothing *but* toadyism. They've all done it to him. I don't know what Johnny expects anymore. If we were going to raid Carson, which we're not, we would have made an offer to Freddie, who—out of the whole thing—is the one I miss: his sheer energy, wickedness, and wit. I miss playing with Freddie. I called him before the announcement to tell him and said, "Of all the people, I want you to know I'm going to miss you." And I started to cry.

How do you feel about Carson now?

I always adored him and I still adore him. He was the one who said, "You're funny." I adored him for that and always fantasized this big, wonderful, warm relationship. I think he's tender, very feeling, very caring; but I also think he doesn't let anybody in anymore—except one or two people—to find that out. He's the money-maker for NBC, so they keep him wrapped in cotton.

The Tonight Show meant everything to me. I really did grow up through that show. I came on as a single woman. I got my fame from that show, I met my husband out of that show, I got pregnant on that show, had Melissa on that show, and America watched the whole thing evolve. But Johnny and I were never personally close. We were a little closer in New York, in the sense that his second wife, Joanne, had two big parties and my husband and I were asked to those. One was his fortieth birthday, which was one of the most memorable evenings of my life. It was the first big star-studded party I ever went to. But we never sat down, the four of us, in the kitchen over a bowl of spaghetti.

You dedicated your book Enter Talking *to Edgar and Carson. Did you get any feedback from Carson on it?*

You talk about hurt! I spent seven years writing that book. The first copy that came off the press, I didn't keep for myself, I had it hand-carried to Malibu to Johnny. Along with it, I sent a long handwritten note telling him how much I thought of him, how much I owed him. He never acknowledged it. Three weeks later, I was going on the show to promote it. The day before the show, they called and said, "Johnny wants another book for the table." So we sent it.

When I sat down with him on the air, we chatted about the first time I was ever on the show, and he said, "Oh, your stand-up was wonderful." I'd never done a stand-up. He didn't even know what I'd done. Suddenly you realize how little you mean in somebody's life. Then Freddie, from off-camera, said to him, "Read the dedication. It's dedicated to you." And then you realize he hadn't even opened the book. They had blown up photographs from it for Johnny to hold up, and he asked, "Are these in the book?" Seven years' work and he hadn't even opened the book!

Is Carson as cold as you imply?

He's very cool. You don't jump at him at a party and tickle him and say, "Guess who?" But no, underneath it all, there is a very warm person. Like I said, he's just so wrapped in cotton by everyone around him.

You've intimated that another network was willing to offer you the moon when you were the permanent guest host. Do you want to say now which one?

ABC. It was two years ago. They came to me and offered me a full-time daytime show, as many specials as I wanted, and the hour before or after the Oscars or Emmys, depending. They said, "We'll make you queen of the network." We had a good laugh about that for a year. The money they offered was phenomenal. We had to hold secret meetings with them at hotels. It was always raining when we met. I wore lots of capes and Edgar disguised himself as a Gentile. [*Laughs.*] I finally said no, because I am not a daytime person and because I felt loyalty to NBC.

Let's see . . . the hour before and after the Oscars—isn't that Barbara Walters's territory? Are you saying ABC was willing to dethrone Walters for a new "network queen"?

Well, here we go again. It's a business. I like Barbara so much, [and] if I had taken what they were offering, it would've meant that she lost what she had. But it can work the other way: If in a year Fox says to me, "You're not working out; here comes Barbara," there's nothing I can do. The men who run Fox, [owner] Rupert Murdoch and [CEO] Barry Diller, did not call me because they liked the way my hair looked. They looked at the ratings over three years, the demographics, and saw success and profit.

Some critics have said you don't wear well; your style is too aggressive. They say it's one thing to do eight weeks a year on Carson, another to do five nights a week all year long. In fact, you once said that yourself, didn't you?

When I was starting out and wasn't as secure as I am now, I may have said that. But, I'm sorry to tell everybody, I may not be the best, but I'm as good an interviewer as anybody else. I can take a show and run it for fifty-two weeks with no problem. As for my abrasiveness, it obviously worked for three years, five times a week. And when we did a version of *The Tonight Show* in London, we were number one. If it doesn't do well, so what? I've got Las Vegas, concerts, another book, a movie.

The press has been tough on you since the Carson episode. How do you react to some of the stronger criticism?

The press will continue doing that until I die—at which time *The New York Times* will do what it did to Lenny Bruce. He was vilified by everybody, all the media. The day after he died, the *New York Times* obituary included comparison to Swift, Rabelais, and Twain. And I said, "This poor slob couldn't get a cabaret card"—which you needed in those days.

Will you be asking your friend Elizabeth Taylor to drop by the new Fox show?

I would never ask Elizabeth to come on the show. I have too much pride for that. But maybe she'll just pop on the show, look smashing, and leave.

Do you think she'll get married again?

I see another two or three husbands for Liz in my crystal ball. The men still love her. But she's having a hard time in Hollywood. All the men over forty have girls of twenty. Even though she's spectacular, she's a bundle. When a man takes Elizabeth Taylor out, he's taking someone he must cater to, and they're not used to that.

Still, Bob Dylan raked up the courage to ask Elizabeth out.

Bob Dylan always makes me laugh. I go way back to the Village with him, when he was Bobby Zimmerman. He was serious then, too. He never wore a coat, always a jacket and scarf—that meant you were serious in the sixties. Now he may write poetry to Liz and sit at her feet, but I don't think we have anything to really worry about as far as Liz and Bobby's making an announcement. She's not interested in a man who says he'll *make* something for her: "Look here, look at this serape jewel case Bob made for me."

How do you really feel about Elizabeth? You've said that when your career took off in the early eighties, it was the Elizabeth Taylor jokes that were the catalysts. You once said, "Liz pierced her ears and gravy came out."

Right. I was always doing the same comedy, always gossipy, but the Elizabeth Taylor stuff really hit a chord. That just turned the whole thing around. I like Elizabeth. She's done some terrific things that I don't think I would have done. When Edgar was in the hospital [with his heart attack], after all the teasing and jokes I'd done, she sent flowers. And she picked up the phone and called. Then we sat next to each other . . . at a charity event, and I liked her. She was very funny. I also like her because I know how hard it is to diet. For me to lose three pounds, I have to undergo a general anesthetic. She also knows who she is. If you're going to be a star, goddamn it, be a star. Get out those white foxes, honey, and walk!

Now, Liz is definitely a man's woman. She prefers to be with men; but then I prefer to be with men too. If I walk into a room with twelve men in one corner and twelve women in another, I'm going to walk over to the men. I think they're more interesting; I have a better time with them.

What do you think men have done for your life—for your self-esteem?

They've destroyed it. [*Laughs.*] Men have taken my self-esteem and flushed it away; it's somewhere in the mid-Atlantic right now. No man, except for my husband, has ever said anything nice about me or backed me up or come to my rescue. I've never been one of those women whom men helped. Nevertheless, I was crazed for men from the minute I saw them. I had my first serious romance when I was four. I apparently went crazy for a boy named Jack, who was sixteen. I would make my parents get into the car and drive past the drugstore where Jack hung out.

You have a stock character, Heidi Abramowitz, who was such a tramp in high school that when she took off her braces, the football team sent a thank-you note to her orthodontist. But in real life, how old were you when you first made love?

Very old. Twenty-one.

Who was the guy?

David Titelson. He was a history student at Columbia and a poet.

Did you have qualms about taking such a big step?

Of course you had qualms. You couldn't go home and tell your mother; you couldn't go to your doctor and get a diaphragm. You really lived on the edge, counting twenty-eight days.

Did you feel when you slept with David that you'd marry him?

Oh, yeah. Whenever you slept with a man, that was saying, "I pledge my troth." That was *it*. However, if we had gotten married, we would've killed each other. Also, I think I was lousy in bed then. In fact, I'm sure I was. I hadn't heard of two thirds of the things you do automatically now.

How many lovers do you think it takes for a woman to get good in bed?

About five. At least it took five for me before I wised up and learned that "Roll over" isn't just an expression you say to a dog. Finally, I got my information from reading books; girls didn't talk to one another. Going down? I never knew what men were talking about.

Weren't the men in your life willing to help you improve sexually?

Not at all. What I didn't know, no one taught me. Did you know that not one man has ever told me I'm beautiful—in my entire life? Not one man.

Not even Edgar?

Not even Edgar—in any circumstance—even with the lights off. [*Laughs.*] They've said other things, like "You're perky" or "You're fun" or "You're good in bed," but nobody has ever said to me, "You're beautiful. I love you and you're beautiful." Never.

Does that hurt your feelings?

Oh, I think that's what's made me the aggressive wreck that I am today.

You're also very bright, a Barnard grad. Are men intimidated by smart women?

Not when you're in bed, because then you're down to basics. You're not doing jokes. And they still never said anything until after sex; then they said, "Honey, you'd better tighten up your thighs."

Has success made you feel sexier?

I got sexier as I had more money to change myself. We don't like that nose? Let's fix it. We don't like these teeth? Let's get them capped. Anybody who doesn't keep working on herself is a fool. If you get fat, a man will say, "That's okay, I love you for yourself"; but if you're in a restaurant, his eye will go to the thinnest girl there.

What, exactly, have you had done in terms of plastic surgery?

I've had my face lifted, my nose thinned; my eyes were done a long time ago, and now I just had a tummy tuck, but that was because I had a hysterectomy. I figured, if you're going to close it up, close and tighten. It's silly to put all that blubber back. And, oh yes, I also had my thighs vacuumed this time around. I figured, if they're going to operate, I want to come out looking better than when I went in.

Do you understand why some people find your obsession with plastic surgery, with changing yourself, an indication that perhaps you don't like yourself enough, despite all your success?

Right. But you must look at yourself objectively and say, "These old things don't look good." If you can make yourself look better and feel better about yourself, that's wonderful. And now that I've discovered vacuuming, it's just the beginning. When I look at my thighs, my arms are now screaming, "What about *us?*"

As for self-esteem, I certainly have more now than when I started, though that's not saying much. I still never feel I belong. I still never feel I have the credentials to work. Very low self-esteem.

Why?

Because of my own childhood. And the long road of getting to where I am now. They're out to shoot you down. They're out to shoot my show down already. The show is not getting a lift from anybody. By the time we go on the air, all the critics will say, "Johnny's still the king."

Speaking of hot items, are Sean Penn and Madonna still in your act?

Yes, and I'm praying for that marriage to work so they can stay in it. They're fun because they're so outrageous. I mean, Sean Penn fighting not to be photographed! Marlon Brando has earned the right; Sean Penn hasn't.

Now that Debra Winger and Tim Hutton are married, will they be giving the Penns a run for their money in your material?

No. They're the poor man's Madonna and Sean. She's an earth mother. Certain women who don't shave their legs or under their arms make men go crazy. "So you don't bathe, Debra. I love you anyway."

The woman's a throbbing bucket of lust. But at least they got married. God bless them. Better to be married five times than to have five relationships.

You've been married twice. First, at twenty-three, to Jimmy Sanger, which ended in divorce six months later. You met your second husband, Edgar, when you were thirty-two and married him four days later. How did that happen so fast?

Edgar was Peter Sellers's best friend. He was looking for a person to rewrite a script that Peter and he were going to produce, starring Peter. Edgar knew the *Tonight Show* producer and asked him if he knew a good comedy writer. The producer said, "We just had a girl on last night who's very funny. Call her." So Edgar called and gave me the script to rewrite. We went to Jamaica to do the rewrite, and four days later, we got married.

Marrying a man after only four days was a very risky thing to do, particularly given your ideas about marriage.

Yes, but I just knew he was absolutely correct for me. He was a businessman, in the business but at the good end of it. He was smarter than I was; I must have a smarter man. And, outwardly, he also had what I wanted: manners, the facade, the credentials to walk into any room. I didn't have to say, "Please take off those theatrical cuff links. Get rid of that twenty-four-karat-gold chain." He was just right for me.

Did you have a big wedding?

We had no wedding. I was working at The Bitter End, and we went to the Bronx, because our lawyer friend found a judge who would marry us. The Filipino navy had arrived the same day and were getting married en masse, so it was the only time that Edgar and I ever walked into a room and were the tallest couple. [*Laughs.*] I'm five-two and Edgar's five-five. Anyway, we got married that night and I went back to work.

We led two lives, his business and mine. I went to the Village to keep honing my craft, and at the same time, we'd be going out to dinner with the Rockefellers. They'd say, "What do you do?" and I'd say, "I'm a comedienne." Peter Sellers would call up and ask Edgar to please take some chocolate mousse over to Princess Margaret in London. After

Carson, I was the hot girl in town. The career moved ahead, but much more slowly than people realized. That's why, when I finally got to host the Carson show, Edgar went to Van Cleef & Arpels and had a little diamond turtle made up for me, because my whole career is like a turtle—it moves very slowly and carefully.

In your act, you joke a lot about Edgar and your sex life—or your lack of one. Is that the truth or just a routine?

Well, things diminish a great deal in twenty years. You settle in with each other and you get to be too comfortable.

Don't you miss the passion?

Of course you miss the passion. But then you also turn around and say, "Here is someone who has stayed downstairs until two o'clock in the morning reading and rereading all the lawyer's contracts." And that's okay with me. I'm lying in bed reading about Louis the Fourteenth and he's downstairs taking care of my business, saying, "I don't want to worry you. I'll call the lawyer tomorrow and take care of this." And we have the same tastes.

Such as?

We're both terrible snobs. We both love the formality of life. If we could afford livery, we'd have it. If we had made *Star Wars*—if my husband were John Edgar Lucas—you'd be talking to me right now at Versailles. I would've bought it and lived my fantasy. We also both read. Our drugs are books: Bookstores love us; we go in and buy, buy, buy. We like and dislike the same people. The only big bone of contention we have is that I like to travel and he doesn't. I don't want to go without him, but I will.

You have an agent and a manager, but you and Edgar effectively run your career together. How much control does he have over you?

I'd say sixty percent. He can control me easily. But I think totally for myself. I weigh everything he tells me and, although it's tremendously influencing, in the long run, I decide. We weigh everything. Nothing is done spur of the moment. With the new show, each talent coordinator's name, each secretary that we decide to put on staff, is mutually decided. Nothing is "Oh, what the hell; let's go." That's why it's working. With Edgar, I've got someone protecting me all the time.

I wouldn't know what to do without him—though when he had his heart attack, there was a good six-month period when I had to run things.

Did you enjoy that?

It was terrific. I found it very heady, exhilarating. I made the decisions, but it was twice the work. I had to be at those meetings. I made a lot of mistakes, because I'm not really a businesswoman. Just the other day, Edgar said to me, "If I die now, at least I know I left you with a great contract at Fox." And he really has. I wake up at night and think, God, I love my husband. I wouldn't know what to do without him. Now he never tells me, "You're beautiful." But that's his English reserve. Yet he'll turn to me and say, "I love you." And I'll say to him, "Then make me a cup of coffee." [*Laughs.*] It's not mushy-gushy, it's just "You're part of my life." I couldn't have an affair and come home, nor could I have a husband who was doing that.

What would you do if you discovered Edgar was having an affair?

It depends. If I found out she was twenty-one and just a boopy-doop who was making him happy, listening wide-eyed to all the tales I've heard for years and am tired of, I'd say, "Well, that's great. That's like Franz Josef. Have your little European fling." But if I found out he was making my friend, I'd be furious: "Don't come into our group with your fly open!"

If something happened to Edgar, would you remarry?

No, I would live with someone. I wouldn't believe that at my age, someone was going to marry me because he fell madly in love with me. He'd be marrying me because of what I have. If it didn't work out, I wouldn't want fifty percent of what Edgar had earned to end up going to some Chippendale dancer.

What kind of men do you like?

I *don't* like old-looking men. I can't lie. I can't say, "Oh, he's sixty-five; isn't that just great?" You know everything's hanging out under that shirt. I love men in their prime—which is forty to fifty-five. That's when they're self-assured; their face is craggy, without that piece of rooster skin hanging. I don't like blondes; I like dark men who look a little beaten up. He could be the Mafia, but he *does* own Standard Oil.

No blondes, eh? How about Don Johnson?

I had him on *The Tonight Show* before he was [*deep voice*] Don Johnson. He was just [*nasal voice*] Don Johnson. He was okay . . . a nice, slim man on a new program called *Miami Vice*. But nothing radiated. The eyes did not lock. Johnny Carson used to have a name he used every time one of these guys—the hot one for that year—came on. Someone told me that when Don was on *The Tonight Show*, Johnny turned to somebody afterward and said, as he walked away, "Erik Estrada."

How about Sting?

He's terrific. But if he had two names, he's be a much bigger star. People don't take him as seriously as they should. To have one name, it has to come from the public's love of you. Bernhardt became Bernhardt—she didn't say, "Call me Sarah." Poor Sting; he should be called Charley Sting. Or, better yet, Sting Bromberg.

Are you a fan of Mick Jagger's?

I would love to meet him. He's fabulously interesting just because of the time span. The first time I met him, we were both doing *The Ed Sullivan Show*. The Stones were in the next dressing room and, for no reason, they ripped apart a piano. . . . I got so incensed that anyone would destroy a musical instrument that I ran in there and yelled . . . that they shouldn't do this. Rough, arrogant English kids. How dare they destroy a thirty-five-thousand-dollar Steinway? "Who the hell are you?"

What men do you find attractive?

Richard Gere, ten years older. John Travolta, if he ages well. Rock Hudson. I know he was gay, but he was a big, good-looking, powerful man. I like all that. I find Merv Adelson, Barbara Walters's husband, attractive, as I do Barry Diller. If I were single, I could easily see myself signing my name Joan Diller. "Barry, honey, your pancakes are getting cold." I also find Ed Koch attractive, because he's funny and smart. I do a joke and Koch knows that I'm doing a joke and laughs at it. Joan Koch, no question about it. "Ed, pancakes."

Ronald Reagan?

He's too old. Turkey neck. Now, Neil Simon is a very interesting man. Funny, good-looking enough, successful, and he gets every joke I make. I love that.

How about Sylvester Stallone? He's dark and rugged-looking.

I love him. I love him because he's vulnerable. When I had him on *The Tonight Show,* he sat there, with thirty-six million dollars in the bank, and said, "I don't think I own my house. No matter what they tell me, I don't think I own it." And I know what he means.

Do you have an opinion on the new Mrs. Stallone, Brigitte Nielsen?

He made a tragic mistake. And I think I should write and tell him. The few contacts I've had with her have not been pleasant. We were going to use her as a guest on *The Tonight Show,* and she insisted on being first guest. First guest is your main star. She should have been thrilled to come on as *fourth* guest. Either she's being badly advised or her ego is totally out of control. Besides, I don't want to hear that any woman left her sixteen-month-old child to be brought up by its father in order to be with another man. You just don't do that. But that's this town. You become successful and you get your tall, cool blonde.

Well, the former Mrs. Stallone, a short blonde, got thirty-two million from Sly in the divorce settlement.

That's not tragic. If you're going to break up, supposedly get thirty-two million dollars; while you're young and good-looking, you can put the pieces back together on the Riviera.

Let's stick with the ladies. Meryl Streep?

An incredible actress but no pizzazz there. When Meryl was pregnant, Cher brought her to meet me. And here was this very quiet, mousy lady. Still, she's the best thing in films today.

Sally Field?

A good little actress. I'd heard she was very hurt by a joke I'd made about her on *The Tonight Show,* and I finally saw her at a party one

night. So I went over to her and I said, "I *like* you, I really *like* you."
She laughed.

How about Jessica Lange and Sissy Spacek—are they stars to you?

No . . . I do wish Sissy would start wearing some eye makeup. They
seem so serious. We all know that acting is an art, not just something
you stand in front of a camera and do; but come on, girls, lighten up.
Enjoy the other part; enjoy the limos; enjoy it.

One more observation, please. Cybill Shepherd?

Lucky, lucky, lucky, lucky. The luckiest woman in the world. A lousy
career to start with, not a major talent by any means, washed up in the
business, and then she moved away to marry an auto-parts dealer in
Memphis—this life none of us wants to hear about. Then, suddenly,
to come back as the glamour lady of television. I hope she knows and
appreciates that she got a second chance. Joan Collins got it, and boy,
does she know it. She's enjoying every minute the second time around.

Where does Joan Collins rank on your list of great living tarts?

Oh, she's the greatest of them all. And having the time of her
life—going to Ascot yet, mixing with the royals, wearing long black
gloves with a bracelet over one glove at a dinner party. It just screamed
Rita Hayworth and old Hollywood!

Who else are the great tarts?

Madonna, of course—very tarty. She raised her arm at the wedding
to wave and I thought Tina Turner was under there. And Cyndi
Lauper.

Bette Midler?

Bette is terrific, because she's really found her niche, which is wonderful, raucous comedy.

Do you feel in competition with Bette?

Oh, total competition. And she feels it with me. Originally, she
didn't want her role in *Ruthless People,* so they brought me in and
were going to give it to me, [then] she heard about it. Immediately, she
said, "I'll take the role." I am to Bette what Tony Randall was to Cary
Grant. If you can't get Bette, send Joan.

Burt Reynolds has said some pretty uncomplimentary things about you. How did this feud start, anyway?

He hates me, and I don't know why. He has said the most evil, vicious, horrendous things about me, but I've always liked him. I like anyone with humor, and he has a great sense of humor. I just figured he had a bad day because his toupee was twisted or his caps might have fallen out or the heels on his boots could've been broken or his dildo may have been pinching. He could have just looked at himself in direct sunlight and realized how old he really is. But, look, I have nothing against him. [*Laughs.*] Another one I don't get is Shirley MacLaine. She's very liberal and worked hard for women's liberation. Yet in Las Vegas, she once headlined and I opened for her. It was a first, a woman opening and a woman closing. But when they offered us four more weeks, she said no, she'd rather have a man open—and this was at the height of her marching for NOW. See, she's a businesswoman at heart and believed it was better business to have a man open her act. I think she's very smart, but I don't trust anyone who talks to people at the bottom of the sea.

Jack Gould, former television critic of The New York Times, *called you "quite possibly the most intuitively funny woman alive." So whom does America's most intuitively funny woman find funny?*

I change, but at the moment my favorite is Robin Williams. There's nobody like him. His mind is just wonderful. I respect him because he does what I do. I've seen him get up at The Comedy Store, work out a whole Carson shot, and then come on Carson and make it look like it's easy. He takes nothing for granted. He knows exactly what he's doing. Robin Williams is one of those people I'll wait in the rain to see. Richard Pryor is another, and I'll also wait for Bill Murray. And Lily [Tomlin], of course. I also adore Eddie Murphy, mainly because he has respect for his elders; he knows I'm going to die. One day we pull into a parking lot and another car screeches to a halt. Eddie, one of the major kings of comedy, jumps out, runs over, picks me up, spins me around, says, "Come over and meet my girl," takes me to the car, introduces me to the girl—and this kid has just made *Beverly Hills Cop* and has seventy-two retainers.

Who responds to you better—male or female comics?

Male comics come in large groups to watch me work—not because the work is inspired but because they are encouraged by me. Female comics seldom come to see me. They don't think that what I'm talking about is pertinent to their lives today. And it isn't. It's pertinent to *my* life; that's why I'm talking about it. They're not a fifty-three-year-old woman with a daughter in college and a hysterectomy. I'm not going to talk about the drug scene, because I'm not into the drug scene.

You do realize that many people find it meanspirited, don't you?

I know, and I stare at them when I hear that, because I don't know what they're talking about. I've said this before and I'll say it again: I do not pick on someone who can't defend himself. That's meanspiritedness.

So all public figures are fair game?

You don't think so? Jackie Onassis, with her eyes on either side of her head like E.T., is not fair game? With her thirty-eight million dollars? But tell me one person I've been mean to that cared.

Well, we understand Princess Anne is in tears.

No, she's just out of breath from pulling the carriage at her brother's wedding.

You were in London for that wedding—Sarah Ferguson and Prince Andrew's. How was it?

Sensational. God bless Fergie for bringing back boobs and hips. Every fat farm girl should kiss Sarah Ferguson's chubby thighs. But she looked great. They had put her in all those things that make you look thin: They had her corseted in, the *V* in front going down and, to cover the rear end, the big bow—the old Judy Garland trick. And, of course, she had her initials over her boobs. The *A* was on the train, but the *S* was on her boobs. *Nobody* can borrow that dress.

How did Diana look?

Too thin. Listen, Diana is ready for that mother-in-law to *go*. She's ready to be queen. Speaking of which, the queen was not happy going in—no smile to the peasants going through that church door—because Sarah was eight minutes late. But she looked great, the queen. The queen mother looked happy, Margaret looked soused, Princess Michael looked like a tall Nazi—just a typical family outing.

You also know that many people find your humor vulgar and dirty.

I watch George Carlin, who's brilliant, and every other word is *fuck, piss, suck,* and nobody says this man is dirty. I walk onstage and say one *fuck* and the whole review the next day is dedicated to "this filthy woman." You want to say, "Excuse me, let's watch Carlin or Robin or Pryor. What the hell are you *talking* about?" But that's because I am a woman. People don't want to hear it from a woman.

You've always been the only woman in the club, the only really commercially successful woman in the man's world of stand-up comedy. Do you consider yourself a pioneer, a feminist?

I didn't realize what a liberated lady I was. I always said, "My life is liberated. Leave me alone. I have no time to join a movement, because I am the movement." I didn't have time to go up to anyone and say, "Go out and make it in a man's world." I just said, "Look at me and you can see what I'm doing." I never wanted to say that, because I was a woman, things were harder for me or I was judged separately. It took two incidents—my book *Enter Talking* and this business about leaving the Carson show—to turn me around. With my book, as I said, women seem to understand it more than men. And when I left *The Tonight Show,* I got such good wishes, such support from women. I didn't realize how nice it was that women were behind what I did. It's wonderful.

I'm absolutely a feminist. When I started doing stand-up, I played these strip joints, these dives all over the country. At Barnard, I had taken a class with Margaret Mead. She was so smart—not a dresser, but so smart. [*Laughs.*] She was married three times, so there was obviously something going on under that grass skirt. Anyway, I called her and told her I was going to play these crummy clubs and said, "Maybe we can find something out for women from this." So she said, "Let's do a little survey." She made up a list of questions that I passed out during each of my performances. Then I'd send Mead back the questionnaires with glass marks on them. [*Laughs.*] The questions were "Who do you think should control the income in your family? Who brings in the income? Who stays with the children? Who makes the big decisions? Do you think women should work? Do you think women should have equal say in money investments in the family?" Very basic things. This was the early sixties. Anyway, when Mead tabulated all the answers, she said, "There's something happening out there, because ladies in Kansas City are saying, 'Even though I don't work, I don't think I should tell him how to invest the money—or wait a minute. Maybe I *should* tell him.'"

Despite what you say about feminism, some people think you don't really like women, that that comes through in your jokes about how a woman should do anything—including undergoing plastic surgery—to get a husband. They say you turn women into objects and therefore degrade them.

But we *are* objects. We're on earth for one reason—to procreate, which means we are sexual objects. The only reason you and I were born is to continue the species. Once we've done that, it's all over and we can wither and die. So we are objects, and there's nothing wrong in saying that. Any woman who's intelligent knows it's true. These women who say I make objects out of them—don't they watch their weight? Are they getting their hair done? You can say I degrade women if you're a woman who's never exercised, never had her hair cut, never worried about how she looks in an outfit. But the only woman who could say that to me and mean it is Mother Teresa.

What if the show doesn't work? What will that say to you about your own style, how the audience feels about you?

It will say that I've got a great contract with Fox and I'm going to be a very rich lady by the end of it. Don't worry. We took care of that end, too; I did not jump into the abyss for nothing.

ROLLING STONE

January 1985

"You need a big ego to do big things."

When Arnold Schwarzenegger married Maria Shriver I was sitting in St. Francis Xavier Church in Hyannis Port. Naturally, I was surrounded by stars: Barbara Walters, Tom Brokaw, Jacqueline Onassis, John F. Kennedy, Jr., Caroline Kennedy, Ted Kennedy, *all* the Kennedys, Andy Warhol (who arrived late but made a dramatic entrance with singer Grace Jones), and Oprah Winfrey (who recited "How Do I Love Thee" during the ceremony).

Just before mass started, Arnold materialized from the side door of the rectory to take his place on the altar and await his bride. In his white tie and tails and sporting a longer version of Bob Haldeman's White House brush cut, Arnold looked unusually small. He also looked nervous. "I am more nervous than I thought I'd be," he sheepishly informed the congregation, and I knew he was telling the truth because whatever he went on to say about that nervousness didn't make a lot of sense. He was that discombobulated. He was also cute.

I mention this because it was the first—and last—time I'd ever seen Arnold apprehensive. For if there's one quality that defines Arnold Schwarzenegger, it's self-confidence. All the stuff that made America what it is—vision, daring, humor—Arnold has in spades. He's what this country is all about. He's the American dream with an Austrian accent.

Americans don't tolerate accents well, especially in Hollywood (where they don't seem to tolerate English that well either). In the old days a bodybuilder with an accent would have been relegated to making Italian muscle movies and selling protein powder. But Arnold took matters into his own hands. He became a genre unto himself. He did what he's done since he won his first weight-lifting contest and broke that mold by merchandising himself as the bodybuilder with a brain. ("I'm a marketer," he announces without shame.) Since he was already a media star, it was only a hop, skip, and bench press to the big screen. Once there, he did the work for producers. He invented the Arnold Schwarzenegger Movie. And he made sure each one made money. Arnold has always paid his own way.

The first time I saw him was the first time he saw Maria. I was covering the Robert F. Kennedy Tennis Tournament in 1977. Schwarzenegger showed up, and that night at the party in the Rainbow Room I saw him dancing with Sargent Shriver's daughter. Ten years later they married. Nobody thought that would happen either. Nobody, that is, except Arnold.

Despite his undeniable qualifications—he's a movie star, he's a Republican, he's rich—the only thing Arnold can't be is president of the United States. It wouldn't surprise me, though, if somehow, he got around this obstacle too. At the least, I suspect, he'll be governor or senator. Maybe king.

What Arnold always had going was that people underestimated him. They assumed that because his biceps were as big as their waists, he probably wasn't smart.

Arnold is smart. He is also funny and warm, ambitious, generous, driven, shrewd, and charming. He's a natural-born competitor who expects to win. And does. Whenever I sit down to face a blank piece of paper, I think of Arnold. Being on television is exciting, powerful, and marvelous for the ego. But I feel about writing the way Arnold Schwarzenegger feels about pumping iron: It keeps me humble.

"No matter how great you think you are, in the gym I am put back to where I was at fifteen, back to the same struggle. There's no comfort. One hundred pounds will always be one hundred pounds. It will never give you a break."

—

For six weeks, The Terminator *was the number one movie in America. Why? To what do you attribute its success?*

Good script. This was the first film I've ever done where, literally, everyone was running around saying, "This is going to be absolutely fantastic."

In The Terminator *you play a robot sent back from the future to kill the woman who, in essence, is the mother of the future. What was it about playing a villainous robot that intrigued you? Certainly it wasn't your lines. You speak perhaps twenty words in the whole movie.*

I have no ego for lines. I can say what I want on television when I do interviews. Besides, the Terminator didn't do his job by talking. He was there to terminate, and for that he was well equipped. He had guns, determination, coordination, and consistency. That's the only thing that counted for this particular part. *The Terminator* is just a futuristic fantasy—a movie that has no message—not a heavy movie, by any means.

Some critics found it overly violent.

The violence fits the story. If you really look at it, there're only two scenes that have actual blood. The hardest part of the whole thing was trying to establish me as a villain. Because of Conan, who was a heroic figure, and because of my own involvement in fitness—working with kids to put them in the right directions, getting them off alcohol and drugs and into fitness and weight training—most people have a pretty positive idea about me. The director, Jim Cameron, was very aware of this and wanted to make sure that the first few scenes really established me as the villain—you know, driving a child's toy truck, pushing in the door and shooting an innocent housewife in a very brutal way. We thought that established my meanness, but when we had the sneak preview, people were still with me halfway through the movie. Even at the end, they were saying, "All right, Arnold! Give 'em hell!" So obviously we were not brutal enough.

How do you think Hollywood regards your career today?

Differently than two months ago. Before, nobody in Hollywood would dare put me in a role like this. It took a young director like Jim Cameron and a young executive like Mike Medavoy [at Orion] with open minds to say, "Let's try something different. Let's make him a villain. Let's use him and not rely on his body throughout the whole film." Now I've gotten my first offer to do a comedy. That's what I call progress, because my idea was always that you should not muscle your way into making an audience accept you as a different character. You have to give people what they want, each time adding a new dimension so they can accept it slowly.

Do you think you're a good actor?

I'm good if given the right role. I know what I can do and can't. But I'm very happy with my work. I hope that each movie is on-the-job training and that they get better and better. It's like bodybuilding competition. The first few years I was competing, although I was on top, I still wasn't where I was toward the end of my competitive years. I hope I grow the same way in acting.

What intrigues you about acting?

Playing other characters. Then the joy when the movie comes out and you get the attention. I'm a Leo. Acting was a nice step from bodybuilding, because you get the same attention, only multiplied by a thousand.

Obviously The Terminator *upped your ante. How much money per film do you command nowadays?*

I never talk about money, because there are too many people out there who don't have it, so it would be wrong to throw it in front of them and make them feel different. But I can tell you that this movie automatically doubled my price. All of a sudden there's a tremendous need for everybody to have me in their films. But I'm booked up for the next year and a half. . . . I want to produce because the acting alone is not enough. By late next year, or the beginning of 1986, I will definitely be producing—acting in my own films.

Which will only make you wealthier. Most people don't realize that you are quite an entrepreneur, that through your bodybuilding business alone you've amassed a sizable fortune.

I make a living.

So it's safe to assume you're a millionaire?

A long time ago. But looking forward to it is always more fun than actually having it. It's nothing. When you look at your financial statement and it says your net worth is more than a million dollars—then what?

What do you spend your money on?

Art, things for the house, some on clothes, and then some on luxuries dealing with travel, vacations. I don't need a lot of money to live. I don't have strange luxuries.

Who are your heroes? You once said your goal was to be the next Burt Reynolds.

I've always loved Clint Eastwood, Burt Reynolds, and Charles Bronson because they were multimillion-dollar actors. Eastwood and Reynolds are always battling to see who [will] sell the most tickets, and I admire that, because the most important thing to me is to sell tickets. Then you have the power to do the kinds of projects you want. . . . John Wayne also ranks right on top of my heroes in film. But I'm also intrigued by Ronald Reagan. I admire him very much.

Why?

Because he's done the impossible—he's never gotten beaten in an election. He's really in touch with the people—which is why he wins.

You seem to put a high priority on savvy and smarts. How intelligent do you think Reagan really is?

Very bright. He doesn't get the credit for it because he's not as intellectual as David Stockman, Milton Friedman, or Alan Greenspan. But he has the ability to delegate, which is important. I met him last summer at the Republican convention. It was midnight—after the convention was over—and he'd just delivered a one-hour speech. I was already tired, and I'm thirty-seven. But he was right there, fast, quick with his answers—full of energy. He appears fifteen years younger than he is. God, when I'm his age I hope I'm still alive. He's remarkable. And I admire his relationship with Nancy. It's so sweet, the way he needs her always to be there, how kind he is to her, and the way they look at each other.

In many ways—your size, your name, your accent—you are unique. A less determined man might have found these insurmountable problems in terms of a movie career, but apparently none of them fazed you.

The worst thing I can be is the same as everybody else. I hate that. That's why I went into bodybuilding in the first place. It was the idea of taking the risk by yourself rather than with a whole team. It becomes a lonely thing in many ways, but you always know that there's one person you can rely on—yourself. You have to.

Your father, now deceased, played a very important role in your life, encouraging you to participate in sports at an early age. How would you describe your relationship with him?

Very solid, with a tremendous amount of discipline but also a lot of respect—respect enough to know the difference between father and child. There was a real wall; he established that wall. In America, parents want to be the child's friend, whereas my father had no patience for that. I always felt I could go to him with my problems, but I always knew that punishments could come up any minute if I screwed up. He used to say, "Sit in front of this book for two hours and read." Lots of times I didn't feel like reading but had to sit there. I would want a bicycle, and he would say, "Get it yourself. Work." It had a great effect on me, because I became very goal-oriented and determined—hungry to get my own things. But I loved my father. He was very affectionate.

What role did your mother play?

She designed the daily routine for my brother and me, let us know when we could play, when we had to study. She took care of the cleanliness of the house, and she was a fanatic. You could eat off the floors. The towels would have sharp corners when they were folded and stacked up. My father wore a shirt one time and she would wash it immediately. The household was a full-time occupation. I have one of the best mothers anybody could have.

We grew up in a very small village. Nobody had a phone except the village restaurant, the priest, and the police station, where my father worked. There was one TV set, in the village restaurant. My father made about two hundred and fifty dollars a month. We were middle-income. There was no refrigerator, no flushing toilet, no doctor—only a radio. For instance, if I got sick in the middle of the night, my mother or father would take me on his or her shoulders and walk over a big mountain for two hours to the main town of Graz. With luck, the doctor would be there.

Your brother was older, a boxer, and was killed at twenty-three in a car accident. Were you alike?

He was different. He was more the thinking type; I was more the physical type. My father was very tough on him. He was more sensitive than I. A typical Cancer—very creative. He did wonderful paintings as a child.

Having your only sibling die violently at such a young age—how did that affect you?

I felt terrible about it. He killed himself drunk-driving. Deep down, I expected something to happen, because he always lived more on the edge than I. I was always the safe guy. To me, sport was the number one thing, so I was living healthy.

Did his death change your life?

Now I wish he were here to enjoy all this with me. Back then I just brushed it off, and a year later my father died. That was a real big surprise. It was the brain, a stroke.

In Pumping Iron, *you said your mother called to tell you he'd died, and you did not go home for the funeral because it was just two months before a big competition and to do so might break your concentration. Your point was that to be a champion, one had to be capable of cutting off one's emotions before a competition. You said, "I trained myself to be totally cold and not have things go into my mind." I must say I found that a bit chilling.*

Yes, but that was not really my story; it was the story of the French bodybuilder. He was so into training that he did not attend his father's funeral. But George Butler, the director of *Pumping Iron,* felt that to introduce another character into the film at that point would be impossible, so I said, "Well, I have to say this as if it were mine. I have to tell this story so people will understand how intense sports gets and how cold you have to be to be competitive." So I said it was my story, but it was not. When my mother saw it, she was very pissed off, because she said I gave the wrong impression.

After graduation from high school in Graz, you went right into the army.

I signed up in the military for three years but stopped after one when it became apparent that what I really wanted to do was get into professional bodybuilding—buy a health club. I won my first championship, the European championships in bodybuilding, the junior division, after one month in the military. I weighed around two hundred and ten pounds. Those were fantastic growing years, especially in the army, because it was the first time I had meat every day. At home we only had it once a week. The meat made my body respond tremendously, because all of a sudden, it got all this protein.

After winning that first title, you obviously knew you had the goods.

No. I felt I did, but I still was not exposed to international competition. I was shocked when I went to the first international competition in London—at nineteen—for Mr. Universe and saw the Americans, tanned, muscular, perfect, having good poses. I did feel I was on a roll and had potential. I knew I would do anything to get to the top. I would train twelve hours a day, eat four hundred pounds of food per day, it didn't matter. When I was fifteen I had a clear vision of myself being onstage winning the Mr. Universe contest, and I was driven by that thought. It was a very spiritual thing in a way, because I had such faith in the route, the path, that it was never a question in my mind that I would make it. Every repetition I did, every set of exercises, every hour I spent on it, was always just one step closer to getting there. It was a wonderful experience to be taken by a higher force and just led there. I didn't say, "Oh my God, the pain. The torture." The pain is

just something that gets you there. Besides, it was just a matter of time. .
And it happened very quickly. I was twenty years old when I won Mr.
Universe.

*In 1968, you finally made it to America. You've said, however, that
1968 was also the worst year of your life. Why?*

Well, I came over here to compete in—and win, needless to say—a
Mr. Universe competition in Florida. But I lost, and that was a shock.
And then I had no money. I had only one gym bag with me, because
I did not plan to move here at that point. I was kind of like a helpless
kid, in a way. It was a real growing-up experience. Finally, I came out
to California. When you're involved in sports, you find people right
away who have the same goals as you do. I walked into a bodybuilding
gym, and everybody said, "Oh, hi, Arnold. How are you?" It was very
pleasant. The only frustrating thing was the language problem. I knew
English, but I couldn't read the paper, because the vocabulary was too
sophisticated. So I said, "To hell with this. I'm going to get with it."
I went to Santa Monica College and took English, grammar, spelling,
and writing classes. I was lonely, because with the language barrier you
couldn't establish the same friendships you had back home. But that
was good. I believe very much in the struggle. It builds character.

In 1975 you gave up competitive bodybuilding. Why?

I was sick and tired of it. But it happened slowly. So I said to myself,
"If that isn't there, get out." But I couldn't, because I didn't have a
replacement for it. I was starting my businesses, and I thought I would
still like to win six Mr. Olympia contests to establish a record that
would be hard to beat. Of course, in 1980 I came back and won the
seventh Mr. Olympia contest after five years in retirement. Actually,
I wanted to retire in 1974, but George Butler came to see me and said
that he wanted to do *Pumping Iron* and that the only way we'd get
financing was if I was in it. So he offered me some money, a percentage
of the film, and asked if I could help him raise money and actively
participate in putting it together. So that's what we did.

Pumping Iron turned you into a hero overnight. The two Conan *films
and* The Terminator *have all made money. Still, your critics contend*

that due to your size and accent, yours will be a limited career, that your physical range far exceeds your emotional.

Who knows? If your physical appearance is dominant, people think you lack emotions. I'm happy others are concerned, because I'm not. As far as I'm concerned, I will, in a few years, be where the top people are now—whether it's Eastwood, Stallone, or Redford—anyone who makes the top salary. I feel absolutely convinced that's where I will be.

Are you tolerant of people who don't share your drive?

Yes, but I'm not tolerant of people who are not efficient. When I work, it has to be with people who are also hungry, driven, want to work.

For the past seven years, you've been dating CBS reporter Maria Shriver. Obviously, you like American women.

Since I've been in America, I've come to appreciate women much more, because I have begun to understand their problems. I love American women because they are independent. I like a woman to be smart. I also love humorous people.

When you first met Maria, at the Robert F. Kennedy Tennis Tournament in New York in 1977, what intrigued you about her? Was it instantaneous attraction?

No—it started very slowly. I thought she was funny and beautiful, so I paid attention to her, but it was nothing serious. That weekend I was invited to go up to Hyannis Port, and I got to know her better, but it was still just one of those relationships where you say, "I'll see you next month when I'm in New York." That's how it started. Not intense, just very natural.

When did it become obvious that you were falling in love?

About a year later. Halloween. I was in Washington on my book tour, and she picked me up in the hotel lobby. She was dressed up all goofy as some kind of gypsy, wearing a lot of weird earrings and stuff, and I thought, "God, this girl is just too much." I loved that. She was also so witty, so "on" that night. I went to Europe then and thought about her a lot. I had a feeling it was reciprocal.

Walking into the Kennedy family, particularly when you're there courting one of the daughters, could be a little intimidating.

Initially, maybe I was a little intimidated, but not after I got there. That first weekend when I went to Hyannis Port, I met just about everybody, and they were all very warm and friendly. Each time I visited after that—even when a stronger relationship between Maria and me was developing—nothing changed. I think they admired me also—that I had accomplished certain things on my own. I was not just some kid running around. [*Laughs.*] It would be tough to walk in there and not have anything going for yourself. But really there is no approving or disapproving in the Shriver house. It's simply, What Maria likes, they will support, so they supported her and they supported me. Although the press wrote many times that they were dissatisfied that we were going out, that they would rather have her with some Washington lawyer, that was never expressed to me. I was always received with warmth and respect.

How do the Kennedys—the premier American Democrats—feel about your being a Republican?

The advantage of being a liberal is that you're open-minded. And they are. There's no animosity. I never argue politics with Maria, because I totally understand that for her to be Republican, having grown up as she did, would be very unusual. My upbringing was different from hers. With my drive toward business, I am more comfortable with an Adam Smith philosophy than with Keynesian theory. But no one is wrong. That is her belief; this is mine.

If you and Maria don't share political beliefs, then what do you have in common?

We ask each other that. [*Laughs.*] We have a lot in common: the idea of family, religion—we're both Catholics—and even politics. We think the same things ought to be done in this country—only our means on how to get them done differ. Professionally, we believe you have to achieve certain things in life, go after them, be dedicated to your profession, and work hard. We're both athletically inclined—love horseback riding, skiing, running, exercising. We both love travel, educating ourselves, reading books and then discussing what we've read. In some ways we are opposites, but that just makes things spicy. Our relationship, I always say, is spicy.

Do you think you'll get married?

Someday we will, yes. We have no plans now. There is no push. Her family doesn't create a pressure. We don't live together. She has her own apartment, I have my own house. Her parents are really the ideal parents to have if you're dating a girl, because they are not blindly behind her. They tell her many times, "I think Arnold has a point. I think he's right." I respect Maria, that she comes from a good family background. When you see that, it has an effect on how you look at the girl.

Do you want to have children?

Oh, absolutely. One day.

You certainly seem to be cutting a much more conservative image nowadays. In the early days, in Pumping Iron *for instance, you were constantly equating bodybuilding with sex, and the finale of the documentary saw you partying away with joint in hand.*

In *Pumping Iron,* when you saw me getting stoned, it was all designed, very thoroughly, to sell the idea of bodybuilding. If you tell people that pumping up feels as good as sex, that you can eat all the cake you want, get stoned, have a good time, and everybody will love you—well, those are sell statements. Sex is something everybody understands, so I compared bodybuilding with sex. In the mid-seventies, my job was to sell bodybuilding to the general public. And I did.

I must say you seem impossibly cheery. Do you ever get depressed?

Yeah. When things don't go the way I want, I get depressed. But I am not a self-analytical person by any means. I don't ask myself why I'm depressed. I don't care, as long as I can get out of it eventually. I'm not going to analyze myself or go to shrinks. I'm totally against those things. To me, the more you analyze, intellectualize, the less you enjoy. Can you imagine going through sex like that? You have to do things with instinct. It's the same with training, business, acting. You can't always expect to be "on"; you just have to take your body and mind and improvise, because it's always different.

When you look at your life now, how far you've come from Graz, Austria, does it surprise you?

Yeah, when I think about it. But I don't think about it that much. I just go on. You have to always immediately make up a new goal— always stay hungry.

Both competitive bodybuilding and acting require a large ego to fuel their respective advancements. With so much success in both fields, you must have an ego as big as your biceps. Any trouble keeping it in check?

You need a big ego to do big things. It's the ego that makes the drive. [*Laughs.*] But I don't have to make an effort to keep my ego in check, because simply going to the gym will do that. No matter how good you think you are, in the gym I am put back to where I was at fifteen—back to the same struggle. There is no help. No comfort. One hundred pounds will always be one hundred pounds. [*Laughs.*] It will never give you a break.

ESQUIRE

December 1986

**"The sexiest thing in the world
is to be totally naked
with your wedding band on."**

Debra Winger paced, her face contorted as she repeatedly raked her
fingers through her chestnut hair. "God, I know I'm going to wake up
tomorrow and regret everything I'm saying," she moaned. "But I can't
help but tell the truth. That's why I never do these things."

She stopped to dig out another filterless Camel from the already
pulverized pack. She lit it, inhaled deeply, and then abruptly changed
gears.

"Do you know Tom Brokaw?" she asked.

"Of course," I said. She knew I worked for NBC.

"What's he like?"

"Charming, smart, funny."

"I knew it." She smiled with secret satisfaction. "You know, I had
the biggest crush on him. When I lived in Los Angeles I used to run
home every day at three-thirty just to watch him on the news. In fact,

in college, I once seduced one of my professors just because he looked like him. And then, every time I fucked this guy, I closed my eyes and pretended I was fucking Tom Brokaw."

Eventually, I told this story to Brokaw.

He was not displeased.

Debra Winger has no shortage of opinions—nor fear in voicing them. She might not like doing interviews, but once there, she gives herself to it—as she does to everything else—uncompromisingly. She is very smart, very funny, and very candid. She shoots from the hip and takes the consequences.

Which were widespread in the case of this interview. Her unusually outspoken assessments of the directors and actors with whom she'd worked set Hollywood on its head. (Three years later, when I finally met Jim Brooks, who directed Winger in *Terms of Endearment* and whom she affectionately described in the piece as "crude, but smart crude," he was still smarting: "I called her up and said, 'What do you mean I'm . . . crude?' ")

To the public, Winger is the bad girl who's been around, who brags she can "drink a sailor under the table," chain-smokes, swears like a minor league ballplayer, and admits she finds women "untrustworthy." Her tough, almost defiantly macho stance has not prevented her from creating, on film, some of the earthiest, most emotionally available women of the decade.

When she was twenty-five, *Urban Cowboy* established her as a performer with uncommon charm and intelligence, as well as a sexual energy that could tame even the most ferocious mechanical bull—or leading man. And she's had some of the best: John Travolta, Nick Nolte, Richard Gere, and Robert Redford. She is, perhaps, best loved for her portrayal of Emma Greenway Horton in *Terms of Endearment,* where she transformed a harried middle-class mother into an American Everywoman. In an era of noble screen women, from Streep to Fields to Fonda, she remains relentlessly flawed and vulnerable. "There's nothing sullen or closed about her," critic Pauline Kael once observed. "She's the major reason to go on seeing movies in the eighties."

But the last word on Winger comes from her pal Jack Nicholson, who always seems to have the last word:

"She's real smart, very dedicated, and extremely resourceful about her work. You put up with her contentiousness because there is always something at the bottom. You get something you wouldn't get otherwise unless you took the trip with her. The girl's got boom."

—

You know, of course, that you have a reputation for being difficult to work with?

I like that reputation because it keeps weak people at arm's length. My argument for that is, if I'm so difficult, why are directors working with me over and over—with, that is, the exception of two: Taylor Hackford [*An Officer and a Gentleman*] and Ivan Reitman [*Legal Eagles*], who will never see my acting ability again.

Why won't you work with Taylor Hackford again?

Oh, he's just an animal. The same thing with Ivan—they're both just crude. Jim Brooks is crude, but smart crude. His sarcasm stings you but it makes you grow. When you're working, no matter how thorough you are, you're vulnerable. I don't need to be worshiped; I just need a little respect.

Is that why you often clash with directors on the set?

I do admit to being challenging, but it's always for the work, it's never personal. I will walk out on a scene [that's] all lit and ready to go if it's not happening. Just because we're on schedule is no reason to shoot bad acting. Someone once said to me, "You're inconsiderate." And I said, "Inconsiderate? Bad acting is the ultimate inconsideration." It's a collective slap to a million faces at the same time. So I'm not afraid of disagreeing—it makes a better scene. It means something is coming to life. Someone once used the word *friction* for what happens, and I say yes, because friction produces heat and you always want heat on the screen. And I don't mean that in sexual terms.

It's well known that you've lived through a "risk-and-raunch phase," as someone put it. Were you in fact that wild?

[*Grins.*] Ask Jack [Nicholson]. [*Belly laugh.*] I've always had to find things out for myself, could never settle for anyone else's knowledge. But I was just looking for fun. It just took *more* for me to have fun—more danger, more turmoil, more everything.

More men, too, huh?

If a man's with a woman, it's not assumed he's sleeping with her, but if a woman's with a man, it's always assumed. When a man is seen with a lot of women it's "Ooh, which one did he grace?" But if a woman is seen with a lot of men, she's just a slut. I'm not a wild sex maniac, but most of my friends do happen to be men. I have a couple of close women friends, but for the most part I find women untrustworthy. Look, I talk man talk. I like to get right down to it, so some women find me offensive—too down and dirty.

Was Shirley MacLaine one of them?

Different worlds. She just behaved badly—like she was competing with me [on the set of *Terms of Endearment*]. I understand that Shirley grew up in a different era, when women had flesh under their fingernails from competing with one another, but I'm not like that. She gave me her book *Out on a Limb* to read as if she had discovered reincarnation. I said, "Shirl, don't give me your book unless you want an honest opinion." And she said, "I do." When I finished it, I said, "My mom will like it very much. It's old news to me. I don't want to hear who you fuck, and I don't think they want to hear it, either." At one point I told her, "Why don't you just strap a camera on your arm and photograph your life? That way you'll circumvent three steps: living your life, writing the book, and then doing the movie of the book." It's sick.

Shirley and you were both nominated for an Oscar for your performances in the movie. She won, of course, and in her acceptance speech referred to your "turbulent brilliance." How did you feel about that?

I thought, Can't you just say, "Thanks, bitch"? [*Laughs.*] She sent me a T-shirt two days after the awards that said: TURBULENT MEANS GREAT. That's for me to wear in the privacy of my home, but for three hundred and fifty million people she'll say I'm "turbulent." I was actually forever grateful when she won because I thought that would shut her up for a while. Imagine my dismay when she just kept having fiftieth birthdays and doing interviews. Jack Nicholson called me up for her second fiftieth and said, "Didn't we celebrate her fiftieth birthday in Texas?"

Thanks to Terms of Endearment, *you and Nicholson became close friends. I asked him to describe you and he said, "She's a lot like me." What do you think he means?*

That's the source of our friendship. We live through each other. If I was a guy, I'd be like him, and he thinks that if he were my age, in my body, I'm what he'd be. We have the same take on life. Jack and I went right to friendship: "I know your story, you know mine; let's not dick around."

Well . . . what was the story with you and the governor of Nebraska? Who ended it, you or [now Senator] Bob Kerrey?

I love Bob and I still stay in contact, but I was the one who made the decision to break it off, although we both came out of it better human beings. And I think he definitely knows that now, but at first he was having a hard time. Plus, he's in the public eye. I had to call him, and he had to have a press conference about it. It's horseshit, but I knew it would happen that way.

It seems only fitting. You two met at a press conference, didn't you?

I was going to Lincoln [to film *Terms of Endearment*] on the train because I wouldn't fly. My press agent told me that since this was the first movie shot in Nebraska in a long time, they were going to meet me. I said, "I am not getting off the train and going to a press conference." She said, "You have to. The governor's going to be there." I said, "Oh, great. The governor of the frigging state's going to be there." And she said, "He's gorgeous, he's single, and you're going to love it." I had no shoes with me. So I said, "I can't go. I have no shoes." My press agent then held up a pair of shoes that were a half size too tight. She said, "You're going." I knew I had to because she had backed herself into something and it was her ass. But I was so pissed. Then Bob called for dinner and I refused every time. One time Jim Brooks was in my trailer when I was returning his call, saying I wouldn't have dinner. Brooks said, "You should go. This man was in the war. You should hear his stories. Who do you think you are?" Brooks totally intimidated me. So I said yes. And after Bob and I walked for five hours over the town of Lincoln, we decided we had things to talk about.

Did you meet Tim Hutton before or after Bob Kerrey?

We met about three years ago, and there was a lot of electricity between us—but we ran. About six months ago we got together and knew instantly it was everything or nothing. It didn't make sense *not* to get married. What were we testing by living together?

So you like being married?

A lot. No one could ever have convinced me that it would change things the way it does. When I used to think about marriage, I thought, When the time comes, I'll make a decision—yes or no. But it didn't come from that place. It came from feeling, You either do this or *die.* It's not a choice. Afterward, I had to answer to a lot of people who said, "What are you doing?" because I had been going along with a philosophy that marriage didn't fit into. But I said, "Sorry, life interceded. And I love it." My married friends told me that when you get married it changes things, and I said, "That's ridiculous." [*Laughs.*] But it's true. It changes everything in a wonderful way.

How has it changed your life?

When we were living together, which we did, privately—no one knew—I had the same commitment. But with marriage you relax. You just *relax.* It's total, complete, unconditional love for the rest of your life. If I didn't feel that way I wouldn't be married, because you're starting your family and your family is built on that. It's great because I've always needed a mate in my life. I moved away from home when I was fifteen, so with the exception of two and a half years when I lived with someone, I've spent the last fifteen years alone. But now it's "Okay, let's go in there. We can open that door together." It's the hottest thing I've ever done in my life. I will say, candidly, that the sexiest thing in the world is to be totally naked with your wedding band on.

Can you explain why this passion overcame you now?

Fate gets up very early in the morning, and it goes to sleep very late at night, and it mostly pays attention to those people who try to nudge it a little bit.

Let's talk about your family. Your grandparents were Orthodox Jews, and you lived with them in Cleveland every summer from the age of six. Did you like keeping kosher?

I loved it. I thought my mother was going to burn in hell when she moved to California and became Conservative. I was a complete freak, fanatical about it. I still love Jewish traditions, although not arbitrarily—and I don't believe in organized religion. My mother's parents had a big influence on me. My grandfather just died this year. He was eighty-six but still driving, still working. I took his death really hard. He lived his life so beautifully. He was the fix-it man—always fixing the neighborhood kids' toys. The day after he died, a little boy knocked on the door with a broken toy and said, "Papa, fix it." He was so great in his life that it gives you a very clear sense of what greatness is: It's not about fame, fortune, how many people you reach. It's about the quality of your life.

His death changed me. It gave me this freedom. My grandfather was one of the few people in the family I always wanted to please. The little girl in me still lived as long as he lived. When he went, I just didn't have very many things to answer to anymore, so anybody who disapproved of my marriage didn't matter because my grandfather wasn't alive. I was married two months after my grandfather died. My grandmother and I haven't talked for a long time. Because Tim's not Jewish, she didn't even come to the wedding.

This isn't the first time you've broken the rules. Yet it doesn't seem to slow you down, not now or when you were a kid. You graduated high school when you were fifteen.

I skipped two grades. I was bored with school. I was a fuckup. I dropped out for most of the eleventh grade. I used to take my books, walk down the street with my mother—she went to work at the same time—and when she turned the corner I'd wave and go to Cal State Northridge, sit in the library all day, and read Nietzsche. My parents never found out. Whenever the principal called, I answered—I had a very deep voice—and I'd say, "I'm Mrs. Winger. Debra's enrolled at another school." At the end of the year I managed to get through only because I went to two teachers and told them I'd write huge papers.

Then you went to Israel, right?

Yeah, I'd worked as a waitress since I was fourteen so I had all this money saved up. I hooked up with a group going to Israel and dropped them when I got there. I lived on a kibbutz and ended up in GADNA, the children's training army, which you can join right out of high school. You can get very worked up in Israel, especially then, when I was only fifteen and everybody was telling me that this was my home-land. I was always trying to figure out why it had to be here—in the middle of the desert—but as a Jew you get used to that. [*Laughs.*] The army was a game. I carried an Uzi around, but it wasn't loaded. It was a time of innocence to some degree, but there was a feeling that you were fighting for your very life and the life of your people. Three weeks into it we were up in the hills above Tel Aviv doing night maneuvers. They were teaching us how to advance behind smoke screens. We'd pull a grenade, throw it, and advance. Our instructor pulled a grenade; it sparked and started a fire. And because of this stupid maneuver, this stupid little training group of children, I watched, with my own eyes, four forests burn down—forests my aunt, uncle, and grandparents had sent money to build. I saw grown men on their knees crying because everything they had worked for was gone. I hated what I saw, so I ran away, went AWOL. I caught a flatboat to the Grecian islands. There was no moon, so you couldn't see the edge of the boat. You just laid there and peed in your pants all night because if you got up, you might fall off. From there I went back home. It's interesting to talk about now, but then it was dirty and scary and hard. There were moments of romanticism, but I could've had them if I'd flown first class and sat in a café in Paris. [*Laughs.*]

Where do you think your spirit of adventure came from?

Not my parents. They don't travel at all. I don't know. I know one story about my grandfather that sounds like me. When he and my grandmother first got married, he had the first Harley-Davidson ever made. And they had this huge fight, and he got on the Harley and rode out to California. He said to me once, "I only made one mistake. I went back." They were married for sixty-five years.

That does sound like you—wild but willing to settle down. When did

*you decide to become an actress? I heard it had something to do with
an out-of-body experience.*

I was working at Magic Mountain amusement park as a teenage troll.
I was under one of those costumes shaking hands with little brats who
were sticking things up my top and saying, "There's a person under
there." They'd poke rattail combs [at me] and say, "Look, George,
that's where their eyes are." They were transporting me from one side
of the park to the other, and I got into a little Cushman car—

And you fell out.

Yeah, I fell on my head, and then my body collapsed on top of me.
I had a cerebral hemorrhage and was paralyzed on the right side. That
was when my life/death moment happened. I saw myself leaving my
body, and as I got farther and farther away, I was more invisible. All
this happened in a split second, a momentless moment when you knew
there was a lot of pain ahead of you and it'd be easy just to let go. But
whatever it was—that need that said I wasn't finished here yet—took
over. The reports of the accident said I had an involuntary muscle
reaction and my arm shot up. My arm shot up because I pulled myself
back. I pulled myself back into my body—that was the moment of
decision. I was in a coma but realized I was paralyzed. Don't ever trust
anything anyone says about a coma. A coma is just suspended anima-
tion. You're still there. I could hear my mother wailing. When I finally
woke up, it was to tell her to shut up. I didn't really want to wake up,
because as long as I could stay floating, I wasn't in pain. I knew that
once I opened my eyes, the trade-off would be a lot of pain, because
my body was a mess. When I told my parents I was going to be fine
they thought it was just me being optimistic, because the doctors were
so negative. I said, "No, no. I'm in my body. I know. They don't know.
They're outside trying to read signs." It was harder on my parents than
on me.

Did you fear you'd be crippled?

I pretty much thought I'd be blind. I studied Braille for a while. I
thought, Maybe it's my karma. [*Laughs.*] When I was a little kid I
thought people would love me more if I were blind or had something
wrong with me. I thought I was getting paid back for wishing it on

myself. You can imagine the guilt I had. Anyway, during that year I said, "If I ever get out of here alive, I'm going to do exactly what I want to do—act full-time." I even thought I would be the first blind actress—just put speed bumps on the edge of the stage so I don't fall off. [*Laughs.*]

How did your parents react to the news that you were dropping out of Cal State to pursue acting?

When I announced I was going to act for a living, my father told me the most enlightening thing. It sounds terrible, but he meant it with all the love in his heart. To them, acting was a hobby; you just didn't do it for a living. Finally, in frustration, my father said, "You can't be a movie star. Movie stars are beautiful." And I said, "Okay, then. I'll be an actress."

Did it hurt you when your father said that?

No, because he was being honest, and I agreed with him. I was nothing special. There was no reason for my parents to believe I could become an actress. No one in our family had ever done this. But I had always had this secret life. In that life, I would go in, close my bedroom door, and act. My decision was a totally selfish one. I acted because I dug it. It was the only thing that made me feel like I was growing as a human inside myself. I didn't think I would ever get paid to do it. I thought I would have to beg to do theater. I never expected to be successful. I never—in a million years—imagined I'd be here.

Like a lot of actors, you started out doing commercials, right?

No, I did a documentary for the police department on why you shouldn't hitchhike. It was called *Vickie the Hitchhiker.* They called me up one day and said they were going to show it, and would I like to see it. And I said, "Oh sure." It was the first thing I ever did on film since home movies. My mother was working, but my father could get free. So he came down. In the movie, a guy picks me up and he tries to rape me and he kills me. He hits me over the head with a rock and there's blood. I decided to die with my eyes open. That was a big choice. And when the lights came on, my father was gone. And I ran out the door and he was in the bathroom. . . . So that was the first time

I thought, Maybe I'm a good actress. You know, If he believed it, maybe I'm good.

It wasn't long before you were doing TV. Your most notable stint was as the younger sister of Wonder Woman. *Somehow I can't see Lynda Carter and you as soul mates.*

Lynda Carter was just a mannequin—only concerned with the way she looked and the fact that I wouldn't wear the same eye makeup as she did. The whole thing was a nightmare. I did two shows and quit. I always go into work thinking I'm going to make something classic out of it, and I thought I was doing a vintage comic strip. I did research, studied the comic strip, believed it could've been great—this camp classic of a cartoon—even though we had to say things like "Wow" and "Golly gee." Then I got to the set and it's "No, no, just do the circle and turn into flames." I said, "This isn't acting. This is prostitution. I'm getting out." But they wouldn't let me out of my six-year contract. So I used all the money I'd made on lawyers, trying to find a loophole. Finally, they changed networks and it screwed up my contract so I was out. And headed for movies.

Urban Cowboy *was the movie that made you a star. In retrospect, how does it strike you today?*

I love it. It was the opening of everything because of the way Jim Bridges worked—the freedom, the collaboration, the end product. It was a slice of life, that movie. I'm real proud of it.

Robert Evans, who co-produced the film, was dead set against you for the role of Sissy, wasn't he?

Yeah, his final line after watching my screen test was "I wouldn't fuck her with a ten-foot pole." So when he showed up on the set, I said to him, "See these marks?" "What marks?" he said—he was standing far away. "These marks. They're from ten-foot poles. Somebody bothered, okay?" [*Laughs.*] Michael Eisner, who was president of Paramount [and is now CEO and chairman of the board of the Walt Disney Company], said, "She's too Jewish for that role. I went to dance school with girls like that." What he was doing in dance school we won't even ask.

Your career has brought you together with some of the sexiest men in the world. How was working with John Travolta?

John's full of talent and magnetism. I believe in him and love him as a human. At that time I probably was a lot less compassionate about his problems than I would like to think of myself as being. But it was good for me. I was right out of the pen, and I saw someone facing all that stuff and said, "I never want to be tortured the way he is." I've avoided a lot of the traps of stardom because of what I saw John go through.

Did Nick Nolte seem to have any of those problems?

The only problem was keeping up with him. He's just a good ol' boy. [*Laughs.*] At that time, cocktail hour began about ten A.M. But I kept up! [*Laughs.*] I lived in my trailer on the lot at MGM—Eloise at the Plaza. I'd been living in the Chateau Marmont for two years until I said, "This is silly. I'll just stay in the trailer. The guard is there—it's safer than the Chateau." So I moved in. About four nights [later] I heard a noise and come out in my pajamas and robe. I saw a light in Nick's trailer, and there he is struggling with two paper bags of clothes. I said, "What are you doing?" "I'm moving in. My wife kicked me out." So we were neighbors. There was this twenty-four-hour bowling alley across from MGM. We used to go there, bowl all night, and then come back for our six A.M. call. But that was in my younger, wilder days.

Were things just as crazy with Richard Gere?

He was a brick wall. He keeps saying nice things about me, and I don't know the man so I shouldn't say mean things about him, but *An Officer and a Gentleman* was a real bad time for all of us. We did whatever we had to do to survive. The producer was the only living person I had contact with, and he was a total pig.

Sounds like fun.

I was surrounded by a lot of macho energy on that film. And there was no collaboration. I got to the point where I'd just play dumb. "You want me to do that? Gee, I don't know. I just can't stop crying. I guess I'll have to cry in this scene." Stupid.

You and Gere had some very intimate love scenes. How did you manage to play them with so little communication going on between you?

It was tough. For instance, in the love scene in bed with Richard, I'm crying. I let myself cry because I know it looks very sexual—a woman crying when she's in bed with a man. So there I am, on top of him, tears coming out of my eyes and people thinking it's because I'm so moved, when actually I'm really crying because I'm so unhappy. I'm thinking, "Oh, God, my career is over, but keep pumpin', honey"—as the sign on the casting director's ceiling says, YOU'VE GOT THE JOB. [*Laughs.*]

You've starred in only six films, and already you've been nominated for two Oscars. That's a pretty impressive batting average. Yet you've been down on more than a few of your movies, including your most recent, Legal Eagles.

I don't regret doing it, but I don't think it stands on its own against good films. It was a nightmare to make. Shooting was supposed to be ten weeks, and it went on for four months. And it was fat—almost forty million dollars—and, politically, I'm opposed to that kind of money unless it's an epic. I took my salary and left.

But at least you got to be Robert Redford's leading lady. How was it?

Everybody was waiting for total disaster, but we got along great. We're so different. I think he was intrigued, and I liked the fact that he was older and set in his ways so I could rouse him up a little bit. I called him the Unnatural, which got him upset [*laughs*], although the people who work for him call him God. When we were shooting, there were times he was a bit diplomatic for my taste, but he was definitely a gentleman.

Was he as disgruntled about Legal Eagles *as you?*

Yeah, but he never said anything. At the end of shooting we both said we'd still like to do a comedy together. [*Laughs.*]

Do you think there are a lot of misconceptions about you?

Actually, I don't think there are any. When I see these things about me . . . that I'm trouble—yeah, that's true . . . or that I'm loud sometimes—yeah . . . or that I ran around—yeah, that's right . . . that I give directors problems . . . I do. I don't feel misunderstood. I have no complaints.

How refreshing. You may be the only movie star who doesn't feel that fame and the press have done her in.

I don't find the media intrusive in my life. I believe you get exactly what you ask for. I've never been attacked by the *National Enquirer.* I've had ratty little things printed—as soon as you get married, you're pregnant—but that comes with the territory. It's so easy to be private. People follow you home, you go around the block and don't complain about it. You say, "Good, next week maybe they'll go and see my movie."

Your movies, sure. But not you. You've said that we will never see the real you on camera. Why?

Because that's not what I do. I'm a character actress. My takes on life are not on film. That's egoistic. I play parts that are written; they're not monologues. I have no ax to grind. I'm obviously living enough in life to get off. I don't have to proselytize my own thing. I'm not attracted to playing anything close to myself.

Don't a lot of American actors feel comfortable only in that role?

I think it's just necessary to drop that. Otherwise, you become a personality, not an actor. And then you get older, and it sours on you. You're afraid to lose that thing that gets associated with your youth and you get all messed up. You can't play parts that are right for you at that time in your life because you can't see yourself clearly. So I never want to be like that. I'm afraid of that.

Will that self ever be revealed another way? Will we ever see a Debra Winger autobiography?

No. [*Loud laugh.*] I've been offered a lot of money to do one [*laughs*], but I've been paid more not to.

I just stopped to think about the fact that most of the big actresses today—Meryl and Jessica and Sally—are . . .

Not Jewish. *Goy* heaven. Those are the girls that my older brother wasn't allowed to go out with.

Would your brother be allowed to go out with a girl like you? You do realize that many men find you very sexy?

That is just hysterical to me, because I don't come from that place at all. If you're simply honest about your emotions onscreen, then it somehow gets translated as sexy. The first time this discrepancy hit me was the way I was perceived in the bull-ride scene in *Urban Cowboy.* I mean, everybody talked about this thing. Pauline Kael wrote a review so graphic that I couldn't go out of the house for two weeks because I was so embarrassed. When I did that scene I wasn't thinking sexually. I was just totally hurt. I was trying to make John Travolta jealous. Now maybe those emotions came out low-rent because of the character I was playing, but I was hurting and I couldn't hide it. When I was riding the bull I was in total pain. If you're too much in love, too much anything, you can't hide it. I don't believe in sexually explicit scenes, because the words mean what they say—explicit about sex. There's nothing I have to say about that. Go see a porno film if you want to see explicit sex. But if you want to see explicit emotion—and maybe you are kissing when you have this explicit emotion—then I'm game. That's interesting to me because in life we're hardly ever doing the thing that we're trying to say. When those times do happen, that's wonderful. That's making love and that's for your private life.

Along those lines, you once said that you love feeling sweaty and sticky. Is that still true?

Still true. Because it usually means you're either fucking or working—and what else is there?

**"This industry never has been,
and I guess never will be,
overpopulated with brilliance."**

All right. Let's get it out of the way right up top. The hair. Ted Koppel's hair. Is it really his? Does that thatch of thick red stuff really belong to him? "Listen, is that his real hair?" was the inevitable question, inevitably asked by men with very little of their own. Well, I'm here to report that indeed it is. Ted's Own Hair.

What surprised me most about Koppel, after the hair, was his car. It was a sporty little Mercedes convertible, very jazzy, very unexpected. On our second day together Koppel suggested we talk over dinner in a Vietnamese restaurant. We were waiting in the parking lot when the attendant came flying up the ramp in this red roadster with the top down. "Is that yours?" I asked with amazement. "Yes," he replied with pride. He gunned down Connecticut Avenue. As we passed someone he knew he honked and waved. "Collins," Koppel cracked, "you've no idea what it's doing for my image to be seen driving around town with a blonde." Or for mine, I thought, to be seen with this particular redhead.

Need I tell you the thought of interviewing Ted Koppel was . . . daunting . . . nervous-making . . . scary? I can't remember whose idea it was, mine or Ed Kosner's, the editor/publisher of *New York* magazine, but one day over lunch one of us thought it up, and the next thing I knew I was writing letters, waiting for replies (the guy wasn't exactly campaigning to get himself on the cover of *New York*), and negotiating for time with the ABC press office. I needed ten hours, I told them.

"Ten hours?" Koppel snorted.

"Okay, eight," I conceded.

"Try six," he countered.

"What? And cramp my style? All right, all right," I finally said, confident I could squeeze in more time somewhere.

Prepping for the interview took over my life. I tracked down professors at Syracuse University, where Koppel had been an undergraduate, and at Stanford, where he picked up a master's. I talked to other reporters—friends, fans, foes—and I worried. A lot. By the time I arrived in Washington I was a Koppel compendium. For an interviewer, questioning Koppel is like playing center court at Wimbledon. I had to be ready.

Not surprisingly, he was a formidable partner. Direct, no-nonsense, not one to suffer fools gladly, Koppel also possessed quirky personal charm, a dry, wicked wit, and a playfulness one might not expect from the nation's inquisitor. And he is more attractive in person. Sexy, actually. He says he jogs religiously, despite a heavy cigarette habit, though I pass both on secondhand, since I saw him run neither nor smoke.

Our conversations took place, for the most part, in his *Nightline* office in Washington. I sat on the sofa, Koppel in an easy chair, during three two-hour-plus exchanges. This was interviewing at its most fun—a fast-paced intellectual volley. I served, he returned; he went to the net, I aimed for the baseline. Outside his door, the constant buzz of the *Nightline* world prevailed.

One night I watched him in action from the vantage point of the vacant Washington bureau newsroom abutting his own roost. Koppel's desk is a plywood facade. The large screen on which viewers see Jesse Jackson or James Baker is a technological mirage. In the studio, the "key screen," as it's called, is a giant scrim affair, rather like a pool table top tacked on a wall, void of actual picture. The image you see at home is created in the control room. Koppel himself watches his guests on three studio monitors planted below the "key."

Sometime after 11 P.M., Koppel dons his suit jacket and heads to the studio from his office. The half hour before airtime, he types his introduction and reviews research, preparing for the moment when "Good evening . . . I'm Ted Koppel" signals that one of America's most respected reporters is on the job. Yet even then Koppel is still on deadline, for it's often only during the six-minute background piece, as he studies the faces of his guests (he can see them, but they cannot see him), that the interview finally gels.

As for our interview, when the three days together were finished and I announced I'd asked my last question, Koppel started to laugh.

"Collins, this is the cheapest psychoanalysis I've ever had."

———

What is the trick to Nightline? *What makes six million people tune in to a news program that keeps them awake until midnight?*

One of the things that makes *Nightline* work is that we focus on one subject; another is that it's live; and a third is that we'll change our program as late as need be in order to do something more interesting than we'd planned. We've even changed the show after we've gone on the air. For example, remember when they went to get the hostages out? We had another program on that night. But when I got home about twelve-thirty, the phone was ringing, and they said, "The White House just announced this rescue attempt." I came racing back, and by two-thirty A.M. we did another show for the West Coast. We've literally changed the show as it's been on the air and as late as ten o'clock at night.

What part do you play in making Nightline *work?*

I think I have a good sense of when people are evasive or getting boring. I also have the necessary lack of tact to cut in at that point and let them know.

Nightline, which officially began in March of 1980, was the offshoot of The Iran Crisis: America Held Hostage, *the nightly news update started by ABC News in 1979. The success of both programs surprised most television news executives, who felt there was no audience for a serious news show at eleven-thirty p.m. What need did—does—*Nightline *fulfill?*

First, there is a fairly substantial group of Americans who are not home at seven o'clock in the evening and therefore cannot watch the news. And even though they know that *Nightline* is essentially a one-subject-a-night program, they also know that if something really important happens, we'll have it. Then there's another fairly large group that wants something more than they get on the local or national news programs at seven P.M. Beyond that, there are the times when there's a running news story—the hostage crisis, the Falklands, the marines in Lebanon—when we fill the greatest need of all. And there's also one other thing—and now I'm feeding you back what I get from others. There's a large group of people in America who feel frustrated by their inability to ever challenge authority. And I think they see in me someone who, within the boundaries of good manners and taste, will challenge people if someone is being evasive or arrogant . . . if someone is just eating them alive.

Although you were born in Lancashire, England, your parents were German Jews who escaped Nazi Germany. What were the circumstances under which they left Germany?

My father had been in prison at least once. Not a camp, just an ordinary garden-variety prison cell. But he was taken prisoner because he was Jewish. He had some influential friends who said to him, "The writing's on the wall; you'd better leave," and helped him get out. That was 1938.

What was your father's profession?

There were three large rubber-tire factories in Germany, and my father had one of them. He was fairly well-to-do when he left Germany, having been invited by the then British Home Secretary to open up another factory in Lancashire. My father was forty-four and my mother forty when I was born. She was very artistic, a piano player and beautiful singer who sang with Paul Hindemith at the time of the great German composers and conductors. In England, my father was interned by the British as an enemy alien. He spent the first year of my life in a camp on the Isle of Man, where they took all German nationals. The paradox was that his German nationality had been stripped. It was an extraordinarily difficult time for my mother because she spoke very little English.

Did you think that your stay in England was permanent or that your family would ultimately return to Germany?

The only reason my father wanted to return was to try and regain what had been his. They couldn't accept the idea of taking me back to Germany and putting me in a German school, so I went to a boarding school in England for three years and hated it. It was pretty medieval. In those days, they still had prefects and fags. A fag was a younger student who would be placed at the disposal of one of the prefects, meaning you made his bed, prepared the toast, tidied the room. And in those days, prefects still had the right to administer corporal punishment. They could beat a fag if they wanted.

Did you get beaten?

Rarely, but it did happen. It was all considered part of toughening you up, learning self-control, and becoming more self-contained. While I would never do it to one of my kids, in retrospect, there is a lot I gained from that experience. I got self-control the hard way.

Growing up in England, the son of immigrants, did you feel as if you were English or a transplanted German?

I was English from my earliest recollection on. When I was a child growing up, Germany was the enemy. There was no ambiguity in my mind about that.

At thirteen, you moved to New York City. How did you feel about coming to America?

What's probably difficult for most Americans today to understand is what an extraordinary vision America still is to people overseas.

America was a country in which anything could happen. And to a thirteen-year-old, that was a very, very seductive dream. I couldn't wait.

Why did you pick Syracuse University instead of, say, an Ivy League school?

I applied to Princeton, Middlebury, and Syracuse as a fallback position. Middlebury accepted me before I heard from Princeton but said, "Send a fifty-dollar deposit." That was a hell of a lot of money, and since I thought I was going to Princeton, I held back on the fifty. Then Princeton turned me down, and since it was too late to send my money to Middlebury, I ended up at Syracuse. However, Syracuse had this terrific live radio station where I could go on air. When I graduated, one of my professors said, "You really ought to get a master's. Why not apply to Stanford?" It was the only place I applied.

At Stanford, in 1960, you met your wife, Grace Anne. She was a doctoral student and today is a lawyer. She is also the mother of your four children and is your closest personal adviser. What attracted you to her in the first place?

She is as much of a scrapper as I am and every bit as bright—maybe even brighter. Certainly a better student. Anytime I got an A minus, she got an A. And anytime I got an A, she got an A plus. That was enough to attract me to her right away—quite apart from the fact she was gorgeous and a fun, wonderful person to be around.

The marriage, in 1963, took some maneuvering because you're Jewish and Grace Anne is Catholic. Your families, I gather, weren't too happy about it.

As my mother-in-law said after eighteen years of our marriage, "Time will tell."

When did you first know you wanted to be in broadcasting?

Since I was seven years old and listened to Edward R. Murrow and Alistair Cooke on the radio in England. Later, I always wanted to be on the other side of the camera. I always thought that the person who wrote the script and delivered it ultimately had more control over the message that goes out. Marvin Kalb, now my best friend, was one of those whom I looked at and said, "Hey, there's a bright guy—probably about ten years older than I am—and I think I can follow in his footsteps." But I couldn't get a job in broadcasting right away. In fact, I couldn't get a job in *anything* related to the media at that point. I still remember flunking the Associated Press test. I ended up teaching English at the McBurney School.

What was your problem in cracking broadcasting?

[*Laughs.*] Well, I was not then the magnificent specimen of a man you see before you today. I looked extraordinarily young, and so people were able to overlook the great potential there. But I knew I was pretty good and would be able to do it. This industry never has been, and I guess never will be, overpopulated with brilliance.

So ultimately you got in through radio?

Essentially, I began as a copyboy at WMCA radio. One day, a friend told me that WABC radio was hiring seven on-air people to do this program called *Flair Reports.* So I went over, and they said they had a radio program that was going to be three and a half minutes, and that there'd be seven of them a day. The pay was three hundred and seventy-five dollars a week. I was earning ninety dollars at that point. They told me to go home and return with two scripts. My wife and I went to the beach that day, and I wrote the scripts there. When we got home, I realized I'd left them at the beach. So I stayed up all night writing two new ones and went in at nine A.M. to read them. They called me back three days later and said, "You're really very good, and we'd love to hire you, but you're too young. Radio news, however, will hire you as a writer for a hundred and seventy-five dollars." I said, "No, I didn't apply for that job. I want to be on this program." After I hung up, I really felt it. To this day I don't really know why I did that, because, God, we needed the money. But two days later they called me and said, "It's radio and no one will know how old you are, so come on in." *Flair Reports* had a wonderful bunch of talent: Charlie Osgood, Stew Klein, among others. Eventually, radio news started sending us out on the street as reporters. But I still knew I wanted to make it into television, because by 1963, television—not radio—was the class act. However, I also knew, being twenty-three and looking sixteen, that radio was a good place to hide out, develop a skill, and become known to the people at the network. Three years later, ABC television called and said, "Would you like to go to Vietnam?"

Wasn't Vietnam a choice network assignment?

They didn't have a hell of a lot of choices. When I joined ABC News, we didn't even have our own camera crews; we were hiring per-diem crews in New York. For a while, ABC was trying to get only unmarried people, while CBS had all their stars rotating through Vietnam.

What were your personal feelings about Vietnam?

I was very dovish and very opposed to the war. I thought we were going to lose it. I was heavily influenced by people like David Halberstam and Malcolm Browne, whose material made a lot of sense to me. They were saying, This is a political war which we're trying to win with overwhelming firepower, even though it's probably not winnable. They seemed to have better answers than the folks who were trying to explain the war on the basis of a basketball game; that is, in the first quarter, can you kill more of them than they can us? If so, let's tote up the number of bodies and we'll be ahead.

You had two stints in Vietnam: January to October of 1967, and January 1969 through the summer of 1971, when, as Hong Kong bureau chief, you went in and out of Southeast Asia. In 1968, you returned as Miami bureau chief. Though obviously rising in the ABC hierarchy, you were, nevertheless, working for a network whose evening news broadcast was the last—in 1967—to expand from fifteen to thirty minutes. Wasn't it frustrating always being the stepchild?

Yes, but one of the great joys of being a foreign correspondent for ABC was when you kicked the crap out of CBS. Now when you do it, it's different because we've got as many producers and correspondents and we're spending as much, if not more, money than they are. Fifteen years ago, when we did it overseas, you were alone with a cameraman who might, if you were lucky, have a sound man with him. If not, you'd be running the sound at the same time you were covering an event. CBS would show up with two correspondents, two crews, and two producers. When I was Hong Kong bureau chief, there was a period of about three months when I was the correspondent, the bureau chief, the business manager, and did the film editing.

In the summer of 1968, ABC assigned you to cover the Nixon campaign. What was your impression of Nixon?

He's a very private man, a little awkward, very smart, complex, and very convinced that no one ever gave him credit for his intelligence. And he's probably right. He wanted as little to do with the press as possible. I once spent two weeks during the campaign trying to capture on film my perception that Nixon was out of sync. At press conferences, he would raise his hands and say, "Sit down." Or he would make a point of emphasis and then hit the table a half second later. Richard Nixon wanted to be president of the United States, but he never wanted to campaign for it. He hated that. He would have loved to be president of Oz, sitting in a little room somewhere where he never had to meet people. He was very reluctant to confront people. I have a lot of sympathy for someone who is not naturally a public leader, and I found him least attractive when he tried to be one. But you have to admire a man who never, *ever,* gives up. That's part of the American fascination with Nixon. Here is a guy who's had a stake driven through his heart, I mean, really nailed to the bottom of the coffin with a wooden stake, and a silver bullet through the forehead for good measure—and yet he keeps coming back. Well, I admire that kind of tenacity in a person.

Why is it that Ronald Reagan seems to get away with things that few others, including Jimmy Carter, ever could?

In that sense, Jimmy Carter and Richard Nixon have a lot in common. There are people like Jack Kennedy and Ronald Reagan who can do that kind of thing all over the place—and I'm not even making reference to amorous affairs—and people would still love them like crazy. Poor old Richard Nixon would have his car spotted behind the hotel somewhere and would be torn limb from limb. Same with Jimmy Carter. Ronald Reagan, like Kennedy, has a twinkle in his eye and he's saying, "I'm one of the guys. Sure, I got blasted a few times, and yeah, I've had a couple of affairs in my life, although we don't talk about that anymore," and he not only gets away with it, but people are charmed by it.

By 1971, you'd been with ABC eight years. Did you, at that point, have a career game plan, or were you simply willing to let serendipity take its course?

I had what I wanted. But our oldest kids were getting accustomed to living overseas and were in danger of losing their roots. There were only two jobs I wanted to return to: either the White House or the State Department. Ironically, we decided on State because I wouldn't have to travel so much. And then a guy by the name of Kissinger came on.

You were a part of the group of reporters who traveled with Kissinger during the dramatic days of shuttle diplomacy—1973 to 1975. Most say that that experience was a landmark in their careers as journalists. Do you agree?

It really was, because above all things Henry is an extraordinary teacher. He loves to teach, especially when he has a good class, and he had a first-rate class traveling with him. He had people who had been covering foreign policy for a long time, who cared about it, and were attentive to everything he was saying. It wasn't a matter of getting a grade; this was their career. You had to listen to every syllable because here was a guy who, all legends to the contrary, rarely, if ever, lies, but is awfully good at misleading. If you listened very carefully and learned to unravel the double negatives and qualifying phrases he puts in, you could read extraordinary stories into what he was telling you.

Many have charged that the close association between Kissinger and reporters was his way of controlling the news.

There is some validity to that. But what was happening in the Middle East was not only being covered from Kissinger's plane. The Israelis—no slouches when it comes to handling the media—were also putting out their stories to our colleagues in Jerusalem and Tel Aviv, while Sadat—again, no slouch—was putting out his version in Egypt. But Kissinger was able to monopolize the news out of the Middle East because even though he was getting only three or four hours' sleep a night, he made sure that at least one hour every day would be spent thoroughly briefing the press. Now consider the risk factor. Here he was, negotiating at the most delicate level in a state of near exhaustion, and then meeting with us. And he rarely, if ever, made a mistake. Now, if he's that good that he was able to manipulate a group of the best diplomatic correspondents I've ever worked with—and I include myself in that group—more power to him. If you go back and read the stories written at the time, they were not quite as syrupy and sappy as people now like to believe. They were pretty accurate.

In 1975, Kissinger offered you—among others—the job as his spokesman at the State Department, did he not?

Yes, and I was fascinated by the prospect. Also terrified, because I don't happen to believe that journalists ought to go into government and then come back to journalism again. My feeling was that if I did it, I would be out of journalism, so I turned it down.

Then you were philosophically aligned with Kissinger?

No, but I find his thinking to be more lucid than that of other people who handle foreign policy. For instance, take the Carter administration. During the first six or eight months, the only theme I could find in the Carter foreign policy was "If Nixon, Kissinger, or Ford did it, we will do the opposite." By the end of their term, they had come back, in most instances, a long way. What I do admire about Kissinger is that he thinks his policies through. Sometimes, from a human point of view, you can take issue with what he's saying. But if you start from the premise that it's the job of the foreign-policy leaders to protect the national interest of this country—and that that is sometimes an amoral job—then you view Henry Kissinger in a different light. And I do. I do think that foreign policy is, basically, amoral.

Why is it an amoral job to protect the national interest of this country?

The people who run foreign policy are charged with one responsibility: to protect and preserve the national interest of whatever country they serve. They have to take into consideration the good of the whole rather than its individual parts. Inevitably, that leads to amoral behavior. It's the only way anyone can ever send troops to war. How can you send young men to die unless you believe it's for the greater good?

Can you understand that some people think you are compromised by your close friendship with Kissinger?

Sure, and I'll have to live with it. But it's a curious kind of friendship. I like Henry very much and have great admiration for him, but we're surprised if we see each other half a dozen times a year. Besides, I find it wrong that Henry Kissinger is put in the same general league with Adolf Eichmann or Attila the Hun. Henry Kissinger is, plain and simple, the best secretary of state we have had in twenty, maybe thirty years—certainly one of the two or three great secretaries of state in our century. Everybody always asks about our friendship. It's as though "Gee, Ted, you're such a nice guy. How can you be a friend of Kissinger's?" Well, I'm proud to be a friend of Henry Kissinger. He is an extraordinary man. This country has lost a lot by not having him in a position of influence and authority. It's a shame we're wasting a talent like Kissinger.

What did you learn from your association with him that you've incorporated into your professional life?

I've learned to listen very carefully. I'm more likely to miss a nuance in the written word than I am in the spoken word. If someone is trying to do a verbal dipsy doodle around me, I don't miss it very often, because Henry Kissinger is the best dipsy-doodle artist in the world.

In 1976 ABC News hired Barbara Walters for one million dollars to co-anchor the evening news with Harry Reasoner. How did that move strike you?

I thought it was dumb, because I didn't think it would work. At that time, Bill Sheehan [then president of ABC News] called me up to New York to ask me about two jobs: One was to be vice president of ABC News, and the other was to take over as executive producer of the Walters-Reasoner show. I, meanwhile, went up to New York to tell him I was resigning. I was going to take a year off and stay home while my wife was taking her first year of law school. I didn't feel I could go in and say, "Give me a year off," so I wanted to make a clean break—resign—and if all went well, come back. Sheehan said, "Let's maintain a relationship," so that year I continued doing radio commentaries and also started anchoring the Saturday-night news out of New York.

You were thirty-six years old, had a steady career at ABC, but were not a major star. Yet you take a year off to be a house husband. That was a very gutsy thing to do.

It was not that gutsy. The gutsy thing is when you do that not really knowing if you're ever going to be hired again. There was no doubt in my mind that I could come back after nine months.

Of course, you weren't the average housewife. You also, during that year, wrote a novel with Marvin Kalb— In the National Interest.

That's why I say there was nothing heroic about it. I knew I had a fixed term. I was going to be off nine months, and then my wife was going to come back and take over again. I was doing something very gratifying to me, because we had a fat advance and had sold the book already. And for the radio commentary, ABC put a line into my home.

What was your average daily schedule?

I got up about five A.M. and read the papers so I'd have an idea for my commentaries. Then I'd fix breakfast for my kids and, if I had car-pool duty, car-pool. Then I wrote my commentary and, at ten, delivered it. I did the shopping, cooking, light cleaning, and occasionally [*laughs*] I did windows and floors.

Did you enjoy doing housework?

It was an awakening. It's not something I would be eager to do again. There's nothing terribly feminine about cleaning a kitchen floor or cooking. What is feminine about chopping up raw meat? In many ways I found that I had to draw on all the reservoir of self-containment that I had. At *Nightline,* it's easy because there's daily gratification. I'm constantly being told how wonderful I am doing this job. Very few people tell you how wonderful you are when all you've done is cooked a meal, put the laundry in, or made beds. What's difficult about it is that it's so taken for granted.

In the spring of 1977, you returned to ABC and the announcement that Roone Arledge, president of ABC Sports, had also been appointed president of ABC News. What was your gut reaction?

I didn't know Roone at all. I had never met him, and I was concerned. I thought he was going to cheapen the news. But let me say he's totally proved me wrong. He's as thoughtful and intelligent a man as I ever hoped to work for. However, there was a period when I was not only ready to walk, but I did. I handed in my resignation.

That was the result of Arledge's firing your executive producer of the

Saturday Night News—*something he did while you were on vacation.
That must have been a blow.*

I was hurt. Not that the president [of] the news division has to ask
permission of the anchor to fire a producer; he can fire anyone he wants,
including the anchor. But I just thought it showed a certain lack of
concern for the feelings of someone who—in my mind—was going to
continue to be a vital part of ABC News. What that said to me was
"Sonny, I don't care who you think you've been here; under me you're
nothing." Roone and I have talked about it since, and obviously it was
not meant that way. After all, Roone had a couple of other things on
his mind. The worst thing I could say now about that was that it was
thoughtless. I'm sure now he didn't mean any cruelty by it, but I sure
took it that way. If he called me in and said, "Look, others may think
you're an anchor, but I don't," you can't argue with that. That really
is a question of taste and perception. Actually, [*laughs*] some people
feel exactly that way about me today. Fortunately, Roone has changed
his mind.

*But he didn't immediately. He ignored your letter of resignation; in
fact, you couldn't even get him on the phone.*

So I quit. I submitted my letter, said good-bye on the Saturday show,
went home, and stayed there. At that point it didn't strike me as
perhaps as extraordinary a move as it did others because I had just come
off of nine months away. For the first time in my professional life I'd
been away from the network and was less seduced by it. I figured one
of two things would happen to me: I'd stay home and ABC would
continue to pay me, or I'd be fired, in which case I could go somewhere
else. After about a month, I was invited to come up and have lunch
with Roone. Roone is a very charming man. When you're in his
presence, he gives you his time and doesn't allow anything else to
interfere. He doesn't push the agenda.

What was your agenda?

I wanted to be an important part of ABC News. There was talk of
this multiple-anchor concept, and I had dreams of being the foreign-
policy subanchor. I wanted to contribute to the magazine show *20/20.*

I wanted to do anchoring to show that I was better than he thought I was. And most of all, I just wanted him to pay attention to me. And, Lord, he was nice enough to pay attention at that point.

But from 1977 to 1979 it was still dicey, wasn't it?

Was I one of the anointed? No. And neither was Sam Donaldson. Sam and I both thought we were a lot better than Roone did. But it was not an unhappy period. It was a period during which we—Sam and I—were sitting in the dugout hoping the coach would send us in to play. But we were on the team, and we were played. We hadn't been sent to the minors.

You said you always knew you were going to be a big star at ABC. But by 1977—fourteen years after you'd joined the network—that still hadn't happened. Weren't you beginning to question whether that big breakthrough was going to happen?

Was I ambitious? Yes. Anxious? No. I was almost thirty-seven, so I wasn't exactly over the hill yet. I still knew the opportunity would come, as Donaldson, Jennings, and Frank Reynolds knew it would come for them. We all looked around and said, "This isn't a matter of being filled with foolish pride." We'd look at ourselves and say, "Be honest, guys. Am I a pile of crap?" And they'd say, "No. You're really good, and one day Roone is going to catch on to that." And he did. The group has done all right. We take a lot of pride in that.

When Arledge initiated America Held Hostage, *anchored by Frank Reynolds, most people thought he was crazy. Did you?*

Yes. Donaldson, Barrie Dunsmore, and I not only thought Roone was nuts, we said it quite openly. When the hostage crisis went on, we thought Roone would ultimately have to give up, but he had no intention of doing that. He was letting everybody know—the viewers, the news division, the network, the affiliates—that a program at this time of night could work. Then it started getting extraordinary ratings. It became clear that if you could do this with the Iranian story, there was something that could be done every night which would appeal to a few million people. All kinds of people like to claim credit for being the guiding geniuses behind *Nightline,* but if there is any guiding genius, it was Roone Arledge.

You were already covering Iran on the State Department beat and began substituting for Reynolds at eleven-thirty. Did you immediately realize this show was the vehicle you'd been waiting for?

Yes—there was no question about it in my mind. I had put in sixteen and a half years with the network, had done almost every kind of story. If ever I was going to do something new and different, this was it.

Arledge again didn't seem to be as convinced. He was still hoping Dan Rather, among others, might be available to anchor Nightline. *Did that make you angry?*

I guess "apprehensive" would be the most honest word, because I really wanted that job. I knew I could do it. But he was looking around elsewhere. Dick Wald [senior vice president of ABC News] does a funny routine about how obvious it was. "Here we have this new nighttime broadcast that we're going to put on the network to go up against Carson and the CBS movie. So obviously we will put some funny-looking diplomatic correspondent that no one's ever heard of in the job, and he will become an enormous success." That took more imagination than even Roone had.

That's very diplomatic, Ted. But with your credentials, it must have been exasperating to have to keep convincing this man of your star quality. After all, you'd proven yourself.

Proven what? That I could handle an ongoing story for which there was a national obsession? It was a very tense time—one of the few times when I felt a little less secure. But it was also not a time to let people know you're feeling insecure. That was the time when, above all, I had to seem more self-confident than anyone around me, because if I wasn't going to be self-confident, sure as hell nobody else was.

Did Roone finally just call up and say, "Ted, Nightline's *yours?"*

No. Roone has a way of not ever doing that. I remember the day precisely. It was my fortieth birthday, February eighth. Dick Wald called and said, "You betcha." Now at that point, I was still earning my regular salary as chief diplomatic correspondent and had about a year to go on my contract. I said, "I guess you're going to want to renegotiate the contract?" And they said, "No." I said, "I really think it would be a good idea for you because now you can get me pretty cheap. A year from now, this show is going to be a big success." And they said, "We'll take our chances."

How does your interviewing technique differ from others'?

It's important to listen and—for me—not to have a bunch of prepared questions. I have half an hour in which to do a show—out of which maybe twelve or thirteen minutes is interviewing. If I come with three or four questions already in my head, the answer to the first question may be so extraordinary that it'd be foolish to use those other questions. Most of the time, if you give people a halfway-decent opening question, they end up telling you fairly interesting things.

Have there been times on Nightline *when you felt you really blew an interview?*

There are times when you're just not sharp enough to ask the right questions. What a viewer means by blowing it is getting an answer that so astounds you that you fall back in your chair and say, "Oh, my God, I never thought of that." That doesn't happen. But we've come close. There was once a Texas husband-and-wife team who censored textbooks and who showed this book in which, she said, "one of the things they show here is how young women can use cucumbers to masturbate." I must confess that took me off. But I only blow it when I'm not ready.

When there's a crisis, Nightline*'s ratings usually go up. Do you ever find yourself secretly hoping for bad news?*

No, but anyone in the business who tells you they don't get a rush of adrenaline when they hear of some major news story—which, by definition, is almost always a crisis—is not telling the truth. If I didn't get excited when that happens, if I didn't feel it was the fulfillment of everything I am, I probably would be out of the business. When you're covering an event, emotions get in the way. People don't pay me to get on air and start crying at the loss of three hundred and sixty-nine lives. They pay me to get on air and put some perspective on the situation.

Yet, ironically, Walter Cronkite's most remembered moment is when he cried upon hearing of the death of John F. Kennedy.

Which simply proves all of us are fallible. You don't see newsmen cry on air in part because it's inappropriate and in part because—if you want to get cruel about it—most of us are cynical enough not to regard things in human terms until much later on. One of the reasons *Nightline* has such loyal viewers is that people get the sense that I can step back and not involve myself personally, that I can be just as argumentative with a liberal as I can with a conservative, that I can give a Russian an opportunity to talk one night, and yet if there's too much garbage coming out, I will hassle him.

Did you ever have a time in your career when you did get emotionally involved and lose it on air?

Yeah, in '65. But it wasn't on air, it was in Selma. I really felt I wanted to march. I didn't want to cover the story, I wanted to be part of it. I called my wife, and we talked about it. And she said, "Look, you've always wanted to be a journalist. The whole idea was to do something good by whatever influence you could. You're a fool to give up the chance now." So I slept on it. The big question was really whether I could step back and be objective when I felt strongly that one side was right and the other was wrong. I stayed reporting.

As one who is being touted as a potential anchor on World News Tonight, *what do you see are the differences between the three network nightly-news anchors?*

The three anchors have never been more alike. They are all urbane, handsome, well read, intelligent. They've paid their dues, come up through the ranks. Dan is clearly a little more energetic, electric, frenetic sometimes. What Dan and I have in common is that we are both great admirers of Edward R. Murrow. I must confess that there was a time in my life when I was doing Edward R. Murrow impersonations, too. Dan does a kind of Texan Edward R. Murrow—clipped—a very effective style, but it *is* a style. You always have the feeling that what you're watching with Dan is terribly important, even when it isn't. Peter is a little more urbane in that sense. When it isn't important, he doesn't pretend it is. Tom Brokaw and I have a lot in common in one sense. Tom is an excellent interviewer. He was terrific on the *Today* show, but the format of a news program doesn't really allow him to display that great talent. I understand why he moved from *Today* to *Nightly News,* but in terms of capitalizing on his strengths, it was probably a mistake.

How much does Arledge get involved with what is seen on Nightline?

We all work for Roone. It would be foolish of me to say, No, he is not the ultimate authority. But it's also foolish to imply that Roone is pulling the strings every day of the week. I was fearful because I had heard all the rumors about this man who cannot keep his hands off the product. But I've got to tell you, in all the years we've been doing *Nightline,* he has called during the program maybe fifty, sixty times, which is a lot. But when he calls, it will be, "Tell him to ask this . . ." It is, literally, the ultimately involved viewer who has a telephone that goes right to the control room. Sometimes Bill Lord [former executive producer] would pass the questions on and sometimes he wouldn't. If it was passed on and I thought it appropriate, I'd ask the question.

Your colleagues say you are the ultimate politician. What does it take to survive in network television?

I don't know. I've told people with whom I negotiate on contracts that I'll always tell them the truth, because I find it the most convenient way to live professionally. But in some way, that has been transformed into the perception that I am extraordinarily manipulative and political. Most of the time, however, it's momentum. As far as my work is concerned, I'm like the guy who tries to keep all the plates spinning. And when he gets to the end of the line and the plate at the start of the line starts to wobble, he goes racing back again. I'm not very well organized, so I'm constantly trying to keep plates spinning. I'm always a last-minute person. I'll be sitting in the studio a half hour before I go on air, gobbling up some last piece of information. In college, I was always the guy who would spend the last three days frantically cramming, always doing well enough to squeeze out a B minus. When I met Grace Anne in graduate school—and there was that competitiveness, when I had someone I wanted to beat—then I made A's.

Have you had to make sacrifices for your career?

Insofar as being away from my family was painful to me, yes. But it was my family who paid for my career. . . . I spent close to a year in Vietnam in 1967, and I would come back to Hong Kong only for a week every two months. Then when I was Southeast Asia bureau chief, I traveled constantly—going six, seven, eight months out of the year, two weeks at a time. But again, those sacrifices were primarily my wife's.

Historically, anchoring major news shows has been the bastion of white male WASPs. You are the first Jew to crack that WASP anchor barrier. Do you think being Jewish has ever slowed your progress in broadcasting?

I don't think it's ever been a factor. Or if it has been a factor, they've been so subtle about it that I don't think they even knew what they were doing.

Still, you are a token in a certain sense. Do you feel the responsibility as a role model?

Yes and no. But I'm hired to be a journalist. If I don't do that, it will be much more damaging to people who have confidence in me, be they Jews or non-Jews, than if I were to suddenly see myself as a representative of a particular religion, political party, or of the males of this world who are five foot nine. I get mail all the time that says, "How can you, of all people, be sympathetic to Yasir Arafat?" I feel that I, of all people, have a responsibility to try very hard not to lean in one direction or another.

How does that consideration come into play when someone like a Jesse Jackson is on the show?

Let's face it—there are an awful lot of bigots in this country, a lot of people who would come down on Jesse just because he's black. So can you blame a man if he takes advantage of the fact that there are a lot of people who are afraid to lay a glove on him because he's black and they don't want to be accused of being racist? But that's another form of intolerance. Jesse doesn't need my protection. He's as tough as they come. I like Jesse, I really do. He was by far the most interesting candidate [in the 1984 Democratic primaries], but he has an appalling lack of knowledge about foreign policy. In the Dartmouth debate, he said he felt the Japanese ought to pick up a larger share of their own defense. But someone pointed out that we were the ones who drafted the Japanese constitution precluding them from having a larger role in their own defense. And he said, "Well, I wasn't alive then." In other words, "How am I supposed to know anything that happened before Jesse Jackson was born?" Come on.

Incidentally, are you a Democrat or Republican?

I'm a registered Independent, and I do that deliberately, because my politics are nobody's business.

Are you an American citizen now?

Yes. I like to say I'm an American by choice rather than by accident of birth, and that's what's still extraordinary about America. I can't imagine this happening in any other country. I cannot imagine going to France at thirteen and being in the equivalent position in French broadcasting today.

Your on-air style has been universally described as "unflappable." Is that an accurate description of you offscreen as well?

People jump to the erroneous conclusion that what they see for half an hour on *Nightline* is what I am as a human being. I wouldn't agree with that term, but I'm paid to be unflappable. Am I unflappable when I'm home with my family? Hell, no.

What makes you angry, then?

Incompetence. I really get angry when people are paid to do something and they don't know how to do it.

How about something petty, like your hair? Do you ever get tired of people commenting on it?

There's not much I can do about it, but I do get tired of it. It must drive some people literally crazy, because they can't seem to get enough of talking about it. I go to a hairstylist and the reason I do is because early on they said, "Ted, you're making enough money now. You're an anchor. Go get your hair cut somewhere where they can do it for you properly." And for a day or two after I get it cut, it looks pretty good. If I somehow just put aside the time every week for a light trim, I think the subject would just go away. But it's never been important enough to me. People will be a lot more forgiving ten years from now, when I'm on the air and bald.

In a rule-infested profession, you seem to have written a lot of your own. Do you, for instance, have an agent?

No, I've never had one. No agent I've ever talked to has ever been able to satisfactorily explain to me how they will handle weighing off my interests against those of their other clients when we are in competition for the same job. I negotiate the terms of my own contract and then have a lawyer go over it. Agents exist largely for those who are embarrassed to go in and say for themselves, "Look, this is how I assess the market, and here's what I think I'm worth."

How confident are you, anyway? People who know you say that your most marked quality is an unusual sense of self. As one man put it, "Ted is the most self-confident person I ever met—but then, I never met De Gaulle."

[*Laughs.*] That's lovely. I like that. It's the most flattering insult I've ever received. Look, no one is that confident in reality, but ours is a business of appearances, and it's terribly important to appear to be self-confident. The minute you give evidence of doubt, people are going to eat you alive. Sure, there are times I have doubt, but people will never know when that is. I lead a very blessed life. I'm married to a woman I love, I have four children I'm crazy about. I haven't gone hungry in any of my adult days, so I don't have a lot to feel insecure about. When you realize that being a success in television is far from being the most important thing in life, once you've got that under your belt and believe it—then what are they going to do? Fire me? Fine. I can survive. And I've never tried to confuse that in the minds of people I've worked for—Elton Rule, Bill Sheehan, or Roone Arledge. Realizing most of your ambitions, you come to the conclusion that there's a lot less to this than meets the eye. The only kind of lasting thing that's left to me is my family, my children, and their children. The only *real* hope I have for lasting beyond this lifetime is through them. The family is a much more important extension of yourself than any work you do. If you don't realize that before it's too late, it can be the greatest tragedy of all.

When exactly did you come to this realization?

In my mid-thirties. I said, "Hey, you're chief diplomatic correspondent. Not bad. So what's left? They make you an anchor. But is that going to make all the difference? So what then? President of ABC News?"

Would you like to be president of ABC News?

No. I love Roone dearly and really empathize with him in that job. But I wouldn't want it for love nor money. In this industry, you realize that being the president of ABC News isn't going to make a hell of a lot of difference fifty years from now any more than being chairman of the board of ABC or even president of the United States is going to make a difference. I don't want to get sloppy or metaphysical on you, but those things just aren't important. What is important is being happy in your life with your family and trying to do a little bit of good. And now I'm in the position where I can do a little bit of good.

THE WASHINGTON POST: HIGH HEELS AND LOW TIMES

It wasn't that I didn't belong at *The Washington Post*—it's just that I signed up for a job I didn't really want to do; I learned the hard way that you can never equivocate about work. I learned that I should have listened to Mama when she told me, "Never pull into a parking space you can't back out of."

As with many of life's big blunders, it all began with sex. In 1976 I was a panel member at the annual journalists' MORE convention in New York, where—along with Liz Smith, John Simon, and Midge Decter—I discoursed on fame and the famous in a panel discussion unfortunately titled "The Private Parts of Public People." When the subject turned to money, I pointed out that, in my experience, people would sooner talk about their sex lives than their net worth. Moderator Jim Brady asked if that applied to politicians as well. I contended it was especially true of politicians since "in Washington getting laid is considered kinky sex." The following week *New York*'s "Intelligencer" column ran the quote along with my picture.

Then I got the call.

I was sitting at my desk at *Women's Wear Daily* explaining to a colleague how she could lose ten pounds in three days eating only watermelon, when the receptionist yelled this fateful directive across the newsroom:

"Nancy, it's Shelby Coffey from *The Washington Post.*"

The editor of the prestigious Style section was calling to ask if I might be available to meet with him on Monday. Available for *The Washington Post*? The illustrious *Washington Post*? Woodward, Bernstein, and . . . Collins? You bet I might. Even if I didn't know what for, I was suddenly heady with a journalist's impossible illusions.

I was escorted through the hubbub of the immense newsroom, a replica of the set in *All the President's Men* (journalism imitating art?), and into the glass-walled office of Shelby Coffey. A thirty-year-old of Virginia pedigree, Coffey seemed the archetype of southern gentility. His courtly, composed manner, I was later to discover, masked a ferocious ambition: He wanted to be the editor of *The Washington Post,* and Style was the first springboard to that end.

Coffey grilled me for an hour on everything from world events to the books I read. Since I still didn't know what I was auditioning for, I took no chances. Proust? *Bien sûr. The New York Review of Books?* Couldn't live without it. *People?* Well, yes, every so often, one had to, right? Right. Here—aha!—I detected Coffey's real weakness, a thinly disguised fascination with celebrity. Immediately I began regaling him with stories of the stars I'd interviewed. I was running out of material when at last he came to the point. The venerable *Washington Post* was thinking of starting its own gossip column.

Gossip column? I was stunned. Gossip column. I was a journalist. I did interviews. I wrote. No, no, no, I didn't do gossip. How had this happened? I had been recommended, Shelby went on to say, by Sally Quinn, Style's most famous and acerbic writer (a.k.a. Poison Pen Quinn) and live-in paramour of *Post* editor Ben Bradlee. She had followed my work at *WWD*, knew I had an A-list Rolodex, and thought I was the one person for the job. I was flattered—but gossip? Not for me.

But . . . wait a minute. Why was I being such a snob? This wasn't just *any* gossip column, this was *The Washington Post*'s gossip column. Who knew where it could lead? You can't play poker until you get to the table, and the *Post*—the newspaper that had brought down a president—was offering to deal me in.

"Yes," I heard myself saying, "that could be very interesting."

From that moment on, things moved very fast. I was whisked to lunch with Coffey and Sandy Rovner, a woman who line-edited (or didn't according to some Washington wags) Sally Quinn's notoriously long pieces. That I gained not only Sally's confidence but her editor portended well. Surely, these people knew what they were doing, even if I didn't. God, maybe this could work out after all.

Within the next three hours, I met managing editor Howard Simons and the legendary editor-in-chief, Ben Bradlee. With his thinning white hair and Coke bottle–thick glasses, Simons was avuncular to Bradlee's dashing. "Why do you want to do a gossip column?" barked Simons, who, it was obvious, disapproved not only of the column but of any simpleton who would want to write it. Since I wasn't sure I did, I babbled on mindlessly, right in keeping, no doubt, with his opinion of me.

My meeting with Bradlee was an elixir compared to Simon's unsympathetic interrogation. Energetic, charming, and iconoclastic, he made it clear that the column was his baby and, by God, his babies worked! By the end of our twenty minutes together, he announced that this would be a snap. "Why, hell—Sal can get on the phone and have this whole town cased in an hour," he crowed. Ben's enthusiasm was infectious. By now I was more than just on board, I was a committed crew member, a believer. "You're right, Ben, I can do this. In fact, I even *want* to do it." As I floated out the door, his voice stopped me.

"Are you tough, kid?" he asked.

"Sure, I'm tough," I said, nearly convincing myself.

"Good," he said with a chuckle. "Good."

On February 2, 1977, I moved to Washington. In a matter of weeks,

I had disassembled my New York life, leaving behind one boyfriend, one apartment, one job at *WWD*, and one unfinished screenplay commissioned by Columbia Pictures and Stanley Jaffe, who, insisting I should write for the movies, had flattered me with sorority rush. (Hollywood might be glamorous, but it was no *Washington Post*!) Ever the researcher, I dug up columns by the rabbis of rumor—Louella Parsons, Hedda Hopper, Dorothy Kilgallen, Walter Winchell, Charlie Knickerbocker, Joyce Haber—and pored over them with the reverent dedication of a Talmudic scholar. Not much fancy writing here, just tidbits of information in straight reporting style. I could do that.

The game plan was simple enough: My first six weeks in Washington ("We'll start when you're ready") were a debutante's dream of lunches, teas, drinks, and dinners arranged, by and large, by Sally, who—just as Ben had promised—was a world-class gossip. To Sal, gossip was serious business. Nothing gave her more pleasure than to get the goods on somebody and then tell everybody else. Although Ben and Sally had fifteen phones in their home, when he asked her what she wanted for her birthday, she answered, "Another one. In the bathroom."

Quinn turned out to be the Stephen Hawking of social discourse, filling the black hole in my head with exhaustive details on the lives, loves, and careers of everyone in town. Oh, the intricacies of the Washington social web! Had every husband slept with his best friend's wife? Sister? Sitter? Was there no end to the number of former assistant secretaries of state from the Kennedy administration still running around? How *did* Pamela Harriman do it? It was intriguing, yes, but altogether daunting. Washington, after all, was unknown territory. I could barely find my way to the White House. How was I supposed to uncover its darkest secrets?

More bewildering were the *Post*'s own internal politics, machinations that could give the KGB a run for its ruble. Although Ben and Sally, the Bogart and Bacall of Washington, had been living together for five years, their relationship was still dense with the heady perfume of scandal. Notwithstanding its international prominence, Washington was really just a small southern town, curiously conservative in its traditions. Moreover, in spite of her live-in affair with the boss, Sally had stayed on in Style, exercising her influence far beyond the feature pages and creating an enormous amount of free-floating resentment among reporters.

"The Gossip Column," as they decided to name it—"Let's call it what it is"—provided the perfect haven for the disenfranchised. It wasn't merely a new feature in the paper, it was a chance at last to choose sides: You were either an ally of Ben and Sally or an ally of Katharine Graham, who, like Simons and Bob Woodward, were opposed to the *Post* descending again into the gossip gutter. (Throughout the sixties and into the pre-Watergate seventies, Maxine Cheshire had wielded serious power in Washington and at the paper with her un-Style-ish, brutally frank gossip column.)

Overnight, "The Gossip Column" took on a weighty significance. It was, to one faction, a question of journalistic principles, to the other, a referendum on the Bradlee/Quinn relationship and its ramifications on the *Post*. As a result, the column was like a political football tossed daily across the newsroom between two opposing camps. My job was to stand in the middle and try not to get hit. In fact, that might have been about as clear as my role ever got. From beginning to end—a pitifully brief scrimmage, as it happened—there was never a coherent direction from the editors. All we had was a name, a debut date, a concept, and me, a person who wasn't sure she wanted the job she had.

Although I hadn't the faintest idea of what I was doing, I spent those few weeks before my March 23 debut prepping myself at a dizzying pace. I took notes on every conversation, filled Rolodexes with names and numbers, wrote practice columns, made calls, and read *Gentlemen Prefer Blondes* because Shelby insisted that (the diminutive) Anita Loos, with her coy twenties style, would've made a superlative gossip columnist. Perhaps. But no one five feet ten wrote like that.

It was Coffey's unenviable job to make the column happen. A workaholic who spent twelve hours a day and weekends at Style, Shelby knew he was being watched, hoped he was being groomed, and realized, when I walked in, that he'd been thrown a grenade with the pen pulled out. If the column worked, it would be a notch in his bureaucratic gun; if it didn't, he would be blamed. Unfortunately, his forte was lyrical, literary prose, not quick takes on the human condition. He could get obsessively absorbed in editing Sally Quinn's reams of copy—"Always put everything in," she once advised me, "because they just might run it"—playing not only to his instinct for a more baroque journalistic approach but to a keener political one as well: Sally was a five-letter word spelled P-o-w-e-r. She had captured the attention not only of the public, but of the man occupying the position Shelby so intensely coveted.

Ultimately, the real problem was even more integral: The best gossip in town was about the *Post* itself—exactly the stuff I could never write about. Indeed *The Washington Star*'s wildly successful gossip column "Ear" had leapt to notoriety prattling irreverently, day after day, about *Post* intrigue. Written by Britisher (and longtime D.C. resident) Diana McLellan, "Ear" was short on facts but long on style and never lost an opportunity to tweak the noses of Ben, Sally, Katharine, Bob, or Carl. Reading "Ear" was like having a conversation with a loopy old friend who never let facts get in the way of a good story. "Ear" made readers laugh, which, I was dismayed to learn, was to be my mission as well. Several days after my arrival, I introduced myself to a sports-writer at the coffee machine. The man nodded gravely. "Oh . . . so you're the one they hired to be the *Post*'s new sense of humor." Whereupon I promptly lost mine.

I didn't openly panic until a couple of days before D-Day. We were still loose on specifics—what length the column should be, what tone should be used—but I still figured they knew what they were doing, even if I wasn't so sure. (Whenever I ran into Bradlee, irresistible in his Turnbull & Asser shirts, his slim barrel-chested physique the envy of even the youngest male reporters, he'd throw out some four-letter epithet, ask how things were going, and invariably chuckle in rich anticipation of the trouble we were going to stir up.) Finally, in despera-tion, I cornered Coffey. "How are we going to do the column?" I pleaded.

"We'll have lunch," he responded—always the Rx for trouble at the *Post*. So off we went to the Madison Hotel, where for the next two hours we agreed how brilliant the column would be. I'd cover not only

Washington but Hollywood, New York, London. That way, a year down the road, when I got syndicated, my stuff would be internationally relevant. It sounded impressive, even as I kept repeating it. But that was the trouble: I was doing all the talking, like a pregnant woman at a Lamaze class reassuring her husband *he* would make it through labor.

Coffey suggested I write up a few items to see how they flew. I first ran the column by Sally, the real litmus test as far as I was concerned. As I sat at my desk and watched her read, her face maddeningly impassive, my stomach did somersaults. Several agonizing minutes later, she looked up and smiled. "These are all wonderful." They were? I thought two, maybe three qualified, half in a pinch, but *everything*? Was she sure? Apparently, and passed the message to Ben. "Great stuff, kid," he confirmed.

The afternoon of March 22, things moved fast. The column, which I had hoped would start small in a bottom corner of Style, suddenly grew big, captivating the imaginations of the gossip committee: Sally, Ben, Shelby, and Sandy. I was boffo, the column was boffo, all thirteen items were boffo. They decided to spread the debut column, like a feature, across the entire upper section of Style.

It was big.

It was splashy.

It was a mistake.

We got creamed.

Why? The items didn't make it? My writing wasn't witty? The *Post* shouldn't have had a gossip column in the first place? I couldn't compete with "Ear"? Who really knew? One local TV entertainment reporter reviewed my debut as if it were a movie: *Heaven's Gate.* Others simply marched up to tell me, point-blank, how much they hated it. My theme song became "Town Without Pity." When a friend reminded me that for its first six months "Ear" had been the butt of considerable ridicule, it didn't register. All I heard was the sound of my career crashing down around my head.

The *Post*'s reaction was reassuring. Sort of. "It's just the first one," said Shelby, a bit too grimly.

"You'll be around long after 'Ear' is gone," Ben declared.

Yet something had irrevocably changed. All too quickly, my glee club lost its pitch. My fan club fired its president. A pall fell on my house, not to mention my desk. In this new light, the truth of my new job became evident. "The Gossip Column" was no mere reporting chore, but a focal point for the identity crisis the *Post* had been suffering since Watergate. By 1978, having run Nixon out of town and been glorified for it on the silver screen, the *Post* had metamorphosed from a local paper to one on the cutting edge of national journalism. Yet it was still determined to compete with the underdog *Washington Star*—even with something as trifling as a gossip column.

Thus, in spite of its inauspicious debut, the column persisted—at least temporarily—and became a major dumping ground for phone tattling. Which saved my life. Give me a lead and a dial tone and I could track down Jimmy Hoffa. (The *Post* even installed a WATS line in my apartment.) I took every call because I never knew which one was going to turn up a story I could use.

In April I reported on David Frost's interview-in-progress with Richard Nixon, the first the former president had given (for a price, of course) since leaving the White House in 1974. I burned up the wires to San Clemente: "Frost was in over his head, the tapings lasted two to three hours a day, Frost lunched with his staff, Nixon ate alone, Nixon had read none of the books about Watergate, including *All the President's Men* and *The Final Days*, Nixon swam every afternoon at five with Pat and changed from a suit into a sports jacket for dinner alone with his wife, and Bebe Rebozo seldom visited California."

Washington ate it up and I learned an invaluable lesson: *You can't miss with Dick.* Anything about Nixon sold. So when, on the day the item ran, I got a call asking if I was interested in talking to someone who had Frost's script detailing his game plan for the Watergate portion of the interview, I knew I'd hit pay dirt. As did my editors. When I produced it, the *Post* decided it wasn't gossip; it was news. It ran on the front page.

While that was certainly good for me—my first front-page byline!— it presented a very real dilemma. What was gossip and what was news? A good gossip column is breezy, trades heavily on innuendo, and sometimes skips lightly over the facts. (In Washington, that could describe any number of political practices and personalities, and so, understandably, the lines often get blurred.)

In the same Frost/Nixon column I also revealed to a waiting world that Hamilton Jordan, Jimmy Carter's chief of staff, "once boasted he never wears, in fact has never owned, a pair of underwear in his life and is proud of it." (How did I know this? In the best tradition of the two-source check, I'd dug up two women who'd been involved with Jordan.)

Frankly, I thought it was nothing more than colorful trivia. I had thrown the item into the column at the last minute, in the heat of a deadline, simply to fill space. Who cared if Hamilton Jordan wore boxers, bikinis, jockeys, jock straps, or all or none of the above? Well . . . all of Washington, that's who.

The next day the capital was abuzz with this "news." Presidential press secretary Jody Powell led off his morning White House press briefing by wryly announcing that "Hamilton Jordan does not wish to respond to questions about his underwear. It is his position that the author of that piece will be the last one to know one way or the other." Instantaneously, the chief of staff's undergarment aversion became the stuff of media legend. Within weeks, *Time, Esquire,* and *The Wall Street Journal* repeated the tale. In the gossip business, I had hit a first-inning home run, an item that had gone national just a month after I had entered the game.

I also struck out.

"You can write about everybody in town, except Mrs. Graham's friends," Shelby told me one afternoon in jest—or so I interpreted this absurd instruction. How was I to know who her "friends" were? And didn't "The Gossip Column," whatever my own deep-seated bias might be, still fall into the category of journalism? No favoritism allowed? There came the day when I revealed that former ambassador William McCormick Blair and his wife, Deeda, had kept their swimming pool heated during the energy crisis. This rather embarrassing information caused Bill Blair, former Kennedy intimate and all around lovely man in saner situations, to call his friend Kay, who called Shelby, who called me into his office to inform me that Mrs. Graham was not amused. Though the source, as he was chagrined to learn, was a prominent *Washington Post* reporter, he was forced to dutifully direct me to run a correction: The Blairs swore they had, in the name of patriotism, cooled it.

Besides this persistent scrutiny, I endured the tedium of having to have my copy cleared by three editors and a libel lawyer. "When I saw that swarm of judges circling your desk," my colleague Judy Bachrach told me, "I knew they didn't want 'The Gossip Column'; they wanted 'The Truth Column.'"

Four months and hours of headache and heartache later, I discovered that writing a gossip column was like having a kid you couldn't get a baby-sitter for. It just never went away. It was always there, demanding nourishment, and, in my case, giving none back.

I knew now my initial instinct had been right: Shelby had hired the wrong person. I was an outsider writing about insiders (not a bad journalistic posture, as a rule, but hopeless for a gossip queen in a town as incestuous as Washington). Friends, I hated this job. I hated the nightly parties. I hated having to chat up the hundreds of people a good gossip columnist must just to stay in business. And, to be perfectly candid, it was not my finest literary hour. Writing short never has been. I just never got the hang of whatever it was the *Post* wanted hung. Still, I wasn't a victim; I was a *volunteer.* I'd longed to work at the *Post,* and now I was. But every time I read the column, I realized it didn't work for me. Then one Tuesday, I found out it didn't work for them, either.

I shouldn't have been surprised that the column ended pretty much in the same manner it began: ambiguously. Shelby Coffey seemed to wish it would just go away, like he wished it had never come. All day he had been prowling, scowling, clenching and unclenching his fists, but I didn't take it personally until a friend who was a Carter operative called. He came chillingly to the point.

"Have they said anything to you about stopping the column?"

Stopping the column? No, of course they hadn't. Why did he ask? He asked because he'd heard a rumor that very morning. Well, I said, incensed, that was piffle. Wouldn't I be the first to know? Obviously, I'd be the first—

"Bull," he broke in. "If they decide to do it, you'll be the last to know. All they're interested in is saving their ass, not yours."

I refused to believe him. They were professionals. We were colleagues. If indeed they ever decided to do away with the column, the very least I could expect was common courtesy, if not a commendation for bravado in the line of duty. I was too exhausted to even broach the subject with Shelby. This had been a killer of a week, and all I wanted to do now was drag myself off to the Fleetwood Mac concert the *Post*'s music critic, Tom Zito, had arranged for me to see.

During his rounds of the section to check copy, Shelby stopped by my desk and said he wanted to speak to me before I left, and I thought, fine—as long as I'm there I might as well go ahead and ask him to clear things up. By seven o'clock the Style section had nearly cleared out, and I was still waiting. By seven forty-five I decided he'd forgotten and stood up to go; at that moment he beckoned me into his office. Stepping into the glass cube, I was taken aback to see Sandy Rovner crammed into a far corner. Well, I damn sure wasn't going to discuss tall tales of my doomed future in front of the Style section's most notorious gossip. I'd address the rumor tomorrow.

Shelby motioned for me to close the door and sit down in the chair facing him. I was cheerful. Only minutes from now I'd be mainlining rock and roll and I was already beginning to feel wired. Obviously, I was the only one. Sandy's face was even more pinched and sour than usual as she stared ahead, refusing to meet my gaze.

Shelby looked downright fierce, his jaw cemented into place, his knuckles gripped white around a ballpoint pen, his back as ramrod straight as the southern military-academy boy he once was. His pale blue eyes, generally genial during our conversations, were deadly cold as he stared me squarely, relentlessly, in the face. Suddenly it hit me: I was facing my firing squad. The bullet came with ruthless speed.

"We've decided to stop the column. Friday will be the last one. It just isn't working and we've decided it's better to end it now." I could hear my gasp, feel my stomach flop as if I were in a plane that got swallowed by an air pocket. "The decision is final. We'd like you to take a couple of weeks off and then come back and cover parties, do the things for us you did for *Women's Wear.*"

A massive wave of relief surged through me.

"Does that mean I'll be on the Style staff?"

"No. You'll be on probation for six months." .

Probation? What was I, a convicted felon?

My first impulse was to tell them, "I quit." My second impulse was to tell myself I needed this job. I could go back to New York unemployed. I could go back to New York embarrassed. But I could not go back to New York broke.

I struggled to keep a neutral expression on my face. On the one hand, I felt numb, betrayed; on the other, the actress in me was riveted by the drama I was starring in, fascinated by the cold-bloodedness with which the bad news was delivered. I suppose Shelby had carried out his mission in the only way he knew how—militarily. But shouldn't Style have more *style?*

"You shouldn't feel bad," he was saying. "You gave it your best shot. You worked hard. I'm not sure I've ever had a reporter who worked as hard as you." (Okay, he was trying to say the right things . . . but why did I know he had practiced this speech in front of the mirror that morning while he was shaving? More important, did *he* know there was a large spot of mustard splattered on the front of his shirt?)

But, oh, wait—now Sandy was speaking up, something about my loving to cover parties. "How many times have you come back here and said how much you'd love to write up a party again?" she burbled. What was she doing here, anyway? Did George Steinbrenner invite the batboy when he sacked Billy Martin?

I stood up. The Tuesday Night Massacre was over. My legs felt weak and my head throbbed. I had to get out of there. Fast. Grabbing my purse, I headed toward Zito. Silently, we walked down the hall to the elevator. Maybe, I thought, I shouldn't go to the concert. Maybe I should have Tom drop me at home . . . in case I lost it. Yes, I'd go home. No, I wouldn't. I wanted to see Fleetwood Mac. I wanted to have fun. Tomorrow was soon enough for reality.

As I walked in the door of my Georgetown apartment later that night, the phone was ringing. It was my pal, the Carter operative, calling from New York, which—unbeknownst to me—was deep in the midst of the 1977 blackout.

"Hey, guess what? Everything here is black."

"Everything *there* is black. You don't know the half of it."

"God, you mean Washington blacked out, too?"

"The blackest. You were right. They axed me tonight. Shelby called me in and announced that Friday was my last column."

"Those sons of bitches."

When I woke up the next morning, I felt down but not out. The thought of facing my colleagues made me want to crawl back under the covers, but I didn't. I had resolve. I don't know where it came from or how I found it, but it was there. I wasn't going to leave *The Washington Post* without making my mark. Somehow I'd beat them at their own game, walk out on the place before it walked out on me. I didn't have a plan, didn't know how or when I was going to do it, but I was. I had six months. I would wait, watch, pick my shot. When I left the *Post* it would be on my own terms.

As I was leaving for my first day as the wayward probationer, feeling like a juvenile delinquent reporting to the detention center, my brother called.

"Nancy?"

"Yeah?"

"Fuck 'em."

"Pat?"

"Yeah?"

"You can count on it."

Sally Quinn's look of distress appeared genuine when I confronted her in the Style section.

"Why didn't you tell me, Sal?"

"Nancy, I honestly didn't know until I got home last night," she said, and I believed her, although I was the only one who did. Everyone else assumed Sally was my saboteur, but it seemed too predictable to simply pit blonde against blonde. Right?

The next two weeks were a blur. I went to California, checked myself into the Ashram, a boot camp of a spa outside Los Angeles, and dragged myself up and down mountain ranges for five days. (The best way to face battle, after all, was with firm thighs.)

Rejuvenated, I dove back into work. I covered ten parties in fifteen days and whipped out my first Style feature (a piece on Sarsfield's, the Carter-crowd hangout immortalized by the underwearless Hamilton Jordan when he allegedly spit amaretto and cream at a female patron).

In mid-September my pieces headlined Style two days running: A GOOD HAIRCUT IS HARD TO FIND explored the problems of celebrated women and their renowned hair; and a lengthy profile of Hodding Carter, press secretary to Secretary of State Cyrus Vance, filled Style's Sunday front page. I turned around the Carter piece in a day, the longest and fastest I'd ever written, to beat out a *New York Times Magazine* cover story. On Monday Howard Simons made a point of telling me he thought it far outpaced the *Times* profile. Ben Bradlee appeared at my desk and cooed:

"I guess nobody in this town's asking what's going to happen to Nancy Collins after this weekend." I was ecstatic. Now that I'd shown them what I could do, I was hopeful we would finally hit a groove.

We didn't. Though they acknowledged my features were good, it was evident they would never ultimately shake their prejudice. Having been a gossip columnist, I discovered, was like having been married to Mickey Rooney. No matter how fast you got the divorce, you would always be the ex–Mrs. Mickey Rooney. I hadn't really been on probation at all. I had merely been given a stay of execution.

"Collins, no matter what you do," Bob Woodward confirmed, "they'll never see you as anything but the girl who didn't make 'The Gossip Column' work."

Woodward turned out to be right. On February 6 I got a note from Shelby. My "probation," as it were, hadn't worked out. As of March

2, I would no longer be an employee of *The Washington Post.* I stared at the memo. *Don't panic,* I told myself. *Don't panic. You'll think of something, you always have. There's still time.* I had three weeks. Not a lot of self-confidence—but three weeks.

The following Monday, I was sitting in the Madison Hotel coffee shop devouring French fries and the news weeklies when I saw the item in *New York*'s "Intelligencer" column:

"In his forthcoming book, *The Ends of Power,* H. R. 'Bob' Haldeman reveals his theories on two lingering Watergate mysteries. According to family sources close to Haldeman, he names Fred Fielding, 38, deputy counsel to Nixon and John Dean's assistant, as 'Deep Throat' . . ."

The Haldeman book. Of course! One of the biggest stories of the year, right on schedule. Bob Haldeman, Richard Nixon's right-hand man, had finally written his version of the Watergate debacle and sold it to Times Books, in those days a division of *The New York Times,* for the then-astronomical advance of $140,000. Declaring its contents "literary plutonium," Times Books had ballyhooed its publication into a real cloak-and-dagger media event. That was it! I'd get the Haldeman book, break through "the tightest security in publishing history," as it was being touted, and deliver it, by hand, to Bradlee. Yeah, that was it. Sounded great. But where did I start?

Intrigue prevailed. The location of the printer was shrouded in secrecy. The usual methods of selling and reviewing were waived. Reviewers allowed to see the book were required to sign a secrecy agreement before opening a copy. The powerful New York Times Syndicate offered serialization rights only to those American and European publications who signed the discretionary pledge—before inspecting a summary of the manuscript at Times Books's New York offices. (Their machinations paid off. At $5,000–$25,000 a clip, the syndicate peddled rights to more than forty national and international periodicals, including Germany's *Stern,* which alone shelled out over $200,000.)

Newsweek, a part of the Washington Post Company, paid $125,000 for U.S. magazine rights to the book, planning to splash it over two successive issues, each twenty-five cents above the normal newsstand price. Although *The New York Times* and *The Washington Star* bought excerpts, *The Washington Post* didn't. Its editors, and, indeed, journalists around the country, took offense at the notion of "checkbook journalism." For those reporters whose publications hadn't committed, it was open season on Haldeman. As a result, the media was rife with reporters trying to get ahold of the book before the official publication date of February 20.

As I finished reading the item in *New York*, I saw Woodward across the room lunching with his assistant, Ben Weiser. Woodward, one of the most adamant opponents of "The Gossip Column," had, in the end, become one of my most ardent supporters. When I landed the Frost-Nixon transcript (and, later, political pollster Pat Caddell's secret memo on Democratic presidential politics, also a front-page story), he'd been the first to congratulate me. There was no one at the *Post* I respected more.

"So, who's Fred Fielding, Woodward?" I teased when I reached his table.

"Collins, that's about the tenth time today I've been asked that question," he groaned. "My phone hasn't stopped ringing all morning. Even some guy from the London Sunday *Times* called."

Accepting his invitation to sit down, I purposefully kept the conversation on *The Ends of Power*. "I'm going after the Haldeman book."

"You ought to," he said. "If anybody can get it, you can."

With that vote of confidence from America's best investigative reporter, my trepidation disappeared. At least temporarily. I raced back to the office and grabbed the phone, calling the two people I knew best in publishing. Nothing. The third call was more productive. Patiently, my source explained the process of producing a book, concluding that a large printing like Haldeman's could only be handled by one of three printers in the country. Where, he asked, did Times Books usually do their printing?

I had no idea. I fetched the Times catalog from *The Washington Post Book World* and leafed through until I recognized the names of two authors. I called both, hoping to pick up some in-house gossip on the whereabouts of the printing plant. No luck. It was the first of many such calls I made that afternoon. Nothing concrete turned up, but with each conversation my enthusiasm soared. If I stayed on the phone long enough, I was confident I'd find that book. For the first time in months, I felt in control of my destiny.

In late afternoon, I apprised Shelby of my project, a technicality from my point of view. Unless Bradlee forbade me, I was staying on the story. Shelby didn't say no, but he didn't say yes. He said he'd check with Ben.

But by now I was on automatic pilot. I got the home number of Joe DiMona, Haldeman's ghost writer, described by a colleague as a "soft touch." I decided to be forthright, hoping to disarm him. Cordial and droll, DiMona was blatantly wallowing in the attention. Identifying myself, I stated I was going after the book. My impudence made him laugh. Inundated with calls from reporters, he admitted I was by far the sassiest. Still, our conversation rendered no new information—only a phone call the next morning from Thomas Lipscomb, president of Times Books. He and DiMona had talked, and Lipscomb was calling to say, charmingly, not to bother. The book, he confidently decreed, was "ungettable." I told him not to be so sure.

The rest of the day was spent with my finger on the dial. Fifty calls later, I'd fleshed out the bare bones: The manuscript was set in type in Bloomsburg, Pennsylvania, at a place called Haddon Craftsmen, Inc., using old-fashioned Linotype machines whose hot metal was melted down as soon as it was used, guaranteeing security. (The plant was manned by uniformed security guards.) The pages themselves were bound at a Haddon plant (more guards!) and the completed books were covered in tough plastic wrappers and stored in locked trucks and warehouses known only to a select few. One of those warehouses, I learned, might belong to Harper and Row, who had their own outlet in nearby Scranton.

Late that evening, as I was leaving the paper, I ran into deputy editor Larry Stern, a man with a marvelous sense of irony and, more important, a close chum of Bradlee's. When he asked what I was working on, I told him.

"The Haldeman book? You and everybody else. Does Ben know?"
I presumed he did.

"Well, I'd forget about it if I were you. You won't get it. Not a chance."

Would this wild-eyed enthusiasm never cease? Did Charles Lindbergh experience such solidarity as he pointed his plane toward Ireland? By the time I got home, I was thanking Larry. His remarks had been the coup de grâce. When I stepped out of the cab, my mind was made up. The Haldeman book was a done deal. (Hear the drum roll?)

The next day, Friday, I put a name with a building, always a good idea. When calls to Haddon Craftsmen produced nothing except cautious secretaries, I rang the Harper and Row distribution center. I asked the operator for the plant manager's name: "Mr. . . . Mr. . . . uh, what's his name again?"

"Scosia. Carl Scosia."

"Right," I confirmed expansively. "Could you put me through to his office?"

A woman answered.

Was Mr. Scosia in?

No.

Any chance I'd be able to reach him on Saturday?

No. He didn't come in on weekends.

Bingo. An absent plant manager. I tucked that information away and tore into Shelby's office. Explaining what I'd uncovered, I asked permission to go to Scranton. He looked, as usual, grim. He'd confer with Ben and get back to me. At my desk, I called Allegheny and booked a seat that night on the plane to Scranton. Whether or not they said yes, I was going.

Later Shelby signaled me into his office. I could go, he said, but there were rules: I couldn't steal or buy any part of the book, and if I got caught doing anything "untoward," the *Post* would disassociate itself. (Did they give this same speech to Woodstein?)

Before I left, I contacted a friend from Scranton. When I'd outlined my mission, he gave me the number of his parents, residents of Scranton, who, he assured me, would help in any way they could, no questions asked. "I'll call and tell them you're a friend of mine. That's good enough."

Around six, as I was leaving, Howard Simons cornered me on the edge of the newsroom. After our first encounter, I'd grown to like Howard, who was warm and paternal. Tonight, however, he was once again The Company Man. When I confirmed I was indeed on my way to Pennsylvania, he gingerly took my arm. Reminding me I worked for *The Washington Post,* Howard stared somberly into my eyes.

"Remember, Nancy . . ."

"Yes, Howard?"

"Don't embarrass the family."

Was I still related?

Back at my apartment I threw a few things into a bag and headed for the airport. When we landed in Scranton, I bused into town, checked into the Scranton Sheraton, and slumped into a chair, the adrenaline that had gotten me this far suddenly kaput. What was I doing here in this barren room with its shag rug on a Friday night? At best, my plan was vague: Tomorrow I'd check out the Haddon printers, the Haddon bindery, and Harper and Row. Beyond that, I hadn't a clue.

The next morning was overcast, dismal, and bitter cold. Dressing for combat, I threw on a pair of faded army fatigues my brother had brought back from Vietnam, a cashmere turtleneck, and black boots—high-heeled. Not *high* high, but heels nonetheless. I was going to need every inch I could get.

I called a cab (with my sense of direction, I knew I'd spend the day hopelessly lost if I rented a car). It was nearly an hour before we reached a large warehouse-type building set off the road on a stark piece of property. When I paid the driver, he looked at me as if I were crazy. As he drove off, leaving me stranded, I agreed with him. I was out of my mind.

I walked to the front door and rang the buzzer. No answer. I headed for a second door near the delivery area, found another bell, and pushed. Ten minutes later, no one had appeared, and I was freezing. Back in front, I tried again. No response. I was about to pack it in when a mail truck came barreling down the driveway and pulled into the loading zone alongside the building. The driver, a friendly kid exactly like a dozen boys I'd grown up with in Montana, jumped down from the lofty cabin.

"Hi. Place is closed," he said. "It's Saturday."

"So I see."

"Can I help you? What are you doing here all by yourself anyway?" he asked.

"Well, I'm just in town for the weekend, visiting my aunt," I lied, gaining speed as my alibi developed. "I'm a graduate student doing my thesis on . . . uh, publishing. And since I was here I thought it'd be a good time to come and see if I could get a tour through a real publishing, uh . . . place. I was hoping it might be open."

It wasn't, he said. But we could check the mailroom to see if anybody was around. We walked inside a storage area toward a sliding door whose windows were partially covered by a canvas tarp. When I pulled it back, I peered into a room devoid of human life. My host, who identified himself as Tom, joined me.

"I don't see nobody." There was no one to see. Just stacks of boxes filled with books. Was one of them written by H. R. Haldeman?

"Place's been under real tight security all week," Tom volunteered.

"Why?"

"They're publishing one of them White House guys' books."

"Which one?"

"Can't remember the name but it must be pretty important because they've been treating it like they was expecting somebody to take it from them any minute."

Mentally, I clicked my heels.

While Tom unloaded his boxes, I finished exploring the place. It was locked up tighter than a tick. Only Houdini could crack this sucker. When Tom asked if I wanted a lift, I accepted, requesting a drop up the road at McDonald's, where I'd call my aunt. This trusting soul saw nothing odd about my being in the middle of nowhere without a car.

No pay phone at McDonald's. Walking across the street to a dingy gas station, I spotted two mechanics, their grease-covered hands wrist-deep in bags of Wise potato chips. The phone, they pointed out, was beside the battery box under the girlie calendar.

"Mighty unusual to see anyone using a cab around here," noted one after I hung up. When the taxi finally pulled into the station, it turned out to be the same man I'd used that morning. The driver seemed unsurprised to see me again, but I was wary. In Hamilton, if a stranger called two cabs in the same morning, the news would be all over Haig's pool hall by noon.

Around midday, I arrived at the Haddon Bindery. Giving myself a quick pep talk, I walked in. Two steps inside the door, I was confronted by a guard—young and unsure of himself. Okay, I thought. I'd found my wedge.

Then I glanced up. Behind him, mopping the stairs, a janitor eyed me suspiciously. I launched into my cover: I was a student, interested in publishing and eager to explore a real publishing facility. The guard started to mumble something about no one being allowed in, but the janitor interrupted.

"Nope, you sure can't come in here. This here building's under special guard," he barked. "You can't get in at all unless you have a pass. They're doing special projects here."

"What special projects, sir?"

"I can't tell you but you can't get in."

Suddenly, a woman toting a canvas bag and wearing a plastic rain hat came down the stairs. As the janitor repeated my request, I watched her expression grow distrustful.

"Oh, no. Nobody can go in there," she said. "How do we know you're not some little reporter?"

"A reporter?" I giggled breathlessly. "I just have to get my thesis done or I'm sunk. But . . . huh . . . I'll come back next week. When you're open."

Before they had time to assess my story, I fled. Outside, cold and discouraged—two down and, so far, nothing—I looked for a place to park myself and think. Spotting a restaurant across the road, I headed toward it. The interior bore an eerie likeness to the diner Jack Nicholson immortalized in *Five Easy Pieces.* Sitting at the counter, I ordered coffee and a hamburger patty. The meat was shriveled and tough. Nevertheless, I polished it off and ordered another. The second I ate more slowly, hoping to nourish my sagging spirits. So what did I do now? Call Woodward? Call Bernstein? Call Mama?

I stood up. I still had another stop. But what if Harper and Row didn't pan out? Did I repeat this whole routine again tomorrow? I couldn't go back to Washington empty-handed. Taxi!

"So, where you wanna go?" asked the diner manager, who insisted on calling for me when I told him his pay phone was out of whack.

"Uh, the Harper and Row plant."

He told the dispatcher, hung up, and gave me a deliberate look.

"Do you work for Harper and Row?"

Alarms sounded in my head. "Uh, not yet. But I hope to. I'm here for a job interview."

"On Saturday?"

"Well, it's the only day the guy who runs the plant could see me." I smiled. Had I said too much? Or was I just paranoid? Did he know the plant manager or, worse yet, *was* he the plant manager doing a Saturday moonlight?

"The reason I ask is that my brother works for Harper and Row," the manager continued. My mouth went dry. "Not here, outta state."

"Really? How does he like it?"

When the cab appeared, I bustled out the door. In the background, the man wished me luck with my job interview.

The cab driver, a new one, was a talker. Wasn't the plant closed on Saturday? I repeated my job-interview story. He seemed to buy it, and I gazed out the window, discouraging further conversation. The ride seemed endless. Eventually, we turned off the main road and drove up a winding incline leading to a large, modern nondescript building. The parking lot was near empty—only four or five cars. Still, this was going to be tricky. At the door, I peered in the glass window and rang the bell. Moments later, a tall, thin man ambled toward me from a back room.

"Hello—I'm here to see Carl Scosia," I said. "We have an appointment, but I'm an hour early. Do you know if he's here?"

The man didn't, but said we could find out after I signed the visitors' book. I scrawled my name; under company I put "WP." Both were illegible.

The guard led me down several halls to a row of darkened offices.

At the end of the hallway, I spotted two doors whose glass panels revealed a roomful of cartons beyond. I could feel my muscles tighten. Somewhere in there, I knew, was The Book. Farther down the hall the guard was standing by another door.

Mr. Scosia, he said, was not yet in.

Well, could I wait?

He said I was welcome to sit in the lobby.

Walking casually to the double doors, I peered in. "What's this?"

"The shipping room."

Inside I could make out rows of cartons, presumably filled with books. I strained to see anything pertaining to Haldeman. Nothing.

"All the cartons look the same. How can they tell which book is where?"

"Oh, they know. People like Mr. Scosia."

"Think I could go in and look around while I wait?"

"No, ma'am. That's blocked off."

"Why?"

"Because it's a special delivery. Top secret."

"Top secret? What does that mean?"

"I can't say," he said with conviction. "But it's off limits."

I laughed. "Well, now I'm dying of curiosity."

He smiled. "If Mr. Scosia wants to explain it to you, he can. That's his business."

Not wanting to alarm him, I walked back toward the front of the building, passing a ladies' room. When we reached the sparsely furnished lobby, I headed for one of two chairs.

"I'm afraid we don't have any magazines or anything."

"Oh, I'm fine," I said, reaching into my bag and pulling out *Time.*

Satisfied that I was occupied, the man disappeared into a side room.

I had to get into that shipping room. But how? I could go to the ladies' room, which would get me near the doors. But how much time could I stay away without raising alarm?

Fifteen minutes later, the guard reappeared.

"I have to make rounds. Will you be all right?"

"Oh, sure. Uh, if somebody besides Mr. Scosia comes should I let them in . . . ?"

"No, ma'am. Oh, I'll be back in thirty minutes. If they don't have a key they can wait."

"Okay."

He walked back down the hall leading to the shipping room, took a right, and disappeared. When his footsteps grew faint, I waited five minutes before getting up and strolling to the ladies' room. My heart was pounding like an out-of-control jackhammer.

Reaching the door, I paused, alert for sounds. Hearing nothing, I glanced quickly to the right and walked to the glass doors. Grabbing a handle, I pulled.

Locked.

What had I expected? A top-secret room to be wide open waiting for me? Flattening my face against the glass, I strained to ascertain the layout. It was useless. All I could see were cartons, stacks of cartons— and no way to get at them.

Wait. What was that door to the left? Maybe.

I hurried back to the lobby and another set of portals on the right. This time when I pulled, they opened into a series of darkened rooms. As I gingerly made my way through the interconnecting corridors, the twilight lighting made everything look foreboding. Where was I going? What if I got lost? God, it was getting so dark. What was that up ahead? A faint light seeping out from under a door? I turned the doorknob. It opened.

Slipping inside, I stopped, listening for noises as I got my bearings. I was in the room with the cartons. Somewhere in here was the Haldeman book. Noticing a few labels, I searched for more. Ah, here was one. HALDEMAN? NO, MUHAMMAD ALI.

Creeping through the stacks, I worked my way toward the back. Look for boxes covered in plastic, I kept reminding myself—they said the Haldeman books were wrapped in thick plastic. Rounding a corner, I suddenly ran smack up against a stack of cartons, eight or nine feet high and sealed in plastic. This had to be it. Nothing else had wrappers. A quick survey revealed no labels. And not one looked open. If I wanted to get into a box, I'd have to cut through the plastic. Was that breaking and entering? Technically, I figured, I was now only in the area of "entering" since I hadn't broken into anything to get here. I needed Edward Bennett Williams to tell me my rights.

Sheer nerves turned my breathing into shallow pants. If I got caught now, what would the *Post* do? Wasn't just being here against Shelby's rules? Not so far, I thought. I hadn't bought or stolen anything. I was simply . . . exploring. "You can't steal it, you can't buy it, you can" . . . I could *borrow* it! That's it, I'd borrow a book, copy some pages, and somehow get it back here. Maybe there was a Xerox machine in the building. The plastic looked impregnable. Was every carton encased? I ran my hands over the boxes directly in front of me. All sealed. I looked up. Everything looked so contained . . . so . . . but wait, on top, a box on top looked slightly askew. Was that brown cardboard I saw peeking through plastic at the end of the stack?

"I think one's open," I whispered aloud. Jumping onto an adjacent table, I found a foothold and shimmied up the stacks. Catching my breath, I crawled to the box in question. Damn! It was sealed after all. Frantically, I ran my hand over its sides. What was this? A flap? Something felt loose. I yanked. And yanked again. The plastic moved. Lifting a chunk, I saw corrugated cardboard underneath. Investigating further, I ran my hand atop what felt like a book. Reaching in, I pulled one out. In the dim light I could just make out the title: THE ENDS OF POWER BY H. R. HALDEMAN. Holy cow! Quickly, I leafed through it . . . Nixon, Kissinger . . . the names leapt from the page. My God, I actually had the Haldeman book in my hands and was reading it! This minute! Somehow, I had to make a copy. There must be a Xerox machine in the building!

Suddenly, I heard voices. Fear shot through me like a quick pain. Get down or stay put? Stay put. I flattened myself on top of the stacks and prayed no one would look up.

Seconds marched by with the speed of Galápagos tortoises sashaying toward lunch. Finally, I heard footsteps. Coming toward me? Retreating?

Retreating.

When the echo quieted, I arose. I had to move fast. Very fast. Surely, an hour had passed! Scrambling down from my perch, I thrust the book into my safari bag. (God, would Ralph Lauren be proud!) Had to get back to the lobby; there must be a Xerox machine in the guard's room.

Nearly running, I retraced my steps. Striding through the doors into the lobby, I glanced at the clock. I'd been gone only twenty minutes? It felt like twenty years. The guard was nowhere in sight. Briskly, I walked down the hallway toward the ladies' room, turned around, and walked back to the lobby. As I did so, I paraded purposefully to the guard's room. No guard. But no Xerox machine either.

Going to the front door, I checked the parking lot. Empty. Black and empty. Momentarily, I heard footsteps behind me. I turned to see the guard approaching me from the far end of the hall. What was the look on his face? Did he know where I'd been?

"Mr. Scosia turn up yet?" he inquired noncommittally.

"Not yet. But . . . uh, I just called him at home. He's going to try to make it in about an hour. It's my fault. I made the appointment at the last minute. I'm only in town this weekend so he's rearranging his whole schedule to fit me in. I'm working around him."

He seemed to buy my story. I went back to my chair. Had to get to a copier. Had to leave. Minutes later, I walked to the guard's room. "I'm getting hungry. I think I'll go grab a sandwich. If Mr. Scosia comes, will you tell him I'll be right back?"

"Sure."

I hurried toward the front entrance, stopping abruptly midway. *Wait a minute, Nancy Drew, you ain't got no getaway car.* I couldn't call a cab again. I needed a car, a chauffeur, someone who knew the area, someone I could trust. My friend's father! I returned to the guard.

"May I use the phone again?"

"Sure."

I dialed the number scrawled in my notebook.

A man answered.

"Hi, this is Nancy Collins." I waited.

"Oh, yes, Miss Collins. We've been expecting your call. How are you?"

"Actually, a little hungry. I know this is real last-minute, but I'm up here at Harper and Row. Do you know where it is?"

"I can find it."

"Could you possibly come and take me for a quick sandwich?"

"Why, sure, I guess so."

"Great. How long will it take you to get here?"

"About twenty minutes."

"Fine. I'll meet you at the turn-off at the bottom of the driveway. . . . Oh and . . . uh, Mr. Smith, uh . . . the car?"

"Oh, yeah. It's dark blue." He laughed. "Look for an old guy in a dark blue car."

He'd read my mind. "Thanks so much."

Out the door and out of sight, I jogged down the hill. Reaching the bottom, I fell to the ground, breathing heavily. Fifteen minutes later, I was getting anxious. I stood up, turned left, and started running down the road. I'd meet him halfway. Besides, even if he got lost, I'd still have to find a Xerox machine somewhere. In the pitch black, I could barely make out trees, fields. Maybe it was euphoria or adrenaline, but it took nearly a quarter of a mile before I realized I was galloping along in high heels. Mmmmm . . . if I stayed in the investigative-reporting racket, I'd have to buy a pair of flats.

Where was he?

Suddenly, behind me, I heard a motor. Wrong direction, but so what? I turned to face an oncoming car, blinded by its brights. A dark-colored compact pulled up alongside me. As I reached for the back-door handle, I got my first clear look at the driver. It was a man, all right, but not old. Jesus!!!! I pivoted wildly, gobbling up the road in fear. The man accelerated. Driving on the shoulder, he tried to force me into the ditch. I skidded on the gravel. Damn heels! Petrified, I clutched my shoulder bag to my side. Did he know I had the book? Had the guard tipped him off? Or was this just some random crazy person?

"Come on," I wheezed aloud, "can't stop now. Run, girl." Suddenly, I saw another pair of headlights. A car coming toward us. I waved my free arm. Please, let it be mine. When it stopped beside me, I lurched forward with my last ounce of energy, flung myself against the door, ripped it open and hurled myself onto the lap of my stunned driver.

"Are you Mr. Smith?" I gasped.

"Yes," replied the startled older gentleman.

"You don't know how glad I am to see you. Let's get out of here." We peeled out.

"I can't explain it, but we've got to find a Xerox place," I said to my accidental co-conspirator. "I've got to make copies and get back here fast. Can we?"

My partner rose to the occasion, flooring it toward civilization and asking no questions. We spotted a motel and stopped. Walking into the manager's office, I said I was a student, in search of a copier for a term paper. There was none. Back in the car, we drove to the next motel. They had one and I could use it: twenty-five cents a page. I started photocopying. At page three the machine ran out of paper. There wasn't more.

I loped to the parking lot. Only one option left: the Sheraton. I knew it had a Xerox machine; I'd seen it that morning. When we got there, I found the manager and asked to use the machine. He walked me into a small office, explained how it worked, and left. I looked at the clock. I had to work fast.

Feverishly, I squashed page after bound page onto the glass plate, resenting the two seconds it took to make each print. What if the cops burst through the door? Would I call Bradlee? Coffey? Would they defend me? Quickly, my anxiety gave way to an odd high, an exclusive exhilaration. Nothing else mattered but the task at hand. My cosmos was compact, decisive, dicey. So this was the "being in the moment" that acting teachers rhapsodized about.

An hour later, I'd photocopied almost 190 pages of the book, but the plant was a distance away. I had to go. Unwillingly, I put the last page through the copier, gathered my work, and found the manager. My bill came to thirty-eight dollars. I paid in cash and got a receipt. The accounting department at *The Washington Post* was ruthless.

My chauffeur and I sped back to Harper and Row. At the turn, I hopped out. Since I didn't know who awaited me, I asked Mr. Smith to park and wait. If something went wrong, I didn't want him implicated since he had no definite idea of what I was up to. I ran up the drive and rang the buzzer.

In a few minutes, the guard appeared.

"Find yourself something to eat?"

"Yeah, took longer than I thought. Did Mr. Scosia show up yet?"

"Nope. You want to call again?"

"I'll wait a few minutes more."

"Well, I'm about to do my rounds."

"That's fine. I'll wait until you get back. If he's not here by then, I'll call."

As soon as the guard was safely out of sight, I returned to the scene of my adventure. Heart in throat, I walked through the dark rooms, the shipping-room door, the stacks, back to the Haldeman cartons. Scaling my own personal Kilimanjaro, I found the box, returned the book, and replaced the plastic flap, leaving it exactly as I'd found it.

Mission accomplished.

Almost.

I tore back to the lobby. When the guard returned I was relaxing in my chair.

"It's getting late. I called Mr. Scosia while you were gone. We're going to try to meet next week sometime. I waited to thank you for your help."

The guard looked askance. Did he believe me?

"Not at all. Just mark your time in the book before you go."

My scribbling was, again, unreadable.

Outside, I walked until the plant was out of view, then broke into a heated gallop. My driver started the engine, I jumped in, and we took off.

Mr. Smith told me he'd pick me up the next morning at 5 A.M. so I could catch the first flight back to Washington. I left the photocopied pages with him for safekeeping overnight. Never knew what awaited me at the Sheraton.

Back in my room I called the only two people I could guarantee would still be working at midnight—Woodward, on assignment in Chicago, and my best friend, Norma Kamali, the fashion designer, the only non-*Post* person who knew where I was that weekend. I reached her on the private line in her Madison Avenue workroom, where she sat sewing sequins on shoulder pads. As I outlined the day's events, her reaction quickly rose to Gregorian-chant proportions:

"Oh, my God, oh, my God, oh, my God, can they arrest you, oh, my God, oh, my God, oh, my God, are you sure they can't arrest you, oh, my God, oh, my God, oh, my God, what have you gotten yourself into? Oh, my god, oh, my God, oh, my God. I'm scared to death. . . . Oh, my God. . . ."

Woodward's response was more restrained. "I told you you could do it, Collins," he said, genuinely pleased. Still, it wasn't over. I hadn't dropped the manuscript on Ben Bradlee's desk. I was black Irish enough to continue expecting the worse. Until I got this baby home, I wasn't talking to anybody.

"Collins, it's eleven o'clock at night and we're the only two people at the *Post* still working." From Woodward, the self-confessed workaholic, it was the ultimate accolade.

As soon as I hit Washington I rang the doorbell of *Post* reporter and Watergate maven Scott Armstrong, per my instructions from *Post* central. When I got off the elevator, Scott met me.

"How are you?"

"How do I look for someone who hasn't slept in days?" I handed him the photocopies.

"How is it?"

"I keep waiting for the punch line, and it's not there. Maybe you can find it."

Scott sat down and started to read. I headed for the kitchen to finally check in with Bradlee and Coffey. Both conversations were short. I told

Shelby where I was and that I'd see him later. Finally, I took the glass of orange juice offered by Karen de Young, Scott's live-in girlfriend and one of the *Post*'s preeminent foreign correspondents. The last time we'd had breakfast together was in New York, when she and I were both guest editors at *Mademoiselle.* Small world.

Karen ushered me into a bedroom to lie down, but it was useless. If I'd downed ten cups of coffee, I couldn't have been more wired. Up until now everything had been in my control. But once the manuscript got into the *Post* system, I couldn't guarantee secrecy. Newsrooms are notoriously loose-lipped. The story had to run before somebody leaked. It might be my coup, but it was Ben's paper. I hoped he'd move fast.

I joined Scott in the kitchen and, together, we read the Haldeman pages until four that afternoon. Before we left for the *Post,* I ducked into the shower, superstitiously climbing back into my army fatigues.

When we reached Ben's fishbowl, Howard Simons was waiting, a paternal smile on his face. "Good work, Nancy," he said with obvious joy. Moments later, Bradlee breezed in. "Well, how is it?" Ben said to Scott.

"It's *The Sting,* the million-dollar *Sting,*" Scott said, indicating he wasn't overimpressed with Haldeman's revelations. Ben was leafing through the pages. "Listen to this," he said, reading aloud from a section on Kissinger. Suddenly, I was petrified. What if, after all this, they didn't run it? What if they decided it was *The Sting . . .* wasn't newsworthy?

I started to speak up, but Ben beat me to it. "Get a copy to Haynes [Johnson]. He'll write the story."

As we stood up, Howard beamed again. "Good job."

"Yeah. Excellent," added Ben. Halfway across the newsroom I turned and walked back into Bradlee's office.

"Ben?"

"Yeah?"

"I told you I was tough."

Postscript:

On Thursday, February 16, 1978, four days before the official publication date of *The Ends of Power*, *The Washington Post* ran the following headline across the top of the front page: HALDEMAN ACCUSES NIXON. WATERGATE BREAK-IN, TAPE GAP CITED. There was no byline on the story, just an italicized box in the middle, composed by Bradlee, reading: "This report was written by staff writer Haynes Johnson from information supplied by staff writer Nancy Collins. Staff writers Bob Woodward and Scott Armstrong contributed to this report."

With that, all hell broke loose. *The Washington Post* had done it again, chortled headlines across the country. Socked it to *The New York Times*! Scooped everybody! What a caper, said anchormen, who smiled when they reported "Scrantongate." One intrepid camera crew even trekked to Pennsylvania to film the room at the Sheraton where I'd stayed. Except, of course, they got the wrong room. ("Next time, Collins," advised Carl Bernstein, Woodward's Watergate teammate, "don't sign in under your own name.")

My caper cost the New York Times Syndicate at least a quarter of a million dollars. Times Books's Tom Lipscomb, who'd bragged that his book was ungettable, admitted he'd been got, and ordered *The Ends of Power* shipped early. And *The New York Times* ran all ten thousand words of its five-part series on Friday, following up with a Sunday editorial huffily dismissing the Haldeman caper as a "second-rate burglary of H. R. Haldeman's memoir of a third-rate burglary."

Closer to home, *Newsweek*'s editor-in-chief, Ed Kosner, stunned at having been scooped by his own employer, called Katharine Graham, who, in turn, shrieked at Ben Bradlee. Ben, it seemed, had neglected to inform Katharine that the *Post* was going with the story on Thursday; he claimed he had been unable to reach her because she was on a plane from Seattle to San Diego.

"I wasn't in San Diego," Mrs. Graham roared to *Time*. "I was at *Newsweek*. It's not a great source of pride to me that the first word I heard was from Sydney Gruson, executive vice president of the New York Times Company, yelling at me. He seemed able to reach me even if the *Post* couldn't."

Meanwhile, back at the *Post,* I instructed the switchboard operators
to transfer all press calls concerning Haldeman directly to me. (Ben,
Shelby et al. were at an editorial conference in Florida, which helped.)
The *Post* hardly had a stake in my future, and since I was the one job
hunting I figured it best to place my own ads. So, when *The New York
Times, Time, Newsweek, Newsday,* and numerous other media called,
I talked to the reporters myself. On-the-job training. As usual.

Most of it turned out okay. *Time* and *Newsweek* did separate stories
on me, accompanied by pictures so ghastly they'll keep me humble
forever. (When your fifteen minutes finally comes, you're going to be
ten pounds overweight.) In a burst of righteous indignation, I informed
a pushy reporter from *The New York Times,* "I will go to my grave
before I disclose how I got the book." (Obviously, I changed my mind.)
But I did shoot myself in the foot and did my bleeding in *Doonesbury.*
One reporter, trying to figure out exactly when I'd gone to Scranton,
asked how long I'd been working on the story. I told him that it "felt
like my whole life." And then I laughed. Only that went unrecorded.
The next week the sagacious Garry Trudeau drew the reporter Rick
Redfern having the following phone conversation with his editor, Howard:

"Howard, are you telling me I'm traveling with Carter just because
of my biorhythms?"

"Rick, Listen! Your physical, intellectual, and emotional waves will
be peaking soon!"

"So?"

"So? The night Woodward met Deep Throat? Triple high! The day
Walters got her Sadat/Begin interviews? Triple high! . . . And you
know that girl who pinched the Haldeman book for the *Post?* The one
who said she'd spent her whole life getting ready to report that story?"

"Triple low?"

"I'm telling you, Rick. It's absolutely uncanny."

Now I knew how civilians felt. And how did I really feel through all
of this? Does "existential" cover it? That I was being both lauded and
fired at the same time? That when people asked how big a bonus the
Post was giving me, I was praying for severance? That in the midst

of the furor it struck me that Ben had neglected to ask how I'd gotten the book—stolen it? borrowed it? embarrassed the family?—until *after* the story ran.

Bradlee, meanwhile, declared his glee over the caper to *Newsweek:* "You gotta admit it's fun. I'm happier than a pig in shit," he gloated. Good for Ben. He was having fun. Shelby, meanwhile, told me he hoped I would use this story to get my next job.

Such were the dynamics when I flew to California in early March to appear on NBC's *Tomorrow* show. Tom Snyder had invited me even though I'd made it clear I couldn't reveal how I'd gotten the book. At the airport I was met by a long stretch limo—complete with color TV and bar—that took me to my hotel. Right away I loved network television.

The next night I was again limoed, this time to the eight o'clock taping of that evening's show, which was to be aired coast to coast at 1 A.M. I was the first guest. An associate producer led me into the studio, where a very tall Tom Snyder, characteristic cigarette in hand, stood beside face-to-face chairs. I sat down, feeling totally relaxed. I loved working without a script.

The first segment went well. Snyder and I bantered easily. ("You're really good at this," he said during the break. How could I be bad? All you had to do was *talk.*) We were minutes into segment two, when suddenly Snyder leaned all six feet four inches forward in his inimitable style, and said, "Listen, this was a big, big, *big* story you got for these people. What did Katharine Graham say to you when she called you up?"

With the camera beading in on a tight head shot, I hesitated just a moment too long and my wily interviewer caught it.

"You mean to tell me Kay Graham hasn't called you?" Snyder said, beginning to laugh. "You mean to say the owner of *The Washington Post* hasn't bothered to talk to the reporter who put her newspaper on the map?"

"Tom, I hardly put *The Washington Post* on the map," I replied, treading verbal water. "And, you realize, owning both *Newsweek* and the *Post,* she's in a very difficult position—"

"Yeah, but don't you think," Snyder bored in, "don't you think she coulda just picked up the phone and at least called and said, 'Good work'?"

Suddenly my Irish caught up with me; the ridiculousness of the moment, indeed, of the entire episode, finally hit me right there on network television. I started to laugh. If only Tom's inadvertent sleuthing had caught the more delicious irony: As far as I knew, I wouldn't even be on her payroll past next week.

A Few Words on Journalistic Ethics:

My friend Ed Kosner, who got his ox gored because of the Haldeman caper but is one of the smartest editors in the business, maintains even today that the Haldeman story was two-pronged: journalism and theft. He claims tracking down *The Ends of Power* was reporting, but "purloining" its contents, as he likes to put it, was simply stealing.

Naturally, I disagree. I believe everything I did was journalism. First of all, news organizations shouldn't pay for news. And, secondly, I did not steal the book. I *borrowed* it. The book I photocopied from is probably sitting right now in someone's library. What I "lifted," and I use this word loosely, was its contents, which, many journalists believed, was "news." And who owns that?

The late Charlotte Curtis, reporter extraordinaire for *The New York Times* and one of my first and most influential heroines, once told me, "Remember, dearie, all you own in life is your own life story." She's absolutely right. My mission and passion has been to assist people in telling theirs in the most complete, interesting way. But what if a part of that life was paid for by tax dollars, by us—as in the case of H. R. Haldeman? In essence, we financed Haldeman's "research," which he, in turn, wrote about and then sold back to us at a hefty profit.

Some of that information happened to be newsworthy. Not the blockbuster inside scandal everyone had hoped for, but good enough that a revered news organization like *6o Minutes* paid Haldeman a reported $100,000 to get his story on television. *The Washington Post* got off a lot cheaper. All they shelled out was round-trip plane fare to

Scranton, some cab rides, a few nights in a hotel, and $38 in photocopying fees.

When I finally got a note from Ben, I expected a summons to his office, a grilling on my tactics. Isn't that how it happened in the movie? But, no, his missive simply said probation was off; I could stay at the *Post* indefinitely. So I did. For a little while. But I'd done what I came to do. I'd, thankfully, gotten dealt into one of the most prestigious poker games in the world and finally held my own, on my own terms, in a tough hand. I learned about corporate and personal politics. But mostly I learned to trust my own instincts. Working at *The Washington Post* was one of the most important lessons of my life. So, despite everything, if I had it to do over, I would.

Both the Haldeman caper and "The Gossip Column" were simply very much in keeping with the "schoolyard ethos," as some like to call it, that operated at the *Post* in the late seventies. Ben Bradlee is a swashbuckler and his paper reflected it. He believes in throwing everybody in the pot and seeing who bubbles to the top. He calls it "creative tension." When my turn in the stew came, I bobbed, sank, bobbed, and finally, with Herculean effort, bubbled.

Like always.

ELIZABETH TAYLOR

TODAY

June 1986

"I was married a virgin."

■

Like most girls my age, I grew up with Elizabeth Taylor's picture on my wall. Or, I should say, picture*s*. I was not merely a fan, I was obsessed. At eight, I was the only third grader in Montana to know that Elizabeth (*never* Liz—she hated that!) boasted lavender eyes and a double row of *natural* lashes. At ten, I could name all her husbands and what she'd worn when she married each of them—information that proved invaluable when I finally met her in 1977 in Washington, D.C.

The occasion was yet another capital cocktail party. Elizabeth was there with husband number six (or seven, if you count Richard Burton twice), Republican senator John Warner. I was there for *The Washington Post,* covering what was D.C.'s glitziest duo. It wasn't the first time. Since starting at the paper, I'd written frequently about Elizabeth, sometimes, alas, in a less-than-flattering light.

In the late seventies, Taylor, as she would confess after her 1983 visit to the Betty Ford clinic, was still drug-and-alcohol-dependent—a condition that often revealed itself in public. When a personality of her magnitude acts inappropriately, a reporter has no choice but to mention it. Although I never said outright that she was drunk, I did note the "erratic" behavior of the senator's wife. (In Hollywood it didn't matter how Elizabeth Taylor behaved at parties; in Washington it did.)

It gave me little pleasure to see my childhood idol embarrassing herself. Yet Elizabeth's escapades, coupled with the *Post's* interest in the new movie star in town, kept the pressure on. What I saw, I reported, even though I realized it was not laughable: Elizabeth Taylor needed help.

When our paths finally crossed at the aforementioned cocktail party, I was standing, notebook in hand, on the sidelines of the room. Suddenly, Taylor, sheathed in one of her voluminous Halston caftans, marched up to me, those renowned lavender eyes boring into mine.

"Why are you writing all those terrible things about me?" she asked.

"What do you mean?" I said, stalling.

"You know what I mean."

"Well, I have to report what I see."

"But why don't you like me?"

"Oh, but I do," I said, unraveling under the scrutiny. "I grew up with your picture on my wall. I know the dress you wore when you married Eddie Fisher at Grossinger's. It was two-toned chiffon—kelly and sea green, cocktail length, with matching fabric worn over your head like a mantilla."

Taylor paused. "I'm not even sure I remember that . . . thank God," she finally said, letting loose with a loud cackle. "That's very good."

And I did like her, particularly at that moment. I liked her candor, her self-deprecating sense of humor, and, most of all, that she had confronted me. Still, I was a reporter, and this was not an opportunity to be missed. "I'd love to do an interview with you sometime. It might be therapeutic to talk about how this town's treated you."

"I love Washington," she said, mouthing the automatic spiel of the Washington political wife. Then the woman who had heard every come-on from the press appraised me skeptically. "Well, we'll see," she said before walking off. Vague, yes, but not a total brush-off. It might take some time and tenacity on my part, but I felt it would happen.

Some time? How about eight years of letters, phone calls, and constant communication, largely with Elizabeth Taylor's primary liaison, her press agent, Chen Sam. An intriguing character in her own right, Chen has represented Elizabeth for eighteen years. They met in Botswana in 1972. Taylor and Richard Burton were at the Chobe Game Lodge, a thousand miles from the nearest hospital, when Burton, then drinking heavily, contracted malaria. Sam, a pharmacist in Johannesburg, not only filled a prescription for the actor, but hand-delivered it, staying on the subsequent seven weeks while Burton went on the wagon. When the famous couple returned to London, Chen went along as Elizabeth's personal assistant. Since then, Sam has been Taylor's liaison to the world. She's seen the actress through husbands, deaths, divorces, boyfriends, tell-all biographies, drinking, drugs, and drying out. The two have a complicated, interwoven, often volatile relationship, but, in the final analysis, Chen Sam is the passkey to Elizabeth Taylor. Period.

Happily, Chen and I got along from the first, especially after she satisfied herself that I wanted to interview, not exploit, her client. Over eight years, she kept my name in play with the scores of journalists requesting interviews. Around Year Three, a standard joke was born: "So, tell me, Chen," I'd say when making my ritual January call, "how does *this* year look?"

By the spring of 1985 I was with *Today* and relieved to learn from Sam that Elizabeth had finally bitten the addiction bullet. She was on her way to the Betty Ford Center in Rancho Mirage, California, to be treated for cross addictions to drugs and alcohol. After completing the program, Taylor returned to Los Angeles and embarked on a strenuous diet, shedding close to sixty pounds. Moreover, she became involved in the fight against AIDS, which is where our story picks up.

I'd now been on Taylor's trail for seven years. Lewis and Clark never knew such diligence. That persistence finally paid off when I got a surprise call. Elizabeth, Chen said, was thinking of giving a television interview. (She hadn't been interviewed on television in three years—

and that had been a promo for her appearance in *The Little Foxes*.)
In 1985 the AIDS crisis was at fever pitch and Taylor was ready to use
her celebrity for the cause, even if it meant going public. Elizabeth and
Chen wanted to do *Today*. Could they request me for the interview?
(Could they?!) There were, of course, caveats. Elizabeth would talk
only about AIDS and wanted a guarantee I'd do an accompanying
piece interviewing the foremost AIDS specialists in the country.

I ran the package by Steve Friedman, *Today*'s executive producer,
who hastily agreed to the conditions. Elizabeth Taylor, after all, was
Elizabeth Taylor. But we both hoped I'd be able to take the conversation beyond AIDS. Quickly, I shot the accompanying segments: interviews with Dr. Mathilde Krim in New York, Dr. Anthony Fauci,
director of the National Institutes of Allergies and Infectious Diseases,
and Dr. Michael Gottlieb of the University of California at Los Angeles.

Elizabeth, meanwhile, agreed to talk during a lunch break on the set
of the movie she was filming, a TV drama co-starring and produced by
R. J. Wagner. Lunch break? Eight years and all I get is . . . lunch? In
the movie business, time is money, and in the case of Elizabeth Taylor,
big money. As producer, Wagner undoubtedly would be counting every
minute. So be it. If that was where and when Elizabeth Taylor was
willing to talk, that's where I'd be. (If she sat on a flagpole in the middle
of the Sahara Desert at high noon, I'd have cameras there, too.)

On the afternoon of the taping, my two cameramen arrived early to
set up in Wagner's office on the Warner Brothers lot. At the last
minute Elizabeth threw a boomerang. She asked that I also interview
Wagner, a conversation to run in conjunction with the airing of their
movie. Though I hated eating into our time, I couldn't say no. Thankfully, Robert Wagner was a pro: charming, polished, fast. Still, when
he and I wrapped after thirty minutes, I was already running late. To
my wonder, Elizabeth, notorious for her tardiness, was waiting in the
adjoining office. Taylor on time? Betty Ford, apparently, cured everything.

Walking into the room, I was astounded by the woman I saw sitting
on the couch, smoking a cigarette. Taylor had shed not only sixty

pounds, but ten years. It was difficult to believe that this tiny person with the taut skin had somehow emerged from the puffery and pound-age of our first encounter. Her size-6 figure was poured into tight black stretch jeans and a white cashmere cardigan that was buttoned allur-ingly over her ample bosom. Her accessories were positively sedate: a pair of large gold earrings and the 33-carat Krupp diamond gracing her left hand. Elizabeth Taylor looked fabulous.

Peering intently into a mirror, she deftly wielded a thin brush, applying gloss to her mix of coral-and-pink lipstick. (It was a routine she would repeat eight times in ninety minutes. Every time we changed tape, she reached for lipstick, mirror, gloss, a reflexive reaction to years before the camera.) Just as we headed for the interview, Wagner reappeared to remind Elizabeth she had to be on the set in thirty minutes. He also said there was someone waiting to meet her, and a nervous Rob Lowe, wearing rump-defining jeans and a white T-shirt, walked through the door. Still seated, Elizabeth extended her hand, glanced provocatively up through that double row of lashes, and gave the kid the Look that had knocked men cuckoo for years. It still worked. Lowe squirmed, his glasses flew down on his nose, he mumbled something about being a fan, and left.

And not a minute too soon. Hustling into Wagner's office, the cameramen did a final lighting check and things got rolling. We talked about AIDS, and when the subject turned to Taylor's old friend Rock Hudson, whose AIDS death made international headlines, I brought up *Giant,* the movie in which the two co-starred. To my eternal gratification, Taylor took the ball and, for the next hour and a half, ran with it. It was magic—one of those rare occasions when the interview not only meets but far exceeds your expectations.

While Taylor was in the midst of reminiscing about Mike Todd, the door opened and Wagner appeared. Out of Elizabeth's eyesight, he scowled at me and motioned to his wristwatch. I acknowledged him with a nod but kept on going. I had no intention of stopping until Elizabeth was dragged bodily from my presence.

Which soon she was. Minutes later the door opened again. This time Wagner was out for bear. His stormy face signaled that, in no uncertain terms, this interview—or my life, if I didn't finish up—was over. Mikes got pulled off and Taylor was rushed from the room, though not before whispering furtively to me, "Do you think it went all right?"

To say the least. When the interview ran on *Today,* Friedman gave it five days.

———

You look sensational. What are you eating nowadays? How did you manage to take off the weight?

It's my own diet. I tried all the fad diets and I've really had a hard time maintaining. Basically, my diet now is low carbohydrates, high protein, and calorie watching. But I wrote a plan for myself, an actual menu, day by day, for a two-week period, which, of course, can be repeated. And you do eat. You don't go hungry. That was one of the things about dieting—I was hungry the whole time. It felt like my insides were eating on themselves. And the maintenance was so boring.

As you know, I've not had anything to drink for two and one half years, but, as a result, I became a chocoholic. When I was feeling sorry for myself or wanted a little reward, it would be the old chocolate. So I lost all the bloat [from drinking] but put it back on in good, solid fat. Finally, I thought since I had cleaned up my act inside, it was time to clean up the way I looked, because I was getting really fat.

Why do you think you got fat?

I was unhappy. I was lonely. Two years ago I lost forty-five pounds but I put back on about twenty-five. You see, I am a very perverse person. My friends were telling me, "Elizabeth, you're beginning to put weight back on," but I didn't want to hear. Five and a half months out of last year I was flat on my back—with my back. There was a lot of self-pity involved. I'd go "Poor Elizabeth. Well, let's have a little reward," and it'd be chocolate, ice cream, hot fudge. People would send me candy and I'd eat the whole box. That was my reward for "Poor Elizabeth." When people would say, "You've got to lose weight," I'd just dig my heels in.

Finally I said, "I've gotta take things out, put them on the table, and decide. It isn't just the pain of being physically immobile. Why am I doing this to myself? Why am I so lacking in self-esteem? If I'm lonely, why am I lonely?" It's individual to each person who has a problem.

I don't know very many jolly fat women—inside there is always a skinny woman crying to get out. I don't know anybody who enjoys fat jokes, and all the fat jokes about myself that I heard only made me more recalcitrant. I would think, "Well, to hell with you. It is my body. It is the way I look. That is my affair." But that is so self-destructive. Finally, after having a good long chat with myself—because I know myself so well—I said, "Who am I punishing? Not the people who are making jokes about me. I am hurting myself. And why am I doing that?" So I stopped. I got the "click." And, my God, the rewards that the scale tells you! When I lost two years ago I went out and bought a whole new wardrobe; being able to get back into size-six jeans is a great feeling. Or better yet, having to take the size six and asking your help to boil them for you and leave them out in the sun so they shrink. [*Laughs.*] Man, if that isn't a reward!

You've always seemed like the woman who has everything. I think most people would ask: "Why would Elizabeth Taylor have a problem with self-esteem?"

Well, I have had everything. I've had my share of joy, pain, luck, rough times. I've had a dose of it all. I've been back and forth like a yo-yo. I hope I've learned from all the experiences I've had. I hope I can channel them in a positive way because it's easy to take all that energy and be negative.

For instance, the energy it took for me to be an alcoholic. Alcoholics really work at being alcoholics. I was never a secret drinker, but I know a lot of people who are, and the lying that it takes is hard work. So the goal is to take all that hard work, turn it around, and make it work for you in a positive, good way.

As a result of changing your life, giving up alcohol and drugs, what do you know about yourself that you didn't know before you went cold turkey?

I'm much more secure with myself than I was before. I used to drink because I thought it would help my shyness. But it didn't—it only accentuated it, as alcohol does. I find I don't have to worry about "Oh, God, what did I say last night?" or "What am I going to say in a second?" I'm much more confident and at peace with myself than I think I have ever been . . . just the knowledge that I can cope with everyday living—working. I have been single now for about five years, which for me is phenomenal. It's the first time in my adult life. And I don't mind it.

Do you like *being single?*

It's not that I like being single—as a statement. I like myself enough not to be afraid to be alone. I don't worry about being alone. I enjoy it sometimes. I still like to share; I still like to give. Giving, to me, is the greatest thing in the world. It is better than receiving—well, you do receive when you give. I haven't shut myself off. I haven't said, "I'm never going to marry again." I probably will one day. But I am certainly in no hurry. I'm enjoying my life the way it is now, my friends, the people I go out with. I enjoy being by myself. I enjoy being introspective, I like my—I call them my "E.T. days," which I take just to regenerate myself.

Screenwriter Joseph Mankiewicz once said about you that some of your best roles have been when you were married . . . that, as a wife, you're capable of totally adopting the life-style of the man you're with.

That's true. I'm very supportive, very gung-ho and one hundred percent with whatever mate I have. And I'll put up with a lot. But when the final curtain falls, I'll still be friends—unless I feel a sense of betrayal. Of course, I'm not putting the failure of my marriages off on anyone but myself, because I'm sure I could've adjusted better in every situation. But you reach a point in relationships where you have to face the truth: It's either working or it isn't—as in my last marriage, to John [Warner]. I tried very hard to make it work. And I love John—he's a wonderful man and a wonderful politician. He's really a super senator. He's completely dedicated. But there just wasn't room in his life for me, for family. The Senate is a very hard mistress to fight, and the competition was too much for me. She was a lady I just couldn't cope with.

What do you think was the most difficult time of your life?

At the time it happened, of course, Mike [Todd's] death. We'd only had thirteen months together and I loved him with my life and had a six-month-old baby. I never thought I'd love again. I remarried, [to singer Eddie Fisher] but . . . [shudders] it was a disaster. I thought I'd never ever have that feeling of being able to totally commit . . . to give and receive . . . the feeling of being in love. But I did know it again. I guess I'm just very lucky because I had it twice. And I had a lot of affection and friendship in between.

That second time, of course, was Richard Burton, whom you subsequently married, divorced, and remarried. Do you have any special memories of him?

Yes, I do. But those memories are mine and I'd like to keep them personal.

Do you have a basic philosophy when it comes to life?

I guess I respect honesty in people. I need honesty more than any other quality.

Of your own films, which is your favorite?

I have two, I guess. *National Velvet,* which was totally me—it was even my horse—and *Who's Afraid of Virginia Woolf?* because that was the most challenging. I was thirty-two and playing fifty-something. I had to change my entire personality, my carriage, my voice, everything. Mike Nichols [the director] suggested I have voice lessons. But I'd never had voice lessons . . . acting lessons . . . anything, in my life, and I was afraid it'd change my natural swing, that I'd start thinking about it too much when I was performing instead of thinking about the intent of the part and the character. So I said, "Mike, will you just let me try and think it lower, give me a chance to do it myself . . . or at least try?" And he said, "Sure."

He also said, "I think you should lose a lot of weight." And I said, "Mike, when I lose weight, I look younger. You want me to look older, so I should *gain* weight." So I put on twenty pounds deliberately for the part, which was not a ball to lose afterward.

When you made National Velvet, *the film that catapulted you to international stardom, did you find it extraordinary—at twelve years old—to be such a big star?*

Oh, yes . . . because it was me. It was my favorite book and I was totally into horses anyway. I ate, breathed, and talked nothing but horses. I had my first horse when I was three. It was the only sport I ever excelled in. Before I went to work in the mornings, I'd go out to the Riviera Country Club and do forty jumps, so *National Velvet* was just an extension of me. I even chose the horse for the film. It was the horse I rode at Riviera, and nobody else could ride the animal because he was so mean . . . but beautiful. Grand Sire by Man o' War—a great jumper. I could jump six feet bareback. It was like flying.

A Place in the Sun, directed by George Stevens, was, you've said, the first movie where you ever had to really work for a director.

Yeah. It was a young-leading-lady part. I was sixteen and had received my own first real live kiss just two weeks before. Thank God I made it! But I was a very young, very immature sixteen.

You co-starred in A Place in the Sun *with Montgomery Clift, who was one of your very best friends.*

Well, he was my best friend. A lot of people like to say that I was in love with him. We were never in love—but we loved each other . . . we were always there for each other. And we had a language that we understood, we could read each other in seconds, even on the phone. . . . It was like an umbilical cord that was transcontinental . . . we could feel what the other was going through.

In Giant, *you co-starred with Rock Hudson and James Dean. During that film, James Dean was killed and you were quite upset about that, weren't you?*

It was the first time that anyone I'd been close to had died, . . . and I did find it hard. He was so alive, so vulnerable, and we used to talk about so much. It was very hard for me—at twenty-three—to accept the finality. . . .

You were only twenty-three when you made Giant?

Yes.

That's amazing, because you played a role in which you aged to a woman of fifty. I didn't realize you were that young. . . . Elizabeth, you did everything so young. . . .

[*Laughs.*] I was married a virgin.

You were?

Yup. [*Cackles.*]

That was to Nicky Hilton, of course. Well, you did once say you'd never even slept outside your mother's house until you got married. So you actually went from your mother's house to Nicky Hilton's house. That was a big house you went to, Elizabeth.

Not big enough. [*Rolls eyes amid raucous laughter.*]

**"I can't conceive of living with
the shame of having backed down
from a challenge."**

When I met Sylvester Stallone he was wildly in love with, but not yet married to, Brigitte Nielsen, the stunning six-foot Danish model, actress, and party girl, whom he'd describe—a mere eighteen months later, when Paradise hit the skids—as "a dark cloud passing over my head." But in October 1985, Brigitte was still the sun, the moon, and the stars, and Stallone was besotted.

He was also a pain in the neck.

Which is not to say he wasn't charming. And even somewhat smarter than you'd expect. As Carrie Fisher put it when describing her parents' charisma: "Listen, these people are stars for a reason." And, indeed, anyone who has managed to stir—not to mention make—millions, has to have something going for him.

But what?

The problems started immediately after Stallone committed to my mandatory four hours—a negotiation that made the Camp David accords look like a day at the beach. I flew to Los Angeles a few days early to hit the library at the Academy of Motion Picture Arts and Sciences. I always try to read everything that's ever been written about someone I'm going to interview. No detail too small for my attention, though in Stallone's case I knew not what awaited me as I trotted up to the academy librarian to request the Sly Files. Twenty minutes later, the woman staggered to my table under a foot-high armload of manila folders. "This covers him up to 1980," she explained, dumping the heap in my lap.

Three days and hundreds of interviews later, my eyes blurred and my brain reeled from the sheer verbiage the Italian stallion had let fly since slipping on his first pair of celluloid boxing gloves. Never had one person said so little while saying so much.

Notorious for canceling interview sessions for no apparent reason and with no notice, he didn't disappoint. Almost daily, Stallone's beleaguered spokesman called with bulletins: "Sly is tired"; "Sly has a sore throat"; "Sly doesn't feel like it today—how about Monday?" As we entered Week Two, I lost patience. Even in the word of superstardom, where time is relevant only to the star and *his* needs, this stonewalling was staggering. I called American and booked a seat back to New York.

It worked like a charm. One phone call later and I was told that he'd see me at his MGM offices Friday at 4 P.M. It was pouring rain as I drove onto the lot and asked the guard for directions. "The Stallone building? Take a left and go past Selznick and Thalberg." (Selznick, Thalberg, Stallone? There goes the neighborhood.) I rushed into the offices, but needn't have hurried. I was left cooling my four-inch heels for nearly an hour before finally being summoned upstairs.

Like most things and people famous, Stallone was smaller in real life. He looked, in fact, like a bonsai version of himself. His biceps and triceps, though Rambo-ian, popped up from a shorter, slighter frame than expected. He was dressed in the same gray hues as his office: pleated trousers and a close-fitting silk shirt, carefully unbuttoned to reveal a meticulously muscled cleavage. It was the first time I had interviewed a man with more décolletage than I.

The first moments of an interview are awkward. This was no exception. With no apologies for the delays, Stallone launched into an attack on the press and *Rolling Stone,* who, he declared, always did him in: "I don't know why I'm letting you guys back to take another shot at me," he mused, shooting a rare glance my way (he generally avoided eye contact, preferring to stare obliquely into space as he talked).

Eventually Stallone relaxed, and there emerged a certain charm, a sense of humor, albeit strained. The more I listened to him, the more I realized he, in most ways, was simply a man who tried too hard, who opted to use (often incorrectly) a twenty-five-cent word where a ten-cent one would do.

Barely had we gotten down to basics when the door opened and the blond head of Brigitte Nielsen materialized, instantly galvanizing Stallone's attention. As the Amazonian body slinked across the room to retrieve a jacket thrown over the back of a chair, he stared, transfixed. As Nielsen retreated, her gaze locked into his, and, before my very eyes, Rocky turned to marzipan. "I'll meet you back at the house," she cooed. "Soon?"

I knew my minutes were numbered.

"Well, what do you think about that?" he asked me, flush with pride.

"She's very attractive, Sly."

"You call that . . . *attractive?*" He jumped up and walked to the window. "I just can't believe her. Everybody wants to talk to her and she could be less interested. She turns everybody down. The last thing she cares about is publicity. I can't get over it," he said with the same tone of genuine disbelief I fear he echoed two years later upon hearing the divorce demands.

Moments later he announced, not surprisingly, that our time was up; we'd continue Monday. On Monday, Sly again was downed by the vapors, but he marshaled a rapid recovery when I informed his press agent I had to be back in New York by Wednesday.

So on Tuesday I found myself cruising through the exclusive Los Angeles neighborhood of Pacific Palisades, looking for the high red-brick wall surrounding Casa Stallone. Once cleared through security, I parked in front of a nice but unexceptional white clapboard house.

The houseman answered the door. Allowing that his employer was in the shower following a workout, he asked if I'd like some herb tea.

Left alone, I wandered through maniacally clean rooms. "A house reflects one's personality," Stallone later explained, "and I like things pretty well in order, neat, clean, and uncluttered." And so it was. But did anyone actually live here? "It's a little much sometimes, because the people who work here take great pride in it," its owner conceded. "They keep the floors so buffed you feel like saying, 'Can we just hover across the living-room floor?' "

In the foyer sat a spectacular Rodin sculpture, one member of an eclectic art collection including Dali, Monet, Botero, and an uncommon array of sketches and paintings of nude women. "I never realized how many I had until I saw them all together. I feel like Caligula."

When a half hour passed and Stallone still hadn't appeared, I explored the main floor: the screening room, the collection of hunting knives under glass, the pool table, the living room with black leather couches snaking through, the den—an afterthought of a chamber where he kept his Oscar and leatherbound copies of his scripts. As I stood by the pool ogling a gigantic Botero, a pool-house-turned-gym, and a curious hutlike affair directly adjacent to the main building, the houseman reappeared.

"Sly's office?" I ventured, pointing to the building.

"No, that's where he keeps his electric polo pony."

Of course.

Thirty minutes later, Stallone walked down the stairs: gray trousers, cardigan, breast-baring silk shirt. Apologizing for the delay, he walked into the dining room, sat at the head of a long mahogany table, and ordered breakfast. For one. We stayed there over three hours. He ate, occasionally puffed on a pipe, and, in the face of some very personal questions, attempted to be candid. He let me throw the punches and he didn't flinch.

Brigitte Nielsen called constantly. (It was her first day on the set of *Cobra*, the Stallone movie in which she co-starred.) Each time, Sly took the call in the kitchen. Finally, her persistent summonses caused even Stallone to roll his eyes. "Gitte," he explained, half-embarrassed, half-proud, "is the jealous type. The idea of me being alone with another woman drives her crazy." I wanted to reassure her I was no match for a Viking.

As we wound down, the phone rang again. Gitte. This time, Stallone purposefully left the kitchen door ajar. "I'm coming over, but first I was gonna stop and buy you a present," he said, facing me. "So which is it? I come now—or come later with a present?" he teased. He paused and then grinned. "You're a smart bitch. That's why I love you."

"Women," he sighed as he walked me to my car. "The women in my life drive me nuts."

"Actually, Sly, I think the women in your life have been very understanding. I was very surprised to read in the paper that Sasha [his first wife] is only asking for twelve million dollars in alimony."

"Twelve? That's just for starters." He laughed ruefully. "Try more like thirty-two million dollars—plus I gotta pay child support and alimony."

That astronomical figure, previously unrevealed, made quite a splash in the gossip columns when it appeared. But that day, as I drove away, Sylvester Stallone was still laughing. After all, what's a mere $32 million when you've finally found the love of your life?

—

You've been living with Danish model-actress Brigitte Nielsen now for ten months. The story of how you met has been highly publicized, but I'd like to hear your version. This lady literally tracked you down, did she not?

I had come into New York for a one-day layover, and my mailbox had suddenly begun filling up with letters from this Brigitte Nielsen. Usually that indicates some fanatic is following me, so I ignored them. Finally, I opened up one letter, and it said that she had been writing to me since she was eleven years old and first saw *Rocky,* and had always wanted to meet me. [Brigitte Nielsen was eleven in 1974; *Rocky* was released in 1976 . . .] I still tore up the letters. I went out to lunch and came back around six o'clock. I had a date with another girl that night. In the mailbox was another letter, only this time she sent over her modeling composite. Now, from the letters I had always pictured her

three feet tall and four hundred pounds, with buck teeth and a horrendous complexion. But what I saw made my knees a little weak. So I
rushed over to her hotel. I went out my door, couldn't find a cab or
a limo, and I'm runnin' down the street in the rain. It was two blocks
away. I pounded on her door, and when it opened I saw this wonderful
vision. She's so imposing when she comes in. She had the flaming red
hair from *Red Sonja,* and she looked extraordinary. I said, "Well, I'm
only going to stay fifteen minutes, but maybe I can stretch it into four
hours." So that was the beginning.

It was love at first sight?

Oh, yeah. But there was also this awkward period where silence
began to erode the confidence in the relationship. In other words, no
one was talking. Both parties were nervous and wanted to say the right
things, so no one was saying anything. So we would have long-winded
battles about not talking, which was so stupid. Eventually, during one
of these, I said, "Well, maybe this isn't going to work out." So she
headed for the door, and I said, "Well, come back. Let's talk about it.
[*Laughs.*] For another week." And that was ten months ago. Since
then, it's been perfect.

Why?

Because she's got it all. She has heart, humor, beauty, athletic prowess, maternal instincts. She's very family-oriented. And she's classically
true to her man—I mean, really dedicated to the maintaining and
prolonging of this relationship. There's a permanency about it. I have
not gone out or *nothing.* It's the same individual—and wonderfully
so—for ten months.

Is that a record for you?

That is definitely a record.

But you were married to your wife, Sasha, for more than ten years.

[*Laughs.*] Like I said, this is definitely a record.

*You mentioned Brigitte's maternal instincts, yet wasn't she married
when you met, and didn't she leave her baby boy back in Denmark with
her husband when she went with you?*

She was actually what we call in American law legally separated. To
get divorced in Denmark, you have to have signed papers that you've

been guilty of infidelity and you have to have your lover sign the papers. So we had to go down to the Danish consulate and sign papers that said we were living together. That severed the relationship. There was a real heavy smear campaign saying that she was an unfit mother. But in Denmark you cannot take your child, a Danish citizen, out of Denmark, period. If the father wants custody, and he's a Danish citizen, he keeps it. No matter what. And that was a real, real painful experience for this woman. I mean, the baby is so young. So she flies back as often as she can, and though it's a very strained relationship with the ex-husband, she does what she can to keep the mother-son bond. [According to the Danish consulate, custody is awarded to the "most fit" parent, and he or she may leave the country with the child. Details of Nielsen's settlement are not public record.]

Will she ever be able to bring the baby over here?

Not unless the husband says so. And he's not whistling "Dixie" by any means.

You're thirty-nine and she's twenty-two . . .

Yeah, poor thing. No one is twenty-two. [*Laughs*] I've got shoes older than that.

So what do you have in common?

If anything, our relationship is based on instructiveness. I try to help her avoid some of the pitfalls of this particular city, give her security, because she's an extremely security-minded person. For being so beautiful she's not interested in flaunting beauty, and she was the biggest model in Europe! So I was very taken by that, especially when most women her age I've known have been so career-oriented. She isn't. She would just as soon stay home, watch television, and have a meal around the fire than go to the hottest club in the world. She's dogmatic, extremely opinionated, and quite gifted in manipulating one's emotions to a positive area. She really knows how to talk to a man, yet again she really knows how to turn on the femininity. I can't pigeonhole her anywhere. She's a whole different brand of woman.

Why? Because she's European?

'Cause she's single-minded about satisfying her man. To her, emotion, love, supersedes everything, and I've never seen anyone that extraordinarily beautiful put all the trappings of wealth in a drawer and go for all the trappings of love. She's ambitious until she gets emotionally involved, and then the work is over. Absolutely over. She cannot work unless she's happy—in love.

As fairy-tale-ish as your meeting was, it looked like a very premeditated move on her part.

It *was* premeditated. I tracked this down, talked to her parents. She had been writing letters to me since she was eleven years old. They have letters at her house that were dated ten years ago but were never mailed. So this was a fixation. She named her son Sylvester before she even met me. It was Sylvester until the husband said, "Over my dead body." So he got named Julian. [*Laughs.*] I guess John Lennon ended up with all the glory. So her meeting me wasn't like, "Oh, he's got *Rambo* and *Rocky* coming out, and I want to meet him." Oh, no, no, no. This was a real fulfilling moment for her. This was like the end of a quest.

The Holy Grail. Why do you think she's in love with you?

I don't know. It's so cosmic, because I would expect her to go for someone younger, maybe more into the party scene. She was drawn to something that is unspoken . . . it goes beyond articulation. I wish I knew what it was so I could get rid of it, but I can't put my finger on it.

Why would you want to "get rid of it"?

Because sometimes you say, "Why do I love someone so much when it hurts so much?" You say, "If I could just figure it out and cut that out." But you can't, because love is in every cell of the body; it's like the DNA code.

Do you think you'll marry Brigitte?

Most likely, yes. I couldn't see anyone else fulfilling the needs plus being so physically perfect. She's a tough act to follow.

Currently, you are, of course, in the throes of a divorce settlement with Sasha, whom you married in December 1974. You two had one of the more highly publicized on-again, off-again marriages in show business. After Rocky, *you separated because of your affair with Joyce Ingalls, your co-star in* Paradise Alley. *You then reconciled. After*

Rocky II, you again left her, quite publicly, to live with actress Susan Anton. After ten months, Sasha took you back again. In November 1984, you two split again, and this time it appears to be final. What ultimately caused this marriage to end? You two certainly seemed to have tried to work things out.

We surely did. I think we were both going through a real sudden change in life. The money had come, the social status had changed, we were getting a little bit more mature. I think she felt that there had to be more to life than what we had experienced, because that had been a pretty trying situation. She had been there from the very beginning, and then there was the difficulty with our child. [Stallone's younger son, Seargeoh, six, is autistic.]

By about two years ago, Sasha and I had run the gamut of emotions. We thought we'd be better off to go it alone and find some new memories, escapades, histories, and friends, because we were in a rut. I didn't like socializing, and she did. It had nothing to do with love gone sour or hate. The relationship was like a tank, and we were on empty. Some things just have a cutoff. You can make it survive if you're willing to establish a new set of rules, which is basically an open marriage. But that really isn't the healthy way to go.

Looking at the numerous times you publicly left Sasha for other women, many people feel she was entitled to walk out—that you had treated her badly.

Outwardly it appears that I was the villain in all of this, but none of this was ever done out of maliciousness. When people say you're cheating, cheating has such a negative connotation. What I was doing, basically, was following my heart, not my mind. And that's when people get into trouble. And I gave in to the weakness, or should I say the strength, of the moment. I just felt I had to be true to my basic instincts, otherwise I was altering the animal. I had flaws, but I was an excellent husband. When I was home, the quality of time was very, very good, giving, loving, and I was an extremely strong family man. But living the life I lead—just like some of my other male counterparts in this business—I . . . we are put into extraordinary situations. Temptation is presented in spades. It's there so much that one doesn't even consider it temptation, it becomes almost a—

Matter of course?

Yeah. A rite of spring. It wasn't as though I was going out looking for women all the time; it was just there. And being put into such a pressurized system of performing constantly, of always worrying if you are going to be around next year, one is always looking for gratification, and usually, physical gratification is the easiest to come by. I'm not saying that it's good; I'm not condoning it, because it is often a dead end. But you get so wound up, it's like, instead of going to a psychiatrist, that becomes the release factor. It has nothing to do with love, nothing to do with true emotion. Basically, I just got married too young.

What if Sasha had decided to seek a little psychic relief and had an affair of her own?

I wouldn't have appreciated that. She needed more, and I can understand that, because I had my fulfillment. There was an open policy that she could go wherever she wanted, whenever she wanted. The world was her playground. It was an interesting transformation, because here was a girl who came, literally, from nothing.

Her father was a steelworker.

Yeah. But I never met her parents.

You were together for fourteen years and you never met her parents?

No. I wouldn't know them if they walked in the door.

Didn't Sasha ever offer to introduce you?

I don't know. This is so hard for anyone other than me to understand. There was an innate shyness about them meeting me, and then after a while it became habit-forming, until there was a kind of shyness about me meeting them, and so the twain never met. Like, I bought them a home, sent one of her brothers through college, and so it was always an amicable relationship. But . . . I maybe talked to the mother three times on the phone.

They never even came to visit their grandchildren?

They never came. Sasha would take the children there. But they would never come. I wanted them to.

Do you think Sasha was ashamed of them?

No, I don't think so. They were pretty tight. They were just shy . . . simple folks. The sister came out, and my ex-brother-in-law, Don, was an excellent man. Lived out here for about three months. But never met the rest. Talked to the father one time. When the child was born. I called up and said, "Excuse me, this is Sylvester. It's a boy." They said, "Oh, that's great." And that was about it.

When did you know the marriage was really over?

When the door was locked. I came home and I was, like, locked out. There was no one there. I said, "Excuse me, hello, hello." But I just heard echoes.

So this time she left you?

Yeah. It's like, there was no more tune to be played on this fiddle. It's over. She wasn't going to take that anymore. When I was doing *Rambo,* the separation gave her time to gather her senses and her confidence and make the move. I don't know what she's doing socially. She's not out flaunting around. I think it was more of a mental thing rather than a physical yearning.

Are you two friendly?

We talk quite often. She lives only a couple of blocks away. Sage, my older child, spends three, four days a week with me. So there is constant contact. But she and I don't see each other.

How do you know that this relationship with Brigitte isn't simply another of your flings and that you won't reconcile with Sasha?

First of all, I haven't entertained the thought. And that's strange right there. Also, I've already been through that, and it's been a very emotional, time-consuming, and painful experience. I'm not stupid enough to do it again. As one gets older, the real thing is harder to find. Nowadays, I find myself retreating more and more into myself, into my past. I feel like I'm trying to pull back and simply look for the little things in life that I have bypassed being on this whirlwind ride for ten years. I really didn't stop to smell the roses. I didn't even stop to smell the fields. I was burning for ten years. Now I want to reestablish some of the basic things I know I'm going to need as I mature, which are stability, love, dedication, loyalty of loved ones, a sense of family that I had lost and am now trying to regain. To regain it, you have to pay the price of having single-minded purpose, especially in the area of love.

What do you think love is, anyway?

I'm not sure. To me love is being able to go to bed with someone and feel better about 'em when you wake up the next morning. It's a sense of growing affection and of putting them first. It's always checking up on them. If they're hungry, you get out of bed and get them something to eat. If you don't do that for someone, you're just having a casual flirtation. You know: "Get your ass out of bed and do it yourself." A real love is one where you develop a sense of selflessness.

And you're developing that selflessness with Brigitte?

Oh, definitely. 'Cause it's been so long. I cannot believe it's been almost ten months.

You were born in Hell's Kitchen in New York in 1946 and lived there until you were five, when your parents moved to Montgomery Hills, Maryland. Your mother had been a cigarette girl and dancer at Billy Rose's Diamond Horseshoe, while your father, a Sicilian immigrant, was a hairdresser. Correct?

My father was first a shepherd.

A real shepherd?

A real shepherd. Then he came to this country. His parents had been involved in the cosmetology business—hair cutting, if you will—in Italy. So naturally their son and all the sisters got involved in beauty school. [Stallone himself attended Wheaton School of Beauty briefly at age fifteen.]

Your parents divorced when you were eleven. You've said of their relationship, "It was earthshaking. She wanted to fly. He wanted to earn money"; and "They stayed together, but . . . it was a war between the black and the red ants." What do you think attracted them to each other in the first place?

There's a real animalistic Stanley Kowalski kind of Neanderthal charm about my father, and I mean that in a positive way. She liked to be dominated, and then she resented it. She really had an extremely artistic bent. She comes from great intelligence. Together you had a combination of the physical and the mental, so there was a real battle there, in a sense.

Do you think they loved each other?

Oh, yeah, in the beginning. Very, very intense, but my mother was extremely bullheaded. For example, when I was going to be born, she was having labor pains five minutes apart and refused to take a taxi to the hospital—which was really a charity ward, because they didn't have money to go to a hospital. She was going to go on the bus and eat a loaf of bread before she got there, period. My father was flipping out. His frustration came because he wanted to be an entertainer—he had a magnificent singing voice—and could have been a good entertainer in the Perry Como mold, but he had paralyzing stage fright. So he would sing in burlesque houses behind the curtain. I guess I inherited the performing needs from both of them.

You've indicated that you were an abused child. You once said, "I know what it's like to be unwanted—an abused kid. I was taken to the hospital many times. I was totally subjugated by my father—pushed under." Were you beaten as a child?

Oh, yeah. I was swatted with great power. I was sent flying, a heat-seeking missile across the room. But I was a difficult child, so I would get difficult spankings. I found myself starting to feel the same kind of anger my parents had toward me. The abused label is not as valid as it was when I said that, because today when we think of abused children, we think of people with acid burns, whipped, tortured with cigarette butts on the heels of their feet. It was never like that. It was just a very, very, very strong upbringing in the sense that if you did something wrong, the hammer fell. But at the time, I felt my father didn't give me confidence . . . like, I always felt the guy down the street was better. I was never good. But I understand my father now. I love him. I see him quite often. I admire the side I inherited from him, which is, if you want, the Rocky or the Rambo. I have a side I don't like to nurture. It's a very volcanic side, a side that has got me where I am. It's an inability to take a backward step from a challenge. I became extremely aggressive because I can't conceive of living with the shame of having backed down from a challenge. That has been my salvation and, if anything, will be my ruination, 'cause I really don't know when to turn out the lights and go to bed.

Your father was the one who said you weren't born with many brains, so you'd better develop your body, a line you used in Rocky. *What does he think about you now? Has he given you any credit yet?*

Yeah, finally, at sixty-five he's come through. I started out so low in this business and never studied in any fine school, and yet went from that to an Oscar. But all he said was "It could have been a little better . . . the fights." But I understand none of this was out of hatred. It's just his nature to be extremely critical.

When did he finally say, "Okay, kid, you've finally done something right"?

Right after *Rocky III,* when he saw me get my shape back. And after the separation from Sasha last Thanksgiving, that kinda brought us together, 'cause we had both come full circle and were both divorcés.

You once said of your mother, "I am the embodiment of her—the male version." What did you mean by that?

I acquired a love for the outrageous from her. And she is a workaholic, too. She cannot relax—she's driven by the need to be somebody, to accomplish something. She's very eccentric, loquacious, and evasive.

She is a frustrated performer; do you think she's proud of your success, or jealous?

Umm . . . good question. A little bit of both. You say, "How can a mother be jealous of her son?" but it goes beyond motherhood. It's just basic human instinct to say, "Hey, I gave this kid everything. Maybe I could've been that, but I guess I didn't have the opportunity or breaks." It's been pretty turbulent. I'd say every smile's been drenched in gallons of tears. It hasn't been all sunglasses and autographs.

Your youngest son, Seargeoh, is autistic. A lot of people feel it was very brave of you to come forward, as you did in the June 3, 1985, issue of People *magazine, and talk about it.*

But I hate people that glamorize. I felt what *People* did was an outrageous breach of faith. They came out here under the guise of doing a story on *Rocky IV* and making *Rambo,* and we spoke for maybe four minutes about the child. That's all I said. I said, "I really don't want to discuss it; you must speak to the mother, not me." And they came and did an entire layout, and everything was aboveboard. When the magazine came out, there was a picture the size of a postage stamp and huge bold letters, SLY'S SILENT SON. The mother called me up, everyone. I was outraged. A lot of people said, "What a brave thing to do," but it had nothing to do with bravery. It was an obvious mission from the beginning to get the inside story, because I had done a cover years before, holding Seargeoh, and they thought, "Wow, what a great follow-up. He's done *Rambo, Rocky*'s coming out, let's zing him this." They brought in things that opened up wounds and used my son's tragedy and illness to sell magazines without even telling me. If they'd said, "This is a story about Seargeoh," I'd have said, "Okay, I will get into that frequency." But it made me look like I was using my son's problem as a selling point to scrounge up publicity.

How is your relationship with Seargeoh?

As good as it can be under the circumstances. I think the way to relate to children with that malady is to go on their level and get into their world. It's a very strange, frustrating ailment. It was one that made me want to go out—and I did—I went out in the backyard and I cursed God. I said, "Why did this happen?" I thought I had paid dues in my life and thought I had tried to accomplish positive things in society, and this was my payback. And I never quite understood it.

Have you understood it yet?

I think so. There are moments of frustration, but overall I think about the challenge of it, say perhaps this is nature's way of trying to focus attention on this ailment, and having a child like this will bring it more into public focus and produce a cure more readily.

The irony is that you, in particular—a man whose business is communication—would have a child with an inability to communicate. It's almost like a slap from the gods, isn't it?

I thought it was a pretty odd thing to happen. But I've never been embarrassed by it. I've never shunned him. I've never kept him away from any social activities. If we're having a party here, he just runs around. But it is a horrible nightmare that the sun doesn't make go away. I mean, it's there all the time. The only way I've been able to justify and live with it in my mind is saying, "Maybe he's happy. Maybe this world isn't such a wonderful place to be all the time. It isn't exactly one beautiful rose garden, is it?" So in his own world, he's protected. He lives by his own rules, goes at his own pace, has the financial resources to be well taken care of. I was walking down this frozen pier in New York thinking about it, and there was this moment when I said, "They'll try to find a cure, but if they don't will you still love and accept him?" And when I came to the conclusion yes, then it was okay.

There is a theory that autism is caused by a shock during pregnancy. In which case, you could feel a bit guilty, if only because during Sasha's pregnancy with Seargeoh, you were leaving her for the second time.

I talked to many doctors about that aspect of it, and they don't buy that theory, but you still entertain it. Again, the answer is that nobody knows.

It's got to be difficult growing up the son of Rocky and Rambo. How's your relationship with your older son, Sage?

Excellent.

Doesn't he play your son in Rocky IV?

He was going to, but I pulled him out at the last second. I thought it might not be good having that stigma . . . him walking through the halls of his school being attacked or praised. I'm worried about him growing up here in California. Also, he's the son of a kind of physical character. People are automatically going to be very challenging toward him and hold him up to very high expectations. He's a very physical kid, extremely strong for his size. I started him training very early. At first he hated it, but then he began to realize that none of his friends could do it. And at nine, you have a child who can do three hundred and fifty push-ups, far and away more than I could ever do. Now I'd like to put a stop on that and say, Let's now develop some gray matter. Let's do three hundred and fifty mental push-ups.

Weren't you taken to a psychiatrist when you were two?

I went to a psychiatrist at four years old, and he said, "There's nothing wrong with the child—I think we should bring in the parents."

That's the way I heard the story. [*Laughs.*] I was just very, very active, extremely emotional, and given to great physical outbursts. I don't know if that came from not feeling loved—you know, you got a lot to give, but there's no place to give it. It's like walking around with a present that no one wants. That's the way I felt as a child. A lot of actors felt that way, I think, and now, luckily, there's an outlet for it.

You once said that you didn't want just to be an actor, you wanted to represent something. What do you think a Stallone movie represents today, in light of Rambo?

I never expected, especially the way I look physically, to stand for something so all-American. Physically, I'm the antithesis of that. What's happened now, I think, is I've assumed the role of the iconoclast—the one not willing to accept the hand that life deals us. If we really try hard enough, we can get to shuffle the deck and get a redeal.

As an artist having the extraordinary power you do at the moment, do you think it's responsible to exploit that violent part of the American psyche?

Here's the unfortunate thing: A man is violent, period. Since the beginning of time we have always said we are peaceful creatures, and that it's always someone else who's provoking us to do dastardly deeds. But to deny that violence is an inherent part of our culture is a lie. What I try to do in films is to explore violence—not so much exploit it, but explore it, use it for a positive means.

What's the positiveness in Rambo?

That Rambo is going against someone who's even worse than you. If the war is over and you're still holding prisoners, making them suffer and torturing them for no other reason than because it's part of that culture's code, that's bad. They deserve to buy it. And that's what Rambo's all about. It wasn't as though he was just going in there and shooting up these little fellows for nothing.

I gather you are a Republican?

I tend to be more conservative by nature. I believe in the hard-work axiom.

As Rambo, *you became America's most famous Vietnam vet, yet you were never in the armed forces. There had been some talk—a column by Mike Royko in particular—that you were less than eager to serve.*

I'm sure this guy is a good writer, but he got his facts wrong on this one. I was here in '67, at the height of the war. I went to Dade College and then the University of Miami. I went for my draft twice, and they wouldn't let me in—once for hearing and once for feet. I have flat feet, fallen arches, superbly fallen, like Rome. And they said no. I went there ready and willing to go. I was very opposed to draft dodging.

Are you by nature a violent person?

Violent? I can be promoted to violence, because I think violence, along with stress, is protective reaction. I see the letters I get from people wanting to point pistols at me. I get deadly phone calls in the middle of the night saying, "We're gonna cut your throat."

Is that why you always have bodyguards?

The bodyguards are used mostly to prevent legal suits. People will come up and want to start a fight. I hit them back and I'm sued. So I need a buffer.

How long can you keep up the pace you've been working at?

You know, I think of the pressure on myself, on Spielberg, on Don Johnson, and I know what they're going through. We're beyond the fast lane. We are now traveling on a starship, and eventually the gravity pulls you down. The thing is not to let it get to you. Because it can get to you. You start to believe it, that it's never going to end . . . or you fall prey into having to make more product, keep working, don't stop. If you stop, they'll forget you, the party's over. Momentum, momentum, momentum. I'm going to try to pace myself and then slowly get off it gracefully. However, the only thing worse than working too much is not working enough. So it's a real vicious cycle.

Isn't there some middle ground?

That's where your private life comes in. That's what your salvation is in this business. If you don't have a private life, then your business life becomes your world, your reality. Frank Capra said something I thought was really extraordinary in his book, and now I fully understand it. He said that for him reality didn't begin until he drove onto the

Columbia lot, that driving home in the everyday traffic was a fantasy. I know exactly what he means, and that's when burnout really happens—when this business becomes your family. Now I'm trying to regather my family, 'cause I kinda let it all scatter. I've had the most extraordinary ten years that any man could ever ask for. But, God, it just seems to me, I know I'm bein' fatalistic when I say it, but it seems like, how much longer can it go on? It's been a lovely ride—I just wish I'd been there to enjoy it. It's been like a blur—like trying to sightsee through a quaint New England town at three hundred miles an hour. I'd like to retrace my steps in the snow and see what I missed. I mean, I've been to Europe ten times in the past ten years, but I can't remember anything. If I didn't have some of the door keys that I took by accident, I wouldn't remember where I stayed. My whole life is door keys.

Have you ever tried to analyze what it is that makes you go into overdrive when it comes to your career?

I believe that I go only so far in solving the mystery and then I back off. It's like the Robert Frost poem: "We dance round in a ring and suppose, But the Secret sits in the middle and knows."

What makes you feel insecure?

[*Long pause.*] The quality of life. You say what is life? Collecting art? Being surrounded by friends? I get frustrated. What if I didn't have what I have, what would I do? Would people be around, would the friends still be there, or would it all diminish? But when it gets down to it, without a loved one, without a couple of people to love, there is nothing. You've got to have someone to share it with. That has been my biggest fear, to go through life with these transitory relationships and, in the end, have nothing but a new face and a different fragrance on your pillow. To me, that is a real depressing thought.

You are a very, very, very wealthy man now. What does money mean to you?

I have this running joke with my accountant, 'cause I asked him, "How am I doin'? Can I buy this, can I get that?" 'Cause I really don't go past what's in my pocket. I have no concept, and they're always laughing about it. They say you can quit tomorrow. You don't have to work anymore ever again. That's a great relief off my mind. Now it's just an exercise in making good movies. I mean, I'm thirty-nine now, and at twenty-nine I was destitute. Really, destitute. I never in my life thought this would happen. I only wanted to be a writer. That's my profession. I like nothing more than going upstairs and challenging that yellow legal pad with nothing. You just look and say, "Okay, baby, let's create a world." That I love.

Do you think you're a good writer?

Yeah, I'm pretty good. I don't consider myself any threat to the classics. What I try to do is to interpret the longings of the everyday proletariat, the blue-collar man.

What do you think is the biggest misconception of you?

I think that people assume I'm some primordial being, wallowing in a morass of mud, carrying a club on my shoulders, and slurring my way through life. I don't think people understand that my life is much more cerebral than physical. I've gotten where I am today only because of mental plan. There are many guys much more muscular than I'll ever be, but mine has been a concerted effort to try to put the two together.

Hollywood is a town brimming with enormous egos. And yet your name keeps coming up as the biggest ego of them all. Why do you think that is?

It's just my time. I started the ball rolling right after *Rocky* by making outrageous statements, and I got a little carried away 'cause I didn't know how to play the fame game, that you're supposed to lay back, let someone else carry the ball for a while. I got burned by that. Let's face it—the first impression is the strongest.

Do you think you're smart?

I think I'm clever. I think my greatest asset is to be able to take a pretty bad or hopeless situation and find some quality in it. Bobby Fischer will never have to worry about me beating him at chess, but I am able to, when my back is on the wall, get my way out of it.

One last question: Do you think you're sexy?

[*Smiles.*] Every guy likes to think he's sexy. He likes to think he's attractive, wanted, and loved. I think I'm physically desirable. Because I take care of myself. I don't think I'm, like, really handsome in the classical sense. The eyes droop, the mouth is crooked, the teeth aren't straight, the voice, I've been told, sounds like a mafioso pallbearer, but somehow it all works, because it's what everybody hopes to be. It's just a little different. All good things have a little bit of imperfection in them. But as for being a sex symbol? I'd say between three P.M. and eight, I look great. After that, it's all downhill. Don't photograph me in the morning or you're gonna get Walter Brennan.

BETTE MIDLER

ROLLING STONE

December 1982

**"My dream—this cheese-bomb,
American crapola dream that I got
snagged by—has beaten me down . . ."**

When I met Bette Midler, her life was the pits. She was living with
a man she didn't particularly love; her singing career had temporarily
bottomed out, and she was still recovering from a prophetically titled
movie, *Jinxed!*, whose hectic filming had driven her to a nervous breakdown.

It was, in short, a tough time to be thirty-five—even if you were rich,
famous, and one of the most talented women in Hollywood.

Five years later she was back on top . . . a movie star, a happy bride,
a new mother. *Down and Out in Beverly Hills*, *Outrageous Fortune*,
and *Ruthless People* turned her into one of Hollywood's top money-
makers. Stockbroker and performance artist Martin von Haselberg—
a.k.a. Harry Kipper—had turned her into a wife and, at forty, a mother,
with the birth of their daughter, Sophie. Her husband had also
smoothed over her "considerable patches of self-doubt and insecurity,"

and urged her to stick with what she did best: comedy. The result was a 1987 *Time* cover hailing Midler as the "Comeback Kid." Sassy but streamlined, Bette Midler sailed into the late eighties as the consummate working mother, the flashy baby boomer who had raced every clock—and beaten them—to have it all.

But in the fall of 1982 these victories lay in the dim future. So dark were those days, in fact, that when Bette Midler became my first *Rolling Stone* cover (photographer Greg Gorman embellished Bette's face with a red clown nose), the cover line summed it up: BETTE NOIR.

It was a sunny August afternoon when I pulled into the driveway of Midler's Benedict Canyon home. Since, onstage, the Divine Miss M. had single-handedly given bad taste a good name, I was taken aback by the attractiveness of my surroundings. The exposed-beam ceilings, stained-glass windows, and a kitchen befitting a Normandy farmhouse were certainly unexpected (and a far cry from her impoverished Hawaiian origins, where, as the third of four children of a housepainter, Bette had grown up in subsidized housing in the middle of sugarcane fields). Yet, like its owner, Midler's digs were a work-in-progress. The house felt oddly uninhabited. Was her life as void as the rooms in which it was being played out?

Escorted into the living room by Bonnie Bruckheimer, Midler's business partner and best friend, I set up shop on a couch facing the stone fireplace (lorded over by a portrait of Mary Pickford). As I adjusted tape recorders, I became aware of a presence. I looked up to see a slight, subtle creature staring back at me. Frankly, I wouldn't have recognized her. Just over five feet, Midler wore her trademark red hair short and mousy brown, the bodacious bosoms lost in a floppy sweater, the famous gams hidden under baggy slacks. She wore a pair of square spectacles and no makeup. She looked small, uncertain, vulnerable. It was only her smile, that dazzling, rabbity grin, that was the giveaway. When she smiled, she sparkled.

Our conversation lasted several hours. Midler was a woman of genuine curiosity with astute psychological underpinnings. A voracious reader, she listened, was very quick and genuinely witty. No doubt she could be prickly; perfectionists usually are. Yet contrary to the outrageous stage persona, this Midler was reserved, a self-proclaimed prude, whose friends call her the Librarian and whose sensibilities were easily ruffled. "When I first read the script for *The Rose* I was shocked because of the language. Can you imagine?" she clucked. "In fact, I put off doing it for seven years because I was so offended. Now I know everyone's going to think, 'Where does she have the crust to be offended?' But I was."

Still on the close side of her collapse (perhaps merely an acute anxiety attack but so debilitating Midler chose to think of it as a nervous breakdown), she was emotionally fragile. One minute she laughed, the next tears welled, especially when recalling her mother. Ruth Midler's life had been a difficult one, cut short by cancer, ironically, on her own birthday. Her existence had been as lean as her daughter's was full— hard work, a retarded son, a daughter killed in a car accident, and a cantankerous husband who refused to acknowledge his daughter's show-business success. (To avoid Fred Midler's wrath, Ruth sneaked out of the house to see Bette in *The Rose.*) Yet clearly she had been the key: "My mother thought I could do no wrong."

With Von Haselberg, Bette met someone else who felt the same way. "My husband," she said, with incredulity, as we sat in a bungalow at the Beverly Hills Hotel in 1986, talking for NBC television cameras, "thinks I'm just perfect, if you can believe that."

Bette was now blond and zaftig, the fallout, she blithely admitted, of happiness. (In a year of marriage, she'd packed on twenty pounds.) And though working with co-stars Richard Dreyfuss and Nick Nolte in *Down and Out in Beverly Hills* had revitalized her zest for show business, it was still Harry she was most wild about.

"He's very attractive," she gushed, describing the man who'd seen neither her movies nor her revues when they married. "Very bright. But what really attracted me is that he's substantial and has a good deal of confidence. I don't have to be afraid when I'm in his presence. He's so much his own person that I don't have to worry about him, which is a great relief. He's very strong and happy to be who he is. That quality is mesmerizing to me. And I like the fact that he likes me, that a man who has that self-assurance likes me. I enjoy that."

And her own self-confidence?

"I haven't got any," she giggled. "That's why I'm so happy. Harry's sort of . . . Thor! And I love it. But he's not macho; he's quite sensitive and treats me with a lot of respect. I can't believe I got so lucky. It's like the forties. We have a real forties marriage going here. Gee, I hope it lasts."

So far, so good.

—

What happened with Jinxed!*?*

Jinxed! was the worst working experience of my life. It drove me to a nervous breakdown.

A real one?

Yeah, I just collapsed and ran to a shrink. I'd never been hurt that badly in my life.

What happened?

I wanted to make the best movie I could, but not everybody else involved felt that way. And they resented me because I did.

For the last twelve years, my work has been solo work. When performers come to work with me, they come because they want to share my particular vision. They come with a certain respect and willingness to work. But this was not the case on this film.

Your co-star, Ken Wahl, openly bad-mouthed you, including stating that, to get through love scenes with you, he had to think of his dog.

Ken was unbelievably hateful to me. All during the shooting he was sending out these *mal* vibes and wanted everybody to know it. That's the kind of guy he is.

The first time I met him, the first thing he said was "I want you to know that I hate niggers and faggots." That was the first thing out of his mouth after hello. I had no idea why he said that, because we had neither of those in our picture. It wasn't as if I said to him, "We're going to introduce you to a lot of gay black people who are going to do your hair and dress you every morning."

And, after that comment, he turned to an Aubrey Beardsley that was hanging on the wall and said, "What the fuck is that?" Now, I had not decorated these rooms. But I felt compelled to tell him, "That's an

Aubrey Beardsley." And I told him about Beardsley and Oscar Wilde. To which he replied, "Well, I don't know nothin' about that fuckin' shit, and I don't want to know nothin' about it. I'm a baseball player." By that time, I knew what particular terrain I had stumbled onto.

Whose idea was it to have him as your co-star? It's a very odd pairing.

To tell you the truth, I suggested him. But after I read with him, I felt it wouldn't work. Originally, I felt Ken Wahl had what we used to call animal magnetism, even though he's a little on the chubby side. And I still feel he photographs beautifully and that there is a place for him in show business, somewhere—although hopefully not in my pictures.

Surely you knew this kind of meanness went on in Hollywood?

I never knew it got so ugly. I never knew it got down to such mudslinging. It was an enormously painful experience, but it was pain about something as trivial as a movie. A movie is, basically, a piece of fluff and entertainment.

How did you know you were beginning to have a nervous breakdown?

Every day, every morning, toward the end, I felt I was holding on for dear life. I would wake up with heart palpitations. And sometimes in the middle of the night I would wake up, not screaming but not being able to breathe. I would just wake up with a shudder and have to pound my back or chest to catch my breath.

On the set, it was as though a wall had come between them and me. I kept thinking, If I can just get through one more day, one more day of having to face them and their awful hatred—or if it wasn't hatred, indifference. Every day I walked between those walls completely alienated and alone and worthless.

Now, I feel very, very proud of myself for having come through it. I feel much bigger, stronger, and more grown up.

Are you still seeing a therapist?

Oh, yeah.

What's the most important thing you've gotten out of therapy?

That it works. I had always looked down my nose at it. I felt it was right for troubled people, but not for me. I've discovered that it does—and can—work for people even with problems as silly as mine are.

What are your problems?

My problems are that my feelings were hurt. And I had never experienced that to such a degree. I had my feelings hurt a lot as a kid and had built up a lot of armor and defenses, which was not a big fucking deal in terms of the overall picture. But I learned that, too. If you're caught up in your trouble, and your trouble is as picayune as my trouble is, then you're just an asshole. And I'm not gonna be that. Don't Be an Asshole—that is my credo.

Let's talk about your singing. What kind of song is too outrageous for Bette Midler?

There's a certain tone you have to hit with radio and business people to get your record played. And that tone is not necessarily what I do. So I've had to make lots of records that are watered-down versions of me. *Live at Last* is about the closest to what I'm known for.

For a long time, I couldn't get on the radio. I got taken off because I slugged a program director who programmed three hundred or four hundred stations in the United States.

Why did you hit him?

He insulted me.

What did he say?

I was at a New Year's Eve party, and I had been drinking, really knocking them back. The whole night had gone badly.

First of all, I was desolate because at my New Year's Eve show, I had done nothing. At a New Year's Eve show, you have to do something. You have to have balloons or confetti—you have to have a surprise. And we had one. We were going to have joints. The marijuana laws had just been changed, and as our New Year's Eve surprise, we were going to have a joint taped under each seat, so that at midnight we could yell, "Happy New Year" and tell everybody to look under his seat.

Well, somebody leaked the plan to the press, and the cops said, "No, that's not going to be your surprise." So at the last minute, we couldn't do it. Oh, I was desperate. So you know what I did? I flashed them. Sitting right there, in the hand of King Kong, I flashed 'em. When in doubt, go for the jugs. But after I did it, I was freaked out because it was so cheap and low. By the time I got to this party, I was feeling pretty down.

At the party, I had another surprise. My label had put out a single about which I knew nothing. My manager, Aaron Russo, didn't tell me they were gonna release it; nobody did. This program director came up to me, waving this record I knew nothing about, and said, "I just heard your new single and I don't like it. It's not very good." I just walked off and started dancing, but the more I thought about it, the angrier I got, until, finally, I walked up to him and said, "Look, you don't like it, don't play it." And I grabbed the record, broke it over my knee, threw it in the fireplace, walked [back] over to him, and just cracked him across the face. And then I walked out.

Where was your manager during all this?

Aaron was back at the hotel, on the floor. He'd taken a bunch of pills, trying to pass out and scare me because I had a date with someone else that night. He was in love with me and didn't want me to be with anybody else. So he was always making it difficult for me to have a love life, even though we were no longer personally involved.

Anyway, when I got back to the hotel, I ran up to his room and banged on the door. "Aaron, Aaron, open up," I said. And from the inside, from this cavern, I heard, *"Aaaahhhhhhh . . . aaaaahhhhhhh."* He wouldn't let me in, so I had to run downstairs and get the concierge. I mean, my dear, this was drama. When we opened the door, there Aaron was, all two hundred pounds of him, in his bathrobe, flat on the floor, with just me and this piss-ass concierge to drag him onto the bed. Lord, what a night that was.

From 1972 to 1978, Russo really ran your career.

He made an environment where I could do my work without strain and tension. He never interfered with the creative part of my life. He interfered with my personal life, my love life. Professionally, though, I was very sheltered. He kept me away from business and from knowing what people really are, particularly in the movie business. I mean, who knew there were such egos on the loose?

Would you say Aaron was your mentor?

No. My mentor was a man named Ben Gillespie. Ben was a dancer

I met when I was doing *Fiddler on the Roof* on Broadway. He opened up the world for me.

Was he also a lover?

Yes, for a good three years. And, oh, I was crazy for him. He really opened up my eyes. He taught me about music and dance and drama and poetry and light and color and sound and movement. He was an artist with great vision of what the stage could provide. He taught me a grandeur I had never known before. He inspired me not to be afraid and to understand what the past had to offer me. I never lost the lessons he taught me.

What happened to the relationship?

Well, with all that wonderfulness, there was the other side. Once the despair and the destruction overwhelm the creative thing, then I always move on, because basically I am a loner. And I always will be.

I like art and I like work. And the whole thrust of my life has been toward those two things, with romance and family and friends and all other human contact simply tributaries of what is the great stream of my life: my work. I still don't know what it is I'm going to wind up saying, but I feel I have to say it. Whatever this river is that I'm on, I just have to follow it to my particular sea.

What was it about Aaron that attracted you?

Aaron was very forceful. And at that point in time, I just wanted to be looked after. I still want to be looked after, but now I know the pitfalls. Aaron, for instance, made me do *The Rose*. He said, "You gotta make a movie, and this is the movie you're gonna make."

There's a couple of versions of your personal relationship with Aaron. You've said you were lovers, but only for six months and only at the beginning. He, meanwhile, maintains you were lovers throughout most of the time he managed you.

What do you think he's going to say? That I shtupped him once and threw him out because he wasn't good enough? That wasn't the way it was, of course, but he has his pride.

Aaron loved me, hated me, fought for me, and tried to destroy me. He brought me to the heights and he put me in the pits. But it evened out completely. And at the moment our relationship was at its most even, I chose to leave.

Why?

Because I couldn't take it anymore. I felt that what he was doing for me professionally wasn't worth what he was doing [to] me personally. I couldn't sleep. I was in a state of anxiety all the time because I never knew what he was going to pull on me next. It was either "I'm dying of leukemia" or "I'm carrying guns because they're out to get me. You're all that's left." It was a lot of mind control. I was going to say mind fucking, but I don't think it's an attractive term for a lovely lady to use. And, always, of course, there was drama—much, much drama.

Eventually, I outgrew my need for drama. At a certain point, when you're thirty-two or so, you just no longer require the raving. You start enjoying pleasant days where there is no drama, where instead you have a little food and some pleasant conversation about wine and books.

Is the Divine Miss M. dead?

Never. *Never.* The best parts about her are still thriving: her outrageousness, her truthfulness, her flamboyance, her devil-may-care attitude.

But, then, saying Miss M. was a character was basically an excuse for that kind of behavior. I didn't want to have to live the life that went along with Miss M., because, if you do, it will kill you.

Take Belushi. I believe John was basically playing a character. He was tricked, and he tricked himself. He wasn't that kind of man at all, yet he forced himself to live that life-style because he felt it was expected of him. And then he died of it. His character killed him.

If you let your character define your personality instead of keeping your true self separate, your character will get you.

Who is Bette Midler's true self?

My true self is a very mild-mannered, gentle person who likes books, certain kinds of music, art, and dance, and who, at this point, just wants a little peace in her life. I'm not saying peace and quiet. I'm saying to be at peace, contented.

I've never been contented. I always used to be dissatisfied. Nothing was ever right, ever good enough. I couldn't sit still, couldn't stand being bored. Now, I live to be bored. I love to just sit and think. Maybe I'm having an early senility, but I don't want to be banged and hammered at anymore.

You said a couple of years ago, "I have no idea who I am. I'm good at shows. But I'm not so good at real life." Have you gotten better at real life since then?

I used to feel guilt about working all the time and about the fact that working was all I was really interested in. I felt it wasn't the thing to do, that my life wasn't the American way. The American way, I thought, was to have a job and then party, play, get laid every night of the week, and be popular. I don't feel that way anymore.

In other words, you've discovered that your work is really a serious career after all?

Exactly. When you hit thirty-five and you're still going at it, then you realize how serious you really are. Did you know, for instance, that Martha Graham didn't even find her niche until she was forty, that she didn't change her style until then? And that she had her biggest success in 1944, when she was fifty? And Lucille Ball. Lucille Ball was not *I Love Lucy* until she was forty years old.

Your career has followed no traditional blueprint. For instance, in 1972, just when you were practically a regular on Johnny Carson and had filled up Philharmonic Hall for your first big concert, you suddenly took off a whole year to rest and eat. And then after breaking records with Clams on the Half Shell, *you took two more years to find* The Rose, *turning down, in the interim, a slew of movies, including* The Fortune, *which, considering how it turned out, was a very smart move.*

Well, I would have loved to work with Nicholson but when I met [director] Mike Nichols, I ended up insulting him because I had just been molested in the steam room.

Yours or his?

The Beverly Wilshire's. I was staying there, and at the time, the masseur was the kind of guy who, if you wanted, would jump on your bones. I did not want, but I guess he thought I needed, to have my bones jumped on, because this guy came on to me and wouldn't let go. He threw me into the shower and started soaping me up. I was very frightened because I'd never had that happen to me before. I was terrified he was going to whip it out and whip it on me any minute. And I couldn't get away. The guy kept me there past my hour, making me twenty minutes late for my meeting with Nichols.

By the time I got back to the suite, I was a nervous wreck. I sat down and didn't know where I was or who this guy was. I looked at Nichols, and all I thought was "Who *is* he?" I wanted to talk about his work, but I couldn't remember any of it. I couldn't even remember his name. . . . He ended up storming out of our meeting, absolutely furious. He told everybody what a cooz I was and how I had no business in the business. But I still think he's a fabulous director.

Is it true you once had an affair with Bob Dylan?

Well, he absolutely charmed the pants off me.

Literally?

No, but close. I tried. Actually, I tried to charm the pants off him. And everyone will be disappointed to learn I was unsuccessful. But I got close.

How close?

Oh, you know . . . a couple of fast feels in the front seat of his Cadillac. He used to drive this hysterically long, red Cadillac convertible, and he couldn't drive worth a pea. He's not a big guy, and he always drove with the seat all the way back, refusing to pull it up to the steering wheel.

He was just fabulous.

What kind of man falls in love with Bette Midler?

He's got a lot of self-confidence, a great sense of humor, likes to have a good time, and likes ideas.

Intelligent?

That's major. But not intelligence of a sneering kind. It has to have some benevolence attached to it. I consider myself intelligent, but I'm no Madame Curie, so I like someone I can learn from. I love a pupil-teacher relationship.

Basically, I want somebody who makes me laugh. I want to giggle my way into oblivion. I want my partner to be on the same wavelength; I couldn't sleep with someone who wasn't funny.

Historically, your relationships seem to run about three years.

I'd say that's a long one.

Where do you meet men?

It's really, really hard. And I know I'm not the only woman out there saying this. It's very difficult. Sometimes you meet nice men when you work, but it's not often. And I can't go to bars. So you depend on the kindness of fate to put someone in your path.

And you're basically monogamous?

I would say so, yeah. I try to be civil and elegant and fair. I do my best not to have my relationships deteriorate into ugliness.

Do you want to get married?

I really don't want to get married. It's not of prime importance to me. It never enters my consciousness.

Yet you always have a fairly intense relationship going on.

Well, I think I—and my work—express what many, many women of my generation are going through.

Which is?

Which is "What the fuck is going on?" We've had our eyes opened, we're seeing life, we're interested in ourselves, and we want to experience all of it—on the one hand. On the other, we still have the tug of home, hearth, and children. We're constantly being pulled and never satisfied. The Cinderella Complex is no lie.

So you're a victim of the Cinderella Complex, too?

More than ever.

Sounds like you're thinking about marriage more than you care to admit—that perhaps a part of you does want the traditional husband-and-children routine.

It's very hard to abandon that. It's million of years of conditioning we're talking about. How do you get rid of it when you're constantly being bombarded in novels and books and magazines? How do you ignore it? It's always in the corner of your mind, always tugging at you.

But I'll tell you one thing: If I were a wife, I'd be a terrific one.

Why?

Because I really have a sense of what being a wife means.

What's that?

It means being an artist on your own planet. You get to have your own home, your own stage, where you get to use your visual and color senses. And, of course, you're real, *real* supportive. If I were a wife, I'd be like Sara Murphy [Gerald Murphy's wife, *Living Well Is the Best Revenge*]. She's my idea of a great wife.

But you have all that without being a wife. You have a great house in Los Angeles that you decorated beautifully, and you have a loft in New York.

Yes, I do. But as a wife, you do it for somebody, not just yourself.

You are quite rich now. What does money mean to you?

It means a good deal. I was always ashamed to admit it, because it's jive. Money is basically jive. But what you can do with it is not jive. Does it give me satisfaction? Yes, because everything in this country is geared to money and how much you make and what you can spend it on. I was never caught up in that. I was caught up in the fact that I was an important enough artist to have people pay top dollar to see me.

Is it true you don't like being called the Queen of Camp?

Honey, I don't care what they call me, as long as they don't quit talking about me. I've been called all kinds of things. Someone in the Midwest once described my show as "an evening with Bette Midler and her unappetizing mammaries." I thought that was funny.

Speaking of which, you've flashed audiences a couple of times during concerts. In retrospect, do you regret doing that?

No. No one was sorry except the guy who wrote about my unappetizing mammaries.

Would you ever do a nude scene for a film?

No, I'll never do a nude scene in pictures, never, ever. They couldn't pay me enough. Because I don't want people judging my parts. I would never give the public a chance to judge me in that personal fashion, to say, "Well, I wouldn't exactly throw my wife out of bed over her." Let them judge my face, but not my parts.

You don't look anything like the Bette Midler of film and concert. Your hair is short and brown, you wear glasses, you're tiny. People probably don't recognize you. Is this intentional?

I can blend into any crowd, and do. I'm not recognizable because I'm constantly changing. I change my hairstyle, the color of my hair, my body, my clothes. The biggest misconception is my height. Everybody thinks I'm six feet one. They're always saying, "You're so short" or "You're not what I expected" or, better yet, "Where is she?" That's always a good one.

"She" meaning Bette Midler—the Divine Miss M.?

Right. Take the other day. My car—I drive a Honda—got stalled in traffic, and I couldn't get anybody to give me a push. I guess it was because I didn't have any Bette Midler gear on.

But I insist upon dealing with the real world, because I have to get out there and get the vibes. Otherwise, the work isn't worth it. Basically, all I really am is a reflection of other people. I take a little from you, a snatch from that person, something else from somebody else, and suddenly I'm a suit. And I shine that suit on the audience as a reflection of what I've picked up from them. So the idea always must be to get out there and get that input, because that's what art is. Or at least that's what my art is.

But you're a celebrity, so the information you're getting is not as firsthand as during the early days in New York.

I know. I must seem like I'm terribly isolated and, indeed, I am and don't want to be. It's insane to get your contact and information from shadows instead of human exchange. I guess I've done it to myself, and sometimes I wake up shrieking, "What have you done? You've trapped yourself!" It's a totally Catch-22 situation. Even though I do stand in line at Pink's [an extremely popular L.A. hot-dog stand] just like everybody else, it's hard to get stimulation and information from the guy behind the counter. So, in one way, I have trapped myself.

My dream—this cheese-bomb, American crapola dream that I got snagged by—has beaten me down . . . because eventually, the very fiber of what I am will shrivel up and blow away without that information and input.

When you decide to get back into character, how long does it take to get Bette Midler together?

About three weeks.

How do you do it?

I call everybody I know, I stop eating, I go back to exercise class, I cut my hair, I do my nails, and I dye my eyelashes. You'd be amazed how much *that* helps. Then I knock myself back into my Bette Midler suit, and there I am. Sometimes I don't entirely get it back, but I fake it.

You've described yourself as a "vicious drunk." Do you still drink?

No. Not at all. My body couldn't take it anymore, couldn't take the hangovers. When I get a hangover, that pit opens up and I might as well just kill myself right then and there. There's no reason to go on. I'm utterly worthless—that's how it affects me.

Did you drink a lot?

At certain periods in my life, yeah.

Would you say you were an alcoholic?

No, I just didn't have a tolerance for it. I'm an extremely cheap drunk and a vocal one. I didn't get enough out of it. It was too high a price to pay.

What's the most ridiculous thing you ever did when you were smashed?

I bit someone's glasses once. Fortunately, they were plastic, but I bit a hole in them. And I've bitten people. That's pretty low.

Did you ever perform drunk?

In the early days, I used to smoke dope and drink stingers before I worked. I had a lot of fun, but I used to lose my voice all the time. At least I think I lost my voice. I was so stoned, I was never sure.

Not long ago I was in New York and ended up facedown in a puddle in front of the Holland Tunnel. I was with some friends—we were on a bender—and we were walking home from a restaurant. Anyway, they just had to pick me up and carry me home. . . . So now I don't drink at all, because I find it extremely destructive.

How about drugs?

Same thing. Basically, I'm not interested.

Have you done cocaine?

I'm not gonna tell you that. I would say no, I've never tried coke.
I don't want people to know my drug habits. I don't think it's anybody's
business but mine. Now, if I had a great one to tell you, if I had a great
tale to spin, I would. But all I really have are a lot of good booze stories,
no great drug stories.

Without vices, then?

I'm working my way toward divinity.

MIKHAIL BARYSHNIKOV

ROLLING STONE

October 1987

**"I like to dream about the future alone,
because the future is clear.
It's an uncomplicated illusion."**

▬

I'd like to tell you I wanted to interview Mikhail Baryshnikov because
I'm a balletomane, a rabid fan, a dance fanatic. I'm not. I'm simply
fatally intrigued by complicated men.

And on that score, nobody beats Baryshnikov.

By the time I got to Baryshnikov in 1987, I'd spent a lot of time with
complicated men and world-class male sex symbols, mostly in the line
of work. I'd discovered that in the beauty-versus-brains department, I'll
always be a sucker for gray matter—though it's nice when both come
in the same package.

With Baryshnikov they do. He is smart and pretty, a delicate man
of almost perfect proportions. He looks, and will probably always look,
boyish, which is deceiving because of his eyes. They are the eyes of an
old soul. They radiate pain and broadcast detachment. They are like

two azure Fabergé eggs set in marble. They say, "Look, but don't touch."

And few have. Particularly women. There was, of course, Jessica Lange, the mother of his first child, and, more recently, Lisa Rinehart, a former ABT ballerina who bore Baryshnikov a son, Peter, in 1989. Red-haired and freckled, the product of a solid, middle-class Chevy Chase, Maryland, upbringing, twenty-nine-year-old Rinehart is simple to his complicated, untormented to his tortured. She was with her paramour in Cincinnati when I caught up with his classy summer roadshow *Baryshnikov and Co.* as it toured the country. Reinhart wasn't one of the ten ballerinas onstage with Misha. She had quit dancing, lacking drive, she explained with an unapologetic shrug. While he rehearsed she spent afternoons shopping with Charles France, Baryshnikov's bigger-than-life, blond, bearded aide-de-camp and alter ego, who walked around cooling himself with a Chinese fan, and whose 1989 firing from the American Ballet Theatre prompted Baryshnikov's earlier than expected exit from the company.

While they bought clothes, Misha and I talked. For almost three days in between rehearsals, we spent lunches, brunches, drinks, and dinners together. Sometimes, since both he and I were addicted to the Iran-contra hearings, we called time-out and watched them on the big-screen TV in the hotel bar. The Russian was intrigued by this American political drama.

He was also a wonderful subject: articulate, professional, complex, manipulative, spoiled, and, in the rare moments when he let go, silly. Goofy, even. At thirty-nine, he was used to being a legend. And though he had fathered a daughter by Lange, he was, when it came to women, notorious for being something of a cad. (This was a time in my life when I still found cads interesting.)

Each session was a subtle, high-powered mental chess game. He delighted in catching repetition. ("You already asked me that!") He made me work for every opinion, perception, reflection. He was a relentless taskmaster, as tough on me as on himself at the barre.

If you want to understand a man, talk to him about his mother. With

Baryshnikov this was particularly true. Though he lived in a world of women, he was deeply conflicted.

In previous interviews, Misha had spoken about his mother in only the sketchiest terms. He said she had died young, but never elaborated on the cause nor the personal trauma it inflicted on him—and it must have been considerable, since he was only eleven. For all intents and purposes, Misha's mother remained as mysterious as he.

I hadn't planned to start our interview talking about her, but as things went, she was the topic almost immediately.

Yes, she had died young, he confirmed, offering no details.

"A disease," he finally added.

Disease?

As he looked away, out the window, he grew distant. There was a long silence. When he glanced back, I saw an uncharacteristically unguarded Baryshnikov. His look was plaintive, the hurt and confusion of an abandoned child, all these many years later, still fresh in his expression. Yet something had been unlocked; he had finally decided, it seemed, to divulge a long-held secret.

"Actually . . ." he slowly confessed, "she committed suicide."

And therein lies the tale.

—

Your first feature film, The Turning Point, *earned you an Academy Award nomination for Best Supporting Actor. The second,* White Nights, *was a popular success. Hollywood has been a very friendly place.*

Very good, very good. I'm reading scripts all the time. The head of a studio just offered me a job, and I said, "Well, what kind of dancing do you want?" and he said, "No dancing," which surprised me.

You were born in the northwestern Soviet Union, in Riga, the capital of Latvia. Were you an only child?

Both of my parents had been married before. I have a half brother from my mother and a half sister from my father. My father was in his thirties when I was born. . . . [My mother's first husband] died in the Second World War. He went to the front, left a kid, and never came back. My half brother was eight or nine when I was born. I grew up with him, but my half sister, who was even older, lived in Leningrad.

Your father, who was a Stalinist, was in the military?

Yes, he was a military commander who taught topography in the academy of flying forces.

How would you describe him?

He was a very difficult man. There was no real rapport between my mother, half brother, and him—no great sense of love and trust. It was not a very happy family. I felt the tension from very early on. My mother was never actually happy with my father. He was extremely impulsive, very nervous, highly neurotic.

Highly intelligent as well?

I don't know about that, but he was a compulsive reader. He had a huge library and read pretty much all of the Russian and Western classics. He would sit alone, reading, into the middle of the night, when he would fall asleep in the chair, waking up only to go in the morning to the job. I remember in the early sixties he ran after Hemingway books when his novels were first published. And Dreiser, too. But at the same time, none of those books went here [*points to his head*]. He would never, what you say, assimilate the information. He was tough, very much a product of the Stalinist era. Obviously, he was a member of the party; his rank was just under general. He was also a big anti-Semite. All Russians were, but it was very accepted in the hierarchy of the party.

I rarely remember him in civilian clothes. Even when he took me to the circus, he wore his military clothes. Summer vacations we rented a house at the beach for a month or two, and there, when he didn't wear his uniform, he was a different man. But still, he walked like he was in uniform.

And your mother—was she a reader as well?

Oh, no, she was absolutely the opposite. My father came from a middle-bourgeois industrialist family; his father and grandfather had a factory in the middle of Russia. But since he grew up in the Stalinist era, he went to military school. My mother came from a peasant background. She was a one hundred percent Russian girl from a little village near the Volga River. She finished beginner's school—that's not even high school—but she could read and write. She did have extraordinary intuition. My father met her in the Volga River area. They fell in love and got married.

Was it a long courtship?

Rather quick, I think. After the war, it was a question of survival for a young mother without any occupation or money. And she also had her own mother on her hands. She had a brother, but in peasant families everyone fights for themselves. I don't know how much of my parents' relationship was love, how much was arrangement.

Your father sounds so austere. Your mother, I gather, was a lighter spirit?

That's for sure. She liked music, art, the theater. She was awfully good-looking, and she tried to dress herself in a very simple but distinct way—very nice, neat. The first time I went to see a ballet, I went with her. I was six.

Did you spend a lot of time with her as a child?

Oh, yes. I knew my father loved me dearly—there was his pride, you know—but I was much closer to my mother. Everybody said, "Oh, he's Mama's son," because I looked very much like my mother. She was blond, blue-eyed, a big woman. But our family was a ball of nerves.

Was there a lot of fighting?

Yes. I don't think my mother was happy. Nothing dramatic happened every day, but it was not a family unit. That's why I fell very much in love with the theater. It was my escape from family reality.

When you were eleven, your mother died. How? She was still a young woman.

I really don't know that many details. She just died. It was an emotional situation, some kind of . . . disease.

Disease?

[*Long pause.*] Actually . . . she committed suicide. . . . She hanged herself.

How was her death explained to you?

"Mommy died." I was at my grandmother's house in the country, near the Volga River. We received a telegram from my father, saying we had to come immediately for the funeral. So my grandmother, uncle, and I took a train. It took two days to get back. And there was a funeral in the Russian way, with the open casket, flowers, the procession, and the orchestra playing Chopin's funeral march. It was a spooky situation.

You were so young. You must have felt abandoned.

No, I accepted her death as a reality. It was a very sad experience, obviously. It wasn't until a few years later I learned how she died.

Who told you?

I don't remember, but I figured it out when I overheard a conversation.

How did your father react to your mother's death?

We lived for a while with my grandmother, my mother's mother, then Father married another woman, whom he'd known in his youth. She moved in with us; I was probably thirteen. A year or two later, I left for Leningrad. She was a very good woman; she had grown children. I had an okay relationship with her. My father couldn't live alone.

As a child, were you an exceptional athlete?

One of the most important things about the Russian regime is the education. When you're young, you have an endless choice of state-supported activities you can join—sports, painting, fencing, chorus— hundreds of opportunities. If you're good in school, do your homework, have decent marks, you could be busy twenty-four hours a day. And if you're good at something, you go to professional school on scholarship. So I used those opportunities. I sang in boys' choir; I was very good at fencing; I played soccer; and I was dancing—Russian folk dances.

At twelve, you were accepted into the prestigious School of Theater, Opera, and Ballet in Riga. At that point, you gave up everything else in favor of dance studies. What did it mean to be a dancer in Russia?

It was a very privileged occupation. If you were dancing professionally, it was good money, security, twenty years of guaranteed work, trips abroad, privileges, and a pension. I dropped everything to concentrate on ballet. It was very much a career choice.

Whose idea was it for you to go to this school?

It was mine. It was the year before my mother died. I said, "I'd like to go to this school. I've applied for the examination next Tuesday."

What was your parents' reaction?

They said, "Why don't you try?" And I was accepted. They were surprised but happy I'd made up my mind.

Did you have a sense, even then, that you were unusually talented?

The first year, I did not know, but by the second year . . . I had a wonderful relationship with my teacher, Yuris Kapralis, a Latvian who was a young dancer with the company. He was not a great classical dancer himself, but he was a great methodist. Very enthusiastic. For him, it was a big challenge to do something with the kids. He worked with us very seriously on a daily basis. He introduced me to the idea of how difficult it is to learn something and how easy it is when you want to do something. We danced with the ballet company when they needed children. So a few times a week, I was onstage professionally.

What intrigued you about being onstage?

Oh, you get corrupt immediately: the orchestra, the lights, the smell of makeup and powder, the audience. It's a sense that you're a very special person, very privileged. There's a moment when you witness the magic of the theater, and you're hooked. There's no way back. I knew I was pretty good, and I started to get all the little children's parts.

What was your body like at that point?

I was more developed, because at seven, I'd started to run and do gymnastics. My muscles were . . . well, I was just like a little man. But I didn't have extremely flexible feet. I was very small, and I had a problem with my pelvis. It turned in a little bit. I worked on it, doing all these stupid, fanatical things. I would sit in a yogalike position and ask people to sit on my knees. You would pull your pelvis and ligaments so badly you couldn't sleep, the pain was so terrible. But I did have good coordination, a light jump, a sense of balance, and I was very eager to please.

So you got attention?

Oh, yes. I clowned for everybody. But in a good sense. I hate children onstage; it's exploitation. But when a professional school offers that kind of opportunity, it's a terrific experience. Professionals give you correction, and you start to have acting lessons. Along with it, we had lessons in historic dances, fencing, history of the arts, music, and piano, which you start when you're still taking the ballet. I wanted badly to play the piano, but I never really had the chance. I play at the level every ballet dancer should. A dancer should read and understand music.

I felt much better in the theater than I did at home. You always looked forward to the ballet class and the evening's performance. Then the days started to shine! My real life would begin.

Did your mother ever get to see you perform?

I remember her seeing me a couple of times. Anyway, I made up my mind that Riga was still a provincial town and school. I knew the art and ballet I was learning was just a beginning.

So what was your plan for advancement?

When I was fifteen, the Riga ballet company took kids from the school to tour in Leningrad. While I was there, I went to the Vaganova school and got introduced to Alexander Pushkin, who had been Nureyev's teacher. We talked, he looked at me and said, "Well, come for the examination in the fall," which I did.

You didn't know it at the time, but Pushkin had already asked that you be put in his class. Clearly, he realized you were special. What did your father say about this?

I didn't ask. I just auditioned, and when I was accepted, I said, "I think I'll go to Leningrad." At first they didn't offer me a scholarship, so I lived with my half sister, who was married and had a child. Once I got a scholarship, I lived in the dormitory like a lot of students from outside the city. I'll always be grateful that my mother and father let me do what I wanted. I think they thought, "Let's see how these decisions work out for him, and if they don't, we can always take him back and put him in normal school." It was not much of a risk.

As for Pushkin, well, he obviously recognized in me some possibilities. He gave me a lot of special attention and worked with me privately. You know, everybody asks about the difference between the system there and the system here. There, it's a different kind of relationship between a master and a student. There's respect and some ethics. People wouldn't take guns and knives to the school. It you don't want to learn, why the hell are you wasting the time of the teacher? I don't understand the system of free education here—this irritates me more than anything else in this country, I must say. It is the lowest of the low. Even with my very mediocre background—I didn't finish special school in university—I think I know much more than a lot of the students in universities here.

Pushkin had an extraordinary influence on you. Tell me about him.

He was a saint and also a very simple person. He was a very strong classical soloist in his time, but he never had a very attractive face—he had a big nose, small head, short torso, and very long legs. Because of his odd build, he was funny-looking, and never succeeded as a principal dancer. From the time he joined the Kirov, he started to teach. He knew his destiny.

What do you think he saw in you?

He liked me. He just liked me, he and his wife. I was accepted in his house. They lost Rudolf [Nureyev] in '61, and somehow, in his heart, I replaced him, because we had similar backgrounds. Rudolf and I came to Leningrad at approximately the same age. Rudy's departure had been tough on Pushkin emotionally.

You studied with Pushkin for about three years. What kind of dancer did he and you think you were becoming at that point?

I was a late bloomer. I never had any problem with ballet skills in general, but I had difficulty finding an identity, because I was a kid, baby-looking, short. Everybody said, "Oh, you're cute," and I hated that, because everyone wants to think of himself as very complex, very bad, just a cool kind of guy. I realized very soon that with my physique and the way I moved, I'd always have a job in any ballet company. I could dance; I knew that. The question was, would I be able to do serious roles? . . . For truly classical dances, especially in the Kirov, you have to be beautiful, tall, handsome. I wasn't. I could dance anything; I had a very strong knowledge of the classical technique; I could take the most difficult step and make it look easy; I had total control over my body. But it was not enough. When I went to the Kirov, I never danced in the corps de ballet. They immediately gave me a solo position. I badly wanted to do more complex, romantic parts. All those years, just to end up as a character dancer! This was not how I had imagined my career. So it was a challenge to convince people to give me those parts, to convince the audience that I could do it. . . . Finally, even with my height, I started to get the romantic roles. They accepted me in repertories like *Sleeping Beauty, Don Quixote,* and, finally, *Giselle.* Then I had the theater in my pocket. I was one of the few leading dancers, and I was pretty much in command. And Pushkin was always a watchdog. He knew everything I was doing onstage in every performance. We would discuss everything at length.

Were you arrogant—having achieved such unusual acclaim so young?

No, no. Listen, success in the theater—it's never enough. It's like appetite. You eat, but the next day you're hungry, so you have to do it again, you have to experience it again. We're all crazy like that. I wasn't too obnoxious. I knew there were a lot of things I didn't know. But it was very clear to me that I wouldn't finish my career in the Kirov, that it wasn't enough. I'd seen some American companies—the American Ballet Theatre and Balanchine's company—when they were touring. I traveled abroad to Spain, London, Japan, Australia.

What was the first Western city you saw? How did it strike you?

It was London, in 1970, and I didn't have much time to think, because I was dancing a lot. I had a big personal success, and I got a lot of attention. I really understood that people liked me not just in Leningrad . . . that they also appreciated my level in the West. I felt, "Well, they're not such barbarians after all."

Were you knocked out by everything you saw around you in London?

I went to see a lot of musicals. I saw *Jesus Christ Superstar, Fiddler on the Roof,* and films like *West Side Story.* I bought my first Simon and Garfunkel record. It was also the first time I actually saw modern-dance companies. I remember the London contemporary theater. I saw my first jazz class. It was a shocking experience. I also saw the Royal Ballet. And then I met Rudolf. He wanted to see me.

You were allowed to visit Nureyev?

No, I was smuggled in a car one morning. I spent all day with him.

What if the authorities had found out?

I'd probably have been flown back to Leningrad and never let out. Natasha [Natalia Makarova] defected on that trip, and I was absolutely shocked. I thought it was the stupidest thing she could've done. It was my second year in the theater; my teacher was still alive. I didn't think I'd be able to leave my country, my theater, my audience. Even when I saw the way Rudolf lived: a beautiful house, Renaissance Italian furniture, paintings. And the wealth, the freedom. He could dance all over the world, but those things didn't trigger in me any feeling that I could do the same.

Did he talk about the defection?

Not at all. And I asked no questions. I wasn't even interested. We talked a lot about choreography, the way people worked in London, how they took class, what technique they developed. He showed me his costumes, how they were designed, built. He asked a lot of questions about his mother, sister, family, about Pushkin, his wife.

He was very emotionally attached; he left more people there than I did. In Russia he was a cult figure. I never created any hysteria. But he had crazy fans following him everywhere, because he was so charismatic. For me, ballet was my job. I can have a million reasons to have a free evening; he has none. Rudolf wants to dance every night.

What was Makarova like in those days? [Baryshnikov reportedly had an affair with her before she defected.]

She left the country very much a young and silly girl. She was not very serious about what she was doing. When I saw her again in 1974, she had progressed in such an incredible way. She changed her body. She was dancing with such security, allure, charm, depth, interest. Suddenly, she was a mature woman. It was a compliment to her surroundings. In Russia, she would've been just another ballerina—probably one of the most talented, but she wouldn't have grown up in the way she did.

In 1970, Pushkin died. That must have been an enormous change for you.

Yeah, that was tough. I realized that I was totally on my own.

But what about your father? Were you in contact?

About once a year. Sometimes I called or wrote a little note. He came to see me about a year before I left Russia for good. He was very proud of me and what I did, but he had a new family. He was happy.

Did you ever talk to him about your mother?

Not really. I was trying to avoid the issue. I had been on my own since eleven. I never thought about the conflict in my family until recent years, when I became more cool and analytical about it. I realize now, trying to build a certain family, that I had an unhappy life in my childhood. There was a lot of misinterpreted, misconducted love.

In 1974 you defected from the Kirov Ballet in a sensational escape that turned you into an instant international celebrity. You've said that almost all the major decisions in your life have been made in a split second. It's somehow difficult to comprehend that a decision as monumental as leaving one's country could be made with no forethought.

It's like when people in a relationship are splitting. Sometimes it takes years for this to make sense, and sometimes, when you realize it's the end, you have to make a decision [instantly], because you can't physically continue to do what you're doing. You must turn from the very firm and nice road to the swamp. I realized that I didn't want to live in Russia; I didn't want to dance in the [Kirov]. I didn't like the way people treated each other. You had to pretend something you didn't feel. They questioned your loyalty to the party, and I was pretty indifferent to politics. I thought the system sucked.

Besides your father, were you leaving behind any personal life? A girlfriend, perhaps?

At that time I was alone. I lived for a couple of years with one girl, a ballerina from the company. She's still dancing there as a soloist. She's very happy, married, with a kid. But truthfully, I couldn't concentrate on my private life. I just wanted to be free.

The moment of truth came in Canada, where you were guest-starring with a Bolshoi concert group. You decided only two days before you actually defected. How did you arrange it?

I had some friends. I asked their help. They contacted a lawyer, Jim Peterson, and introduced me. He was a general lawyer; he didn't have any previous experience of this kind. We talked; he was very articulate. He asked, "How firm are you in this decision? Do you understand what you are doing?" He wanted to see that I wasn't crazy, that I wouldn't change my mind.

You decided to finish your performances in Toronto [the troupe was to go on to Vancouver]. *The night of the last performance, Peterson parked a car two blocks from the theater. After the program, you came out the stage door, surrounded by fans. Suddenly you broke into a dead run. The fans thought you were running from them, and followed. You, however, were running for your life. Finally, after thinking you'd lost the car, you found it, jumped in, and sped off. I must say that I am still stunned by the sheer bravery of that act.*

But that was not the most difficult thing to do. More difficult was to go through the performance. I went to the theater, and I danced the whole evening. I knew that I'd definitely made up my mind. So when I started to run, I didn't feel my legs under me, I just felt fear and empty stomach. I almost threw up when I jumped into that car.

For several years after your defection, you wouldn't talk about it. Why?

Emotionally, it took me a few years to adjust. I left friends, everything I was brought up on—a lot of emotional and geographical attachments. I had moments of sadness and loneliness that I didn't want to talk about. I will never be able to talk about it openly.

Were you fairly confident that the ballet world would, in effect, take care of you once you landed in the West?

Oh, I could do anything. I had an invitation from every major company in the world to come and dance. So I went to Germany, France, Italy, Australia. My interest was more to work with choreographers, to explore certain horizons which I'd never had the chance to do.

Your first American appearance was with the American Ballet Theatre. Why not with George Balanchine and the New York City Ballet?

I was invited first to dance with the ABT by Natasha Makarova. She phoned me to say she would like to dance with me and could I come. I knew I had an open invitation from the ABT, but I didn't want to belong to just one company. As for Balanchine—at that time all I knew [how] to dance was classical, period.

How did you cope with the environmental change?

Well, I was paid quite well, and I wasn't going to spend the money, because there was nothing much to buy. I didn't need anything. I had my clothes, my music. A very generous friend of mine lent me his apartment, a beautiful penthouse on Fifty-seventh Street [in Manhattan], so I didn't have to think about rent. I was just lucky to be surrounded by people like that. Beyond that, everything was dancing, theater, language, television, movies. I watched everything. I went out every night—sometimes alone, sometimes with people—to see something else.

Did you get lonely?

Yes, there were a lot of lonely moments, but I called my friends in Russia.

In 1974 you signed on with the American Ballet Theatre, where you stayed for four years. In 1978 you shocked the ballet world by announcing you were going to work with Balanchine. The time spent with Balanchine is regarded by many as an interesting, but not stellar, time in your career. Would you agree?

Again, that's people's perception. I had a very good time in that company. It was a great experience just to be next to Balanchine, just to see the way he ran a company, treated people. It was very much a master-and-student relationship, because he discovered all his people. He taught them, appointed them, choreographed them. They went through their whole artistic life with him. It was one man's theater.

He had many personal problems, too. He would be married to one person, involved with another. He was very vain and at the same time a very proper man. Also a very gentle man. He taught his ballerinas what to wear, what kind of perfume to use, what kind of hairdo to have, what jewelry to wear. . . . He conducted every moment of their lives. Balanchine had his own problems—that's for sure—but at least *he* created them. [*Laughs.*]

How did he treat you?

He was wonderful to me. He asked me all the time to his apartment. We talked, had a little vodka, a little schnapps. He was a great gourmet; he went to good restaurants, tasted the wines. After dinner we talked, but we never really talked much about ballet. He liked to talk about old Russia. Also about music. He was a truly great musician. He played the piano like a professional. [He] revived some ballets for me; he rehearsed with me a lot, but he didn't really separate me from anybody else. In interviews he was asked about me, and he always said, very coolly, "He's a good dancer. He has good feet."

Is there anything in your life that you would have done differently?

I would have gone to Balanchine a little earlier, maybe a couple of years earlier, when he was in good health. If I had, that relationship would've been more fruitful, from my point of view. But I have very few regrets.

Any personal regrets?

Yes. I regret that my relationship with Jessie [Jessica Lange] didn't work out the way we'd wanted and planned. It's a big regret that will be there for the rest of my life. She was—and always will be—one of the very few women I have loved in my life. But now we are very good friends. In fact, we have a much better relationship now than we ever had before.

How did you meet?

At a party at Buck Henry's house. Milos Forman introduced us. I said to Milos, "Who is this?" And he said, "King Kong's girl." And I said, "Who is King Kong?"

Was it love at first sight?

Yeah, very much so. We were very attracted to each other.

For about five years you lived together off and on. Why do you feel this relationship ultimately didn't work out?

Because it was the wrong time. We weren't adult enough. She was in the middle of her career, and I couldn't change my life and my career, which was dragging me everywhere. But you can't blame our careers and our drives in different directions, because this is not an excuse. She was rising in her field very rapidly, and she had to make a lot of personal choices. You cannot keep a relationship when you're six, seven months apart sometimes. You cannot live together on the phone—this is ridiculous. And then she met Sam [Shepard] and fell in love.

Were you surprised when she and Sam got together?

Oh, sure. But she has to go on with her own life. And with Sam, the situation is much more flexible, secure. They're working together; they're together all the time. I'm very happy for them. And I am very happy that I figured out how to be happy for them, because I love this woman very much—not just as the mother of my child, but as a human being. I am very proud of myself that I found this trait—to be happy for them.

How long did it take?

[Laughs.] Quite a few years.

Do you and Sam get along?

We didn't know each other that well. I met him a couple of times, just on social occasions. I think he is a terrific, very talented man, but I don't know him personally.

It's healthy you feel this way, because this man is going to have a big influence on your own daughter.

I hope a good influence. I think this man stands for all the things I admire. He's decent, he's not corrupt, he's very solid, he's straightforward. These are the qualities I admire in a man.

Despite the state of your relationship, it was a very adult thing to have a child.

It was wonderful for both of us.

Was this a planned baby?

Not really. It just happened. It was kind of a shock for a while, but I was very happy about it. In general, our future together was a question mark, but there was no question about keeping the baby. It was a natural decision.

Your daughter has had a great influence on your life. What have you learned from her?

You learn certain reasons for life, and suddenly it becomes the most important reason—to be a father. She's the one person I have, and this is the truth. It helps sometimes in the bad days. It's nice to know you have somebody who needs you.

She said the most perceptive thing. Apparently, she was visiting you, and when she talked to Jessica on the phone, she said, "I went to the theater today. And I saw the stage where my daddy lives." Does she accept the fact that Daddy dances for a living?

Oh, Daddy dances. People around her work in the movies, write, or dance. It's normal. But she lives the life of a normal kid. She's just a loving girl with a wonderful heart.

If she one day says she'd like to be a ballerina, will you encourage her?

No. I would discourage her. It's a tough life.

Do you find yourself more readily attracted to dancers because they understand your problems?

Not at all. Women are women. Dancers are a very special breed of women [*laughs*], but they are all pretty much the same. . . .

What attracts you to a woman?

Two legs. [*Laughs.*]

And?

I'm not that finicky. . . . But I'll tell you this. I'll work with any son of a bitch, but I won't sleep with a bitch.

I suppose you know that you have a reputation for being rather tough on women.

I won't comment on that, but I really don't care what people think about me right now, and I think it's a wrong observation. Yes, I have had relationships in my life. Some were very long, some quite brief, but all were very meaningful and wonderful from my point of view. I wouldn't dig into why some last longer than others. I guess it's just the chemistry between people. I never took advantage of any young lady. There was always very much a free choice to get into the relationship. I don't think I should say more than that.

Perhaps you're a man who has trouble with commitment?

I stay committed when the emotional side of the relationship still is at a high level. If it's dropping down, there's no commitment, because it's torture for both partners. I don't believe in working on a relationship. It's nonsense.

Do you think you might ever marry?

I have my hopes, my doubts. Maybe I'm not that kind of person. Maybe I'm too selfish, too demanding, too impatient. I'm not an easy person. I know myself. I'm very moody and unpredictable, but I'm fighting this myself, too. I know my weaknesses; I don't hide them.

Isabella Rossellini said of you, "He's a very lonely man. And quite sad."

I don't know about sad, but I like to be alone, because then you can face yourself. You can talk to yourself. When somebody else is next to you, you are automatically involved. It's already a relationship, whether it's a friend or a lover.

Have you always been comfortable being alone?

Yeah. There's a bittersweetness to it. I like to remember the past, all the beautiful and sad moments. I like to dream about the future alone, because the future is clear. It's an uncomplicated illusion.

So you are as moody as everyone claims?

I am.

Is it something you can control?

It's uncontrollable. Genetic, maybe.

So how do you get out of these deep Russian depressions?

You dig into your memory, into certain books that you like, certain things that you already know work better than extra-strength Tylenol.

What books work, in that case?

Oh, I don't want to discuss that. This is an invasion of privacy. Mostly poetry, because it's so abstract and so antiromantic, if you want to know. Rhyme destroys romance, somehow.

When you're in these moods, how do you treat the people around you?

Nobody can stand me for a long time. I just try to avoid people, period.

Who's your best friend?

This is a private matter. The difference between Americans and Russians is that Americans go to the shrink, and Russians go to their friends. There are probably two people in the world to whom I can really address myself seriously.

Do you trust people easily?

I have a few people in my life whom I trust more than I trust myself.

Somehow, I don't believe you trust anybody more than you trust yourself.

I do trust a couple of people. And there is no difference between them and me. . . . I never use people. I never blackmail. I can't do that. If I did, it was not intentional.

You've always been a public person.

Yes, but I like it less and less. Unfortunately, I seem to be doing more and more interviews, which I sometimes find a very unpleasant part of my existence. I pretty much have said everything. I haven't had a chance to start a new life and accumulate new emotions. Maybe it's just hitting forty that makes me feel this way, because there's going to be a new life, and I know it.

What do you think that new life will be?

I don't know. It's a question of stopping dancing, a question of being a man in general. Dancing doesn't excite me the way it used to. I did it all.

Does it bother you to see your body get older?

Not yet, thank God. [*Laughs.*] I still take a ninety-minute class every day; if I miss one day of exercise, I feel I punish my body. But the body memory is stronger than visual memory, and sometimes—in the mirror—you catch your body pushing in one direction and you see a reflection of somebody else. Then it's a philosophy of how to age and what to do with it. For instance, I don't have that much elevation now, and I fake some steps because of my physical problems. But I'm a better dancer now—maybe less sensational, maybe less people will be jumping from their chairs—but I am a smarter dancer. I dig into different aspects of dance, which I didn't have a chance to do before—like duets with women. [*Laughs.*]

Have you ever looked in the rehearsal mirror and been totally satisfied?

Some moments are more satisfactory than others . . . [*laughs*] but I don't recall any rehearsal I ever loved from the first second—isn't that interesting? [*Laughs again.*]

Is having money important to you?

I want to have enough money to do whatever I want to do. I don't want to have to someday go to Duluth and teach a local ballet company how to dance because I need money. I have certain responsibilities to my daughter. And I must say I'm very spoiled by the way I live. If I want to go to the Caribbean and rent a house for a month, I have to have a good one right on the water. If I want to catch a Concorde, I will catch one any second and not even think about how much it costs. And if my close friends need money, it's theirs.

I think everybody assumes that you're probably very, very wealthy.

What's "very wealthy" from your point of view? Do I have a few million dollars? Yes, I do. It's a lot of properties.

When you were in Russia, did you ever think you'd be a millionaire?

No, I never really thought about it. I didn't even notice the first time I had the first mil. My lawyer said to me one day, "You know, you have more than a million dollars in assets." I said, "Are you kidding?"

As a former citizen, any feelings about glasnost?

Listen, I know nothing about it; I haven't been in that country for a long time. It's definitely a very welcome mood. And I think it's the beginning. I hope Gorbachev sustains his position. But he's got to change the key players; the bureaucratic system is very strong.

What's your take on him?

He's a very impressive figure. He's definitely a new generation. It was always unthinkable to have someone so young. Before, the leaders were all in their seventies, living in paradise behind the Kremlin walls. But this guy really travels; he sees, talks, functions, takes action. The biggest question is, Are the people ready for that kind of change? I have a suspicion it's going to be tough, even from a middle-class point of view.

Will you perform in the Soviet Union?

I said I'd come with pleasure, but I'd like to come with my company. I don't think it'll happen in the near future.

Wouldn't you like to go back while you're still dancing?

It's not really necessary. All my films and tapes are there on the black market anyway. They've seen them all.

Are you a happy person?

Me? Happy? No. No. There are moments when I'm with my daughter, when we're playing games, and I forget everything and am happy, but in general, I'm not the happiest person in the world.

But you've got so much—what keeps you from contentment?

Possibilities. You create problems for yourself; you're solving problems. You think it's possible; you think it's not. Would I do it? Can I do it? No matter how good you feel, there's always the next project. I want to do it first. Will it be fun? Will it not be fun? You're too old to do that; you're not strong enough to do this. You're not talented enough to do this, but that definitely is not your cup of tea. You don't have time; you can't afford it. It's endless. Then you get depressed. I wouldn't know what to do with myself if I was . . . *happy*.

ROONE ARLEDGE

NEW YORK

August 1983

"I like to run scared."

■

Where would America be without split screens, instant replays, and *Monday Night Football*? Where would America be without Roone?

Roone who? To anyone in the media business he needs only one name. He is Roone—the man who invented modern television sports coverage and who's now reinventing TV news as president of ABC News.

Arledge is a busy man. You have to be prepared to grab your minutes where you may. Anytime, anyplace, under any circumstances: talking while eating, talking while flying, talking on split-second notice. Before I even got to him, I was prepared to wait.

On two counts. He was occupied and I was desperate. I'd just begun free-lancing and decided to specialize in interviews. Most magazines didn't take the format seriously. I was determined to prove they should. My new career depended on it. I convinced Ed Kosner to give it a try at *New York*. I also convinced him I could get interviews with people as elusive as Roone Arledge.

"Move over, Oriana Fallaci," said I.

"Show me," said he.

When the legendarily evasive network chief agreed to talk to me, I figured I'd won half the battle. How was I to know I'd not yet begun to fight? Arledge is the Howard Hughes of broadcasting, a mysterious presence, notoriously hard to pin down, whose fingerprints permeate his product. He invented *Nightline* and the Olympics as we know it. He put the company's money on Peter Jennings, moved David Brinkley to Sunday morning, and firmly established Barbara Walters as America's foremost Mother Confessor. He dreamed up *The Wide World of Sports* and foisted Howard Cosell on an unsuspecting nation. But, most important, he proved to a stadium of doubters that a guy who came out of sports could not only do news—but make his network number one.

Anybody who's tried to grab five minutes with Roone knows that he runs on something I came to call *A.T.*—Arledge Time. Vaguely aligned with Mountain, Pacific, and Central, A.T. trails at least an hour behind each. Arledge is a dreamer of dreams, a natural conversationalist. And since each takes time, he, invariably, falls behind in the pursuit of both.

The Keeper of Arledge Time is Nancy Dobi. As Roone's assistant, Nancy is arguably one of the most powerful people at ABC. She's certainly one of the few people in the universe who knows not only where her boss is, but just how far behind himself he's running.

To talk about Arledge is to talk about Nancy. To get to Arledge is to bond with her. Sometimes I called her three times a week, sometimes daily. We'd lock in an hour only to get locked out by a terrorist attack, a correspondent crisis, a flood. I'd be all revved up and ready to go, my adrenaline pumping like Spindle top, and the phone would ring. Nancy's apologetic voice: "Roone's so sorry, but it's the Gaza Strip again . . ."

Resolute, I tracked the man as if I were Daniel Boone. I knew no shame. I sent him pleading telegrams. I crisscrossed from Los Angeles to New York and back. On the notion that propinquity is power, I came to New York (I was living in L.A.), checked into a hotel, checked in with Nancy, and told her I'd be available anytime Arledge was. For a week I lived on room service and hope, but nothing materialized. Undaunted, I tried to book a seat next to Roone on a coast-to-coast flight—but even there there was a waiting list.

Finally, in April 1983, he addressed thirteen hundred affiliates in Los Angeles. I was in the audience. Afterward, I made a beeline. "Roone, I'm Nancy Collins." I thrust my hand into his.

"Oh, yes." He smiled. "I'm so sorry about all these delays . . ."

"Any chance we could get together while you're here?"

"Uh . . . yeah. Why don't you call me later?"

"Progress!" I said as I was submerged in a sea of enthusiastic station managers.

That night I called Arledge's room, but he wasn't there. I left my number, sat by the phone, waited, and then eventually called again. Nine . . . ten . . . eleven . . . finally, an answer.

"You're persistent," he acknowledged. He suggested lunch the following day. There was a God.

The next morning I called Nancy in New York for moral support. "Do you think he'll actually make it?"

"He'll try. He *wants* to do this interview."

At 9:30 A.M., taking no chances, I walked into the hotel lobby, stationed myself by the house phones, and rang his room until he answered.

"Hi—Nancy Collins."

"You caught me just as I was walking out the door."

"We're still on for lunch at twelve-thirty?"

"Oh, yes. I'll meet you in the restaurant. Call me when you get here."

"I *am* here."

At twelve-thirty I sailed into the café and perused the room. A red-haired man in a navy-blue suit sitting alone and scanning a newspaper. *Arledge in the flesh.* I wanted to weep. He greeted me with a relaxed smile. No fidgets, no watch-glancing, no hurry.

For the next three hours I had Roone Arledge's undivided attention. The president of ABC News and ABC Sports, ruler of thousands, acted as if time were of no consequence. Within minutes the waiting and stewing was all but forgotten. The man was a charmer: articulate, intuitive, thoughtful, unstructured, and vulnerable—surprisingly so, a person easily wounded by criticism. When he spoke he seemed to take *you* into *his* confidence.

Even after a nervous ABC messenger materialized to remind his boss that ten people awaited him in an upstairs suite, Arledge lingered over his coffee. I felt bad, but not that bad. Had they waited six months?

Before he left, he vowed to make time to continue. While I never doubted his intentions, I knew this wasn't going to be easy.

With a renewed sense of mission, I charged to New York. Every day I checked in with Nancy. Every day we looked for an opening.

"Not today—sorry," she finally told me around noon one Wednesday.

"You're sure?"

"I'm positive," she laughed. "Take the day off."

So I did. Dumping my only dress-for-success suit at the cleaners across the street, I jumped in the shower to wash my hair. Then the phone rang.

"Nancy, it's Nancy. Can you meet Roone for lunch?"

"Today?"

"Today. Some time just loosened up. Say one-thirty?"

It was already twelve forty-five. My hair was wet, I had no clothes, and it was at least a half hour across town to the restaurant.

"No problem. Tell Roone I'll be there."

I hung up and streaked to the dry cleaner in jeans and T-shirt.

"Hi," I panted. "I just gave you some clothes ten minutes ago. I need them back."

The woman behind the counter looked confused.

"Mmmm . . . well, I don't know . . . I think maybe these already went down . . ."

"Could you please look?"

By now I'd pole-vaulted over the counter and was rummaging through the drawstring bags myself.

"You're in a hurry, I see."

"Listen, I'm sorry, but I have to wear those clothes. Now. I'm a journalist. . . . I have an interview I have to do in thirty minutes. . . ." I was blabbering.

"So you go to work in dirty clothes with wet hair?"

"They're not that dirty. There's only one *tiny* spot on the skirt. Nobody can see it but me. . . . I . . . I . . . ." I must be crazy. Why was I explaining my dry-cleaning habits to a stranger?

The woman sashayed to the back of the shop, picked up a white bag, and dumped it on the counter. "Let's see now . . ."

"There. *There.*" I grabbed my things and headed for the door.

"Hang on, honey. That'll be eight dollars."

Who had time to argue?

When I reached the apartment it was after one. I had twenty minutes, max. Wouldn't you know?

Miraculously, I arrived at the restaurant before Roone. I collapsed into my seat, asked for a double espresso, and tried to collect what was left of my wits. I repaired to the ladies' room to see if I was still in one piece.

The woman in the mirror looked fine. A little flushed, but at least I'd made it. As I reapplied my lipstick, I took my reliable Sony tape recorder out of my bag. New batteries. Extras in the bag. Plenty of cassettes with one already in place. Let's just try it to be sure: "One, two, three, four, testing."

Oh, no. Oh, no.

"Oh, no," I groaned aloud to the empty room.

My trustworthy, never-failed-me-before Sony had just bought the ranch.

Roone Arledge was finally on his way to talk to me and I had nothing for him to talk into. Maybe . . . maybe . . . maybe . . . I could run out and buy a new machine. I opened the powder-room door just as Arledge walked in the front one.

Too late. I had to cope. I had to punt. I had to . . . take notes. God, how long had it been since I'd done that? Four hours later my hand looked like a claw. I'd recorded every single word he uttered on every single scrap of paper I had (old envelopes included). Thinking, writing, maintaining eye contact, and staying one step ahead of my subject had thrown my adrenaline into overdrive. My brain was tapioca.

But, so what? I'd won. I'd gotten the interview!

A month later it was a moot point. In July, Frank Reynolds, anchor for *World News Tonight,* suddenly died of cancer. No one had expected it, least of all Arledge, who'd spent much of our conversation swearing that, despite Reynolds's low ratings, he was going to keep him in the job.

Thus, much of our conversation was now dated. Which meant I needed more time with Arledge, whose personal problems had also multiplied: He and his wife, Ann, announced their separation. In the ironic and often cruel way the media works, both events suddenly made the Arledge interview an even hotter ticket. That I held the chit made *New York*'s heart leap; that I had to corral Roone one more time made mine sink.

Suffice to say, I made it happen, via an L.A.–New York telephone call one summer night. When we said hello in late afternoon, Arledge was on Long Island, sitting by his pool. Three hours later, he was still sitting by his pool—in the dark. Essentially, we redid the interview. It was a completely generous act on his part. There were no easy answers in Roone's life that balmy night, but he tried.

The next morning I jumped on a plane for *People,* to follow Prince Telal, a half brother of Saudi Arabian King Fahd, as he traveled around the country on his private jet for UNICEF. I wrote the Arledge piece in San Francisco, filed it in Seattle, and by Chicago was arguing about cuts with Kosner over the phone.

On August 15, *New York* ran its first-ever in-depth interview on the cover. It featured a picture of the president of ABC News and Sports under the following headline:

A LONG TALK WITH ROONE ARLEDGE BY NANCY COLLINS.

Arledge Time.

—

What's made Peter Jennings your first choice to anchor World News Tonight?

Peter's been around, has experience, marvelous credentials, all of the on-the-air appearance anyone would want, as well as a desire and interest to communicate. I think people will be astounded the first time there's a public event—particularly anyone who didn't see him do the pope's funeral or the royal wedding or Sadat going to Jerusalem. Peter has the potential to be the best describer of live events in television.

Peter, however, is not an American. He's Canadian. Isn't that something of a drawback, particularly since Dan Rather and Tom Brokaw are so American? Don't Americans like to hear their news from Americans?

I think that's true. But Peter's been around so much, and people know him. Canada is foreign, but not really. Besides, he might become an American. He hasn't up to now because his Canadian passport has been of great use to us, as lots of countries won't accept U.S. passports. But, in effect, he's been working for ABC News for nineteen years.

Was Jennings the first choice, or did you ask Ted Koppel first?

No, I did not ask Ted. He is the logical choice. He's a bright new star in the news. At any other network, they'd have put Ted onto the news when Frank Reynolds got sick, but we were not going to risk *Nightline* for a substitution. *Nightline* is perhaps more important to us than *World News Tonight,* because it's the program that makes us different from anybody else. We have an hour-long news program. Nobody else does that. And it's very profitable. Of course, everyone bad-mouths it. They did the same thing with the specials we did during the hostage crisis, but the truth is they—particularly CBS—would give anything to have a half hour, let alone an hour, every night.

Did Koppel want to anchor World News Tonight?

No, but that wouldn't enter into it. Ted loves what he does, but we have the right to put him anywhere we want to. The only thing I gave him in his contract was that I wouldn't make him do *World News Tonight* and *Nightline* without both of us agreeing to it.

Is Tom Brokaw strong enough to carry an evening news broadcast by himself?

Really hard to tell. I think Tom—like Ted Koppel—is the kind of guy who's going to get better as he gets older. But whether he's old enough now, I don't know. With Jennings doing it for us, you'll have three network-news broadcasts with people who are roughly the same age. I toyed with the idea of doing a David Brinkley evening news and going exactly the opposite from the young guys—that, having gotten Cronkite and Chancellor off the air, we could come back with a counterpunch with an elder statesman. But David doesn't want to do the news.

How would you describe the strengths and weaknesses of ABC, NBC, and CBS News right now?

I'm biased, of course, but I think ABC is basically the best. Probably because of our anchor setup, people perceive the news as being the star of our program. We do about twenty percent more foreign news than the other two; we do fewer features and give much more background information, covering the stories from three or four angles. On the other hand, CBS has the tradition, and Dan Rather is very good. NBC, I can't say. We'll have to see what happens when Tom Brokaw really has a larger input, although they've tended to be the least predictable and the least distinguished.

Why do you think Dan Rather and the CBS Evening News *consistently beat the other two networks?*

CBS has a built-in tradition, and they've earned it, although I don't think they are what they were several years ago, whether in strength, reporting, or seriousness of purpose. The other thing is that Dan Rather is an extremely hardworking, very dedicated, will-do-almost-anything-to-succeed-and-to-win kind of person. Also, he could not have been the White House correspondent under Nixon and had the kind of confrontation they had—as well as been on *60 Minutes* for six years—without developing a major following in this country. I'm not knocking this, but if you add it all up, then figure that you have an anchor who, if he has to wear a sweater, will wear a sweater, and if he has to lead with a more spectacular story, will do that too, then that's a powerful combination, not to mention the fact that CBS stations around the country are traditionally very strong.

The hardest thing in the world is to change the habits of watching news programs or buying newspapers. The terrible part about the evening news is that it is so dependent on local lead-ins. If every station you had across the country were number one, then you could put a robot on as your anchor and it wouldn't matter. That's too strong a statement. You couldn't put a robot on.

What are the most important things that CBS News president Van Gordon Sauter and NBC News president Reuven Frank have done for their respective networks?

Reuven, I don't know. That's hard to tell. Van I think has been responsible for changing CBS's priorities to include a lot of things we've been accused of at ABC. I have been responsible for making ABC News try as much as possible to put aside ratings and simply become, hopefully, the best news organization in the world. Van has taken a hell of a good news organization and made it much more commercial and competitive in terms of ratings.

Someone at CBS News told me that what Sauter has done is "bring CBS into the Roone Arledge age."

In a sense, that's true. He did the same thing in sports. He took a lot of the techniques we used and applied them to CBS Sports. He also hired a lot of our people. It seems to me his mandate—if that's the right word—is different from any other incoming president of CBS News. Until ABC became competitive, everybody was happy with the way things were. There had been only two or three physical changes in the pecking order of TV-news history—when Huntley-Brinkley made NBC number 1, and then when CBS took it back again. But now it's a three-way race, so the role of president of CBS News is much more that of a competitor. I'm proud of the fact that most of the things we've accomplished we've done without a marvelous image to build on—first in sports and now in news. That's the great advantage Van Sauter has. He can come in and do commercial things, because he is working in an area where he has an image already established. It'll take a while before anybody criticizes him for anything.

It's been rumored that you offered CBS's Diane Sawyer a job.

I have never met Diane Sawyer, nor have I talked to her agent.

Would you hire her if you could?

Yeah, but I don't know what she'd do. She is very good, but I lost a notch—not a major notch, but a notch—of respect for her when I watched the last *CBS Morning News* she did with Kuralt. On that day, she sounded exactly like Kuralt. Then that Monday I tuned in—when they had changed to Bill Kurtis and were trying to copy our *Good Morning America*—and Diane was joking back and forth with the weatherman, the sports guy. . . . Critics of television who like to say that newspeople act on the air had only to look at those two programs to see how a personality changed over the weekend and their questions would be answered. Her credentials are good enough, however, that people are not going to accuse her of being phony. But then, until recently CBS has been exempt from a lot of the criticism that we're subject to.

Why?

Because there's a certain clubbiness to any profession, and at a certain point, people are canonized. Bill Moyers has been certified a saint. He may irritate people because he's too liberal, but he is not going to be criticized very much. Geraldo Rivera, on the other hand, has been categorized as a villain, so he can do the most incredible piece of journalism and it's going to take a courageous critic to praise him.

Geraldo's brought much of that criticism on himself. Many journalists, including those at ABC, find Rivera insupportable and wonder why you've been so loyal to him.

I am very well aware that there is a group in both TV and print journalism to whom Geraldo is a symbol of ABC far more than he should be. I'm not going to defend everything he's ever done, but by and large they're wrong. He's done good work, but he's also been his worst enemy. It has taken him a while to realize you can't solve all the problems of the world by reporting on them. But he's matured. He wears suits and ties, his hair's shorter.

Jessica Savitch's contract with NBC expires this month. Would you hire her?

I'm not a big fan of hers. It would depend on what she wanted to do. I wouldn't hire her as an anchor. I'm not opposed to her; I just don't think she's in that group of top correspondents—Lynn Scherr, Sandy

Vanocur, Jim Wooten, Richard Threlkeld—who are a cut above the rest.

Two of the most outstanding things you've done at ABC News are the rejuvenation of David Brinkley and the rediscovery of Ted Koppel. Koppel had been at ABC almost twenty years without emerging as the star he is now. What did you do?

When I came to ABC, he was part of a group I didn't know, and he didn't know me. He was ready to leave. In fact, he wrote me a note saying he was leaving ABC, and I just ignored it. I wouldn't let him resign. Finally, we had lunch. I got to like him tremendously, and he saw I didn't have horns. I said to him, "Tell me what you do other than what I've seen you do." So he sent me some tapes he'd done at past conventions. We started having him substitute on *Good Morning America.* And he did part of a series—that turned out to be one of the things that helped us take over second place.

How did his participation in Nightline—*his real debut, so to speak—evolve?*

I was at Lake Placid one day about five days after the hostages were taken. I came back and found out we weren't doing a special that night. I said, "Why?" And they said, "Because there's nothing new." And I said, "I have not met a person today who wants to talk about anything else but that. I'll make the decision for you. We will do a special every night until this is over."

People must have thought you were crazy.

CBS and NBC in particular. Obviously, we didn't expect it to go on as long as it did. At first, people tuned in to see if Peter Jennings and Bob Dyk would come back alive from Iran. When it settled down, we were able to do long pieces on Islam and Iran. That's when we proved serious people would watch when it wasn't "Are they dead or alive?" Frank Reynolds did the first half of the specials, but when it became obvious that this was going to be a long haul, you couldn't have Frank do the evening news and the specials, so I put Ted in, and he was wonderful. One night we had this hookup with Vladimir Pozner in London, Harold Brown in Washington, and some Republican senator, and we discovered Ted had this ability—which we'd never seen—to keep all this conversation going in a way that everybody followed and listened. So we built a program around that ability.

You're opposed to the TV ratings system; what have you done to fight it?

A couple of years ago, I tried to get all three networks to agree not to count the ratings of prime-time documentaries. CBS and NBC both said no just because I proposed it—rejected it out of hand without even thinking about it. So we did it by ourselves for a while. But that just became an empty gesture, so we stopped it. To compare a serious documentary about the black labor unions in South Africa with a half-hour situation comedy is nonsense and maddening. We have common enemies in this country—people who would like to repeal the First Amendment, to silence unpopular criticism or boycott advertisers who sponsor anything controversial. But we are not enemies; we need to help each other.

Have you found the Reagan White House cooperative?

Yes and no. If it's something they can't avoid or that's not going to hurt them, they're fine. But there's two or three instances where they have threatened us right down to ten minutes before we went on the air, trying to kill a story. We had an instance recently. The United States was moving the aircraft carrier *Nimitz* off the coast of Lebanon at the time Muammar Qaddafi was planning an invasion of Egypt. We had flown AWACs to Egypt, and Libyan troops were massing on their border. We held off reporting the story for a full day. We were going to go with it, but the White House called and said lives were at stake. We went over everything we could think of that might endanger lives and finally did what we had done before—call them, read them what we were going to do, and ask what in there would endanger lives. Their answer was simply that the whole story was wrong. At that point we knew they were just trying to kill it because it was embarrassing for them, so we went with it, although there was a lot we didn't put on because it would have compromised some security people within the Qaddafi government.

When you took over as president of the news division six years ago, many people were surprised. What do you think you personally brought to ABC News?

I think I brought a sense of purpose and self-assurance. When I came, ABC had a defeatist attitude. They had withdrawn into this mentality that "since we're never going to be able to compete, we'll be purer than anybody. We'll knock what the other guys do instead of doing something on our own." I brought in enough new blood to stimulate the good people and prove to them they could succeed.

What surprised you most once you got there?

At ABC News there were two extremes: One was how good some of the people were and the other how terrible. And a lot of the terrible people were in key positions.

Beyond that, even though I expected criticism, I was not prepared for the virulent rewriting of history that took place, the viciousness that some of the critics and columnists had toward me. Once I took the news job, it was suddenly all show biz—Howard Cosell, *Battle of the Network Stars*—the showman coming to desecrate the temple. Is *The New York Times* judged by the crossword puzzle? What troubled me the most was that people totally forgot what I'd done in sports. There I had a career where ninety percent of what we did was acclaimed. I won every award there was. There was never any suggestion that we trivialized things. We were the first people who refused to let organizers name or approve announcers; the first to be critical of athletes and not treat sports like a religion; the first to deal in any kind of sports journalism, particularly anything that required standing up and being counted.

Of course, a lot of the criticism was normal. You know, "Who the hell is this guy to be running a news division?" And a lot of it was genuine concern on the part of the people who didn't know me, people who when they finally met me would say, "Gee, you're not what I thought at all." I remember *US* magazine—which, to my amazement, is still being published—wanted to do a bio on me, but I refused. So *US* just made it up. They made it look like they had interviewed me, took some old pictures and quotes, and made it sound like I was some sort of hippie, wearing shirts open to the waist with gold chains.

Were you, in fact, wearing gold chains and open shirts?

Only if I popped a button. But I did want people to know I was a hands-on executive. So I used to go down to the editing room a lot, where you naturally wear different clothes than when you are speaking to affiliates. Sally Bedell came to interview me one day when I was editing and had a sport shirt on. By the time she got done describing it, it had turned into a polka-dot shirt, and from that time on, anytime people did a caricature, there I'd be in this polka-dot shirt. In her recent book, *The Evening Stars,* Barbara Matusow has me wearing a medallion—whatever that is—at a meeting in Montauk. She also has me coming into a police station with a Scotch in one hand and a walkie-talkie in the other.

The point is that these things feed on themselves. Of course people say, "If it makes you colorful, what do you care?" I care only if it reflects on my seriousness. If you're trying to do a serious effort, like [running] a news division, it can diminish you in the eyes of the people you want to work with. Once an impression is made, it takes forever to break it down. But it's a wonderful experience for the head of a news division to go through, because it makes you much more sensitive to what inaccurate portrayals of people mean.

You do care what people think about you, don't you?

I don't give a damn what certain people think about me—but there aren't very many of those. I do care what most people think. I don't want them to idolize me, but I don't want them to think I'm something I'm not. I never mind criticism if it's intelligent. But when people attack either your character or your taste, that's part of who and what you are.

I guess it goes along with my compulsion to explain things. Dave Burke [former ABC News vice president] said that my idea of hell must be that I'm trying to explain something to somebody and they don't understand me and walk away.

What frustrates you most about your job?

One of the most frustrating things is that myth about my flamboyance. People are constantly writing that I love publicity, love to get my name in the paper. But they don't see the inconsistency right before their noses—that someone like Van Gordon Sauter creates it. He dresses eccentrically—sweaters, pipes—just to look different. He gives speeches and more interviews than I do, and yet no one writes things like that about him. Maybe it's because he followed me in sports and news. They also like to write that I like to collect celebrities, that I ingratiate myself with the Kennedys. I was accused of hiring Pierre Salinger because he was a friend and I wanted to bring back Camelot. But he's a godsend.

Then you wouldn't call yourself flamboyant?

I don't really know what flamboyant is. I'm rarely thrown out of nightclubs at four A.M., and I certainly don't recall running down the beach nude.

Where do you think these misconceptions got started?

I'm not a hundred percent sure. A lot had to do with me putting Howard Cosell on the air—people thought Howard and I were alike.

Did you feel great pressure to turn the news division around immediately?

I'll tell you a wonderful story. I talked to a number of people before I took this job—Walter Cronkite, Morley Safer, Jack Chancellor. Morley said, "It'll take you seven years before you're even on the table." Chancellor said five, and [ABC president] Elton Rule one day said to me, "I want you to understand we're not expecting miracles. It might take a year." Finally, at the affiliates' meeting in May—before I even officially took over—the head of affiliate relations grabbed me and said, "Hey, if we could turn this news thing around in a couple of months, there's about six stations I could get for us."

One criticism of you is that you are not a good administrator. You don't return phone calls or write memos and you often miss meetings. Are you a good administrator?

I'm a different kind of administrator. I pick the very best people around me, and I delegate things. You can't take sports—always a loss leader at other networks—and make it one of the most profitable divisions at ABC, or take ABC News, which never made a profit, and make it profitable, without some idea of what you're doing.

Now there is always a certain amount of untidiness that's necessary in the business we're in. It's not IBM or Mobil Oil. Out of organized individualism comes order, although at a certain point you have to say, "Okay, this is what it's going to be." I encourage a free-form work atmosphere, but you can't have a good organization without discipline. Lots of times I suggest people take a day off and just go home and think or look at cassettes or answer the mail if they can't get it done in the office. I'm totally intolerant of systems that don't allow for last-minute changes. You've got to have rules, but when you find a better way to do something, if the situation allows you to do something better, then you've got to break the rules.

Then you don't think you're elusive and hard to reach?

Compared to what? Who? I told ABC when I took the two jobs that I could not run two divisions—daily—and also attend every meeting, write memos, and always be available to answer phone calls. The bottom line is that everything gets done. We operate at a profit. It's a matter of priorities with me. They pay me to make programs and find ways to excel in areas I'm involved in. As for not returning phone calls, that's overplayed. I've never trusted anybody who's always available to return calls. If they've got time for that, they're probably not doing their job.

What's your typical day?

In New York, I get up at seven, seven-fifteen, watch the news, *Good Morning America,* and read five or six newspapers—*The New York Times,* the *Daily News, The Washington Post, The Wall Street Journal, USA Today,* sometimes the *New York Post, The Christian Science Monitor.* I get the *Financial Times* every day and then everything else from *The New England Journal of Medicine* to *Opera News, Architectural Digest,* and *Sports Illustrated.* I also try to do about an hour of exercise. Usually I'm in the office by nine-thirty or ten, although I generally get trapped on the phone at home. After I get to the office, it's up for grabs. I'm always in the office until around eight, and some nights I have a function. There are weeks when every night gets filled, and I hate that because then going out becomes just an extension of your day, instead of an event. When do I see my wife? Dinner, weekends, lunch. We try to have dinner with as few interruptions as possible. I always watch *Nightline,* during which I sometimes ride my exercise bike.

When people you've worked with talk about you, especially as a television producer, they say you have the "feel." What is that?

Basically, it's a sense of what people are interested in, being not too far ahead and not too far behind the public. You have to do what pleases you. It's a sense of curiosity—"What would I like to know about this?" The first quality I look for in anyone is curiosity. . . . You have to constantly be saying, "What would happen if I tried this?" That's the difference between those who are very good and those who are mediocre. First, to be curious, and second, to say, "What if I tried this?" I always try to act as if I'm seeing something for the first time.

What drives you?

First is a desire to excel and make a general contribution to an area that's important in the world. Beyond that? You know, when athletes talk about the game, they usually say they're not afraid of getting hurt, they just don't want to embarrass themselves. I guess I feel that way. In my job you have to be very well informed in an awful lot of areas. You have to keep up, to keep reading newspapers, looking at cassettes, talking to people. That's half your job. Power itself doesn't interest me, although I suppose I wouldn't like the lack of power. My Achilles' heel has always been that I'd rather do something of quality than make a lot of money.

What's the biggest turkey you were ever involved with?

The opening program of *20/20.* I've taken responsibility for it. I let the program go on the air, even though deep down inside I knew it wasn't ready. I let myself get talked into it. The Howard Cosell variety show was also not a success, although a lot of talented people came out of it. Beyond that [*laughs*] there was the very first program I ever produced on NBC, called *Sunday*—a Sunday version of the *Today* show produced on no budget. *Variety* called it "an abdication of programming responsibility."

How did you get into television in the first place?

It was an accident, really. Originally, I wanted to write for *Time* or *Newsweek* because I was interested in music and politics and theater— all of which they seemed to have. After graduating from Columbia I went to the School of International Affairs [also at Columbia] to study the Middle East, until I found out that learning Arabic wasn't something I wanted to spend a lot of time doing.

My dad, who was a lawyer, was involved in some real estate representing Equitable Life with the old Dumont network. And it struck me that television might also be a place where these various things also existed. So I got an interview at Dumont. I worked my way through several interviews, until finally I was to meet with the head of programming.

And now I have to flash back. During the summers I was in college, I worked at an inn in Chatham, on Cape Cod, as a waiter. One night this family drove from Brockton to Chatham, but when they got there the dining room was closed, and the hostess—I was headwaiter—said, "I'm sorry—we can't handle you." But I said, "I can't let you be disappointed. Come in, and I'll wait on you." So they sat down—the place was deserted—and began rushing through their meal. I kept saying, "Take your time. I want you to enjoy your dinner." They were very grateful, and before they left they took my name. The day I walked into the office at Dumont television, the guy in charge of programming looked up and said, "How's everything at the Wayside Inn in Chatham?" And I said, "What do you mean?" And it turned out he was the person who had driven down for dinner that night and had never forgotten that I stayed to wait on him. From that instant, I had the job.

How would you compare sports with news?

Sports is much more difficult than news. In news you can get a credential. By and large, if we want to cover the Democratic convention, we call, get a credential, and send a correspondent. In sports, you have to buy the rights to something. Therefore, the organizers have tremendous power because they can give it to whomever they choose. For a long time they felt the purpose of a telecast was to be the publicity arm of the league. And no one ever criticized anything. For years the NFL had a rule that they could approve announcers. NBC and CBS—particularly CBS—would never show fights on the field. If a fight broke out, they'd pan around the field because the league didn't want mothers at home thinking their boys were hurt.

For nearly twenty years you've line-produced every broadcast of the Olympic Games. Obviously, they are very important and personal to you. Why?

During the Olympics, it's inhuman. It's like being in a war twenty-four hours a day for two weeks. I'm most proud of the Innsbruck Olympics of 1976. Fred Silverman was just coming to ABC, and they were just getting momentum at the network. *Variety* had a big headline claiming that the Olympics were going to kill that momentum and Fred was also running around telling everyone that. At that time there was not a single athlete Americans had ever heard of, except for maybe Dorothy Hamill. I went over to Innsbruck on New Year's Eve to find out what the hell we were going to do to make this interesting. I ordered a helicopter and flew around the mountain until finally I said, "I'm going to send a 'postcard' back to the United States. We'll do it to 'The Sound of Music,' featuring the Alps." So we did. We were on the air every night until four or five in the morning—responsible for the entire prime time of ABC for two weeks. Everybody was absolutely exhausted. One night we had signed off the air and had our production meeting for the next day, and I was on my way home, trying to figure out how I would end the final broadcast. Two associate producers were editing something—they said it was an idea of how to end the Olympics and would I look at it the next day? Well, God, that was the last thing I wanted, because what if it was something I hated? The next day I was dreading the meeting, but when I saw what they had done, I sat there with tears streaming down my cheeks. They had taken Beethoven's "Ode to Joy" and edited it together with the highlights of the game. We ended up opening our final broadcast with it and have used it at every Olympics since. There I was with the tears, not only because it was so wonderful but because of the idea that people who were so exhausted had the mutuality of purpose to be there on their own at five-thirty in the morning to try this idea they had and then be willing to show it to me and suffer rejection if I didn't like it. To me it embodied the kind of spirit you have to have in any organization. You've got to give back the same kind of love they give you. This may sound corny, but I believe it.

You appear to be unusually secure about taking chances other executives won't. What makes you insecure?

That's a hard question. First of all, I'm a very shy person, not psychotically shy, but much shier than people realize. I'm a good speaker, and yet I hate to give speeches, because I don't want to disappoint people. I guess I'm insecure about my own life. This is a business that takes a lot of your energy. When I first took over this job, I was in pretty good shape. I played golf. I went hunting, fishing. Then I got out of shape. I said, "This is ridiculous. What's the point of accomplishing something if I'm losing the person I am?" Things that give other people pleasure are my work. It is not recreational for me to go to a professional football game on Sunday. Yet, so much of my life is a fairyland, anybody would want to be doing it—going to Henry Kissinger's birthday party, election night in London. Still, I find I had more fun as a producer when I could just take off and go on a safari for a month. Now if I did that, two days into it there'd be four hundred calls and they'd be sending cassettes in on elephants' backs.

It's important not to let the fun go out of our lives. I was at a dinner one night with Secretary of State Shultz, and I asked him if he was having any fun. He said, "I didn't take this job to have fun." I said, "I know, but do you go home at night feeling enjoyment from what you're doing, feeling that you did something unique and important?" He said, yeah, he guessed that he did. Well, for me it's very important to feel that a lot.

The television business is tough on personal relationships. Dan Rather once told me in an interview that the toughest thing he's ever done is make his marriage work. Do you think your first marriage was a casualty of your career?

Probably part of it. I don't know if I would've remained married or not. You sacrifice a lot of home time in this job. My kids probably suffered more from my not being around, but I'm not sure what effect it had on my marriage. [Arledge's second marriage also ended in divorce, in 1986.]

When you're not involved in television, what else interests you?

I'm a generalist. There's nothing I hate more, in fact, than one-dimensional people. I hate making small talk; to me it's an insult to someone. Hostesses like Liz Rohatyn and Ethel Kennedy always get annoyed because if I go to a party I try to find out beforehand who's going to be there so I can get a bio on them and be able to make intelligent conversation. You can't imagine how people look upon that as a form of rudeness.

I don't believe most people know that you love to cook and that you are also a classical-music buff, collect art, and love ballet.

Probably not, but as one friend said, "Keep that quiet. You'll blow your image."

From your association with the Kennedys and such, I would assume you're a Democrat.

I rarely root for teams; I root for close games. In this business you try hard to be objective, so I try hard not to get involved on a personal basis. My dad was a Democrat. And in the early days I would've been, but these days I seem to spend more time with Republicans—Pete Peterson, Kissinger, Jeane Kirkpatrick, Bill Simon.

When all is said and done, what do you want to be remembered for?

I guess that I left every place better than I found it—in life and work. That at ABC Sports, which didn't even exist, and ABC News, which practically didn't exist, I made things that I and many other people are proud of—through innovation, experimentation, recognizing value in things other people didn't see, and working with people with a mutuality of respect. In a creative business, you cannot order people to do things. You have to have people who are willing to build with you; you have to respect them and let them know you respect them.

Describe Roone Arledge.

[*Long pause.*] Essentially, I think I'm a decent person. I like to run scared . . . like not to take things for granted. I'm more reflective than most people think, but the nature of my job is that I'm always putting out fires. Beyond that . . . I think I'm kind and considerate of other people—maybe to a fault. I've screwed myself up a lot trying to accommodate too many other people. This is going to sound ironic, given my reputation, but I tend to be too available to people. Jim McKay once told me that it takes a while to get to me but once you do you've got my total attention.

KIM BASINGER

INTERVIEW

February 1986

**"I always just figured that I'm
gonna go get what I want because
in this life there isn't anything
that's so hot it's ungettable."**

■

"Kim Basinger? Come on, Mark, give me a break." I was talking to an assistant editor at *Interview* magazine and knew I sounded impatient. I was. For fifteen minutes he'd been trying to convince me to talk to actress Kim Basinger, a former model whom *Interview* had decided to splash across its February cover. The hook was *9 ½ Weeks,* the controversial film about an obsessive love affair, featuring Basinger as erotic comrade-in-arms to Mickey Rourke. It was a script that had been floating around Hollywood for years, titillating the troops but never getting made. Until Basinger. *Interview* wanted me to talk to her about it, but I wanted no part of it.

"I've had that conversation a hundred times already."

"But you said you've never interviewed Basinger."

"I haven't, but I've talked to every other model-turned-actress. I know the story."

"What story?"

I took an exasperated breath. "Beautiful-girl-who-makes-megabucks-off-her-looks-hates-modeling-and-is-convinced-by-someone-usually-her-photographer-or-rock-star-boyfriend-that-she-can-act-and-ought-to-take-all-those-emotions-she-puts-into-pushing-pantyhose-and-put-them-in-front-of-a-camera-that-actually-moves. So-she-goes-to-L.A.-and-takes-acting-lessons-and-after-one-shot-in-a-James-Bond-movie-decides-she's-ready-to-play-women-of-substance-(the-kind-of-roles-that-Meryl-gets)-so-she-and-the-boyfriend-who-has-now-quit-photography-to-manage-her-career . . . Got it?"

"But Kim's supposed to be different . . ."

"She may be, kiddo. She may be Susan Sontag, but I'm just not interested. Count me out on this one."

Two months later Kim Basinger was knocking on my door at the Chateau Marmont in Los Angeles, ready to be interviewed. I hadn't changed my mind about models-turned-actresses, I'd just changed my mind about Basinger. The girl had waged an impressive campaign.

"Kim only wants to do the interview with Nancy," her press agent kept insisting to my editor.

"Who's she kidding?" I kept telling my editor to tell her press agent. "I'm sure Kim doesn't even know who I am."

"Yes, she does," she declared. "She only wants you."

Right.

Try as I might, Kim Basinger simply wouldn't go away. Finally, a sucker for tenacity, not to mention flattery, I finally said yes, and then had to cancel; I said yes again and canceled again. This behavior was totally out of character for me; once I commit, I am feverishly obsessive. My heart just wasn't in it. Unlike millions of men, I didn't want to be in a room alone with Kim Basinger. Secretly I hoped *Interview* or Basinger would get fed up with my scheduling problems and go with someone else.

They didn't. Finally, a third date was set in New York—only to be preempted by Sylvester Stallone. With suitcase in hand, I called *Interview* from the airport, just before I boarded the plane to L.A. and

Stallone. "Please tell Kim I'm terribly sorry but I don't want to tie up her time anymore. Perhaps you'd better use someone else."

"We can't," cried Mark. "Kim only wants to talk to—"

"I know."

By now, of course, I was intrigued. Most times it was I chasing them. (Mick Jagger had read my clips, one of the few stars to ever do so [and you wonder how he's controlled his image for twenty-five years?], and said no because my questions were "too hard.") Still, with due respect to Basinger, she hardly struck me as a woman who remembered bylines. What was the deal?

In Los Angeles, two days turned into two weeks, as Stallone played hard-to-get, leaving me with time and tape recorder on my hands. Antsy and anxious to work, one Friday I found myself impulsively picking up the phone and calling *Interview*. "Look, if Kim can be here at three on Sunday for a couple of hours, I'll do the interview," I announced magnanimously. A fast phone call later and it was set: Basinger would be there.

At that point the only thing I knew about Kim Basinger—as did anyone who could see—was that this was an extraordinarily beautiful woman. Georgia-born, she'd shipped out early when, at seventeen, she won a national Miss Breck [shampoo] contest. That brought the atten-tion of Eileen Ford, head of the Ford Model Agency, who signed Basinger and talked her into coming to New York. Within months, the teenager was making a bundle modeling and doing television commer-cials. But she hated the work. One morning, she kissed New York good-bye and headed to California to pursue acting.

When I opened the door at the Chateau, I saw a face that had obviously opened hundreds of doors on its own. This woman was ridiculously good-looking.

"Hi—I'm Kim Basinger," she said in a deep Georgia twang. She'd arrived unescorted, and unencumbered by things a less attractive woman might feel she needed—like makeup and beautiful clothes. The Basinger body, so provocatively undressed in *Playboy*, was camouflaged under a baggy black sweater, pedal pushers, and white crew socks accordioned up to her knees and crunched into moccasins. An orange plastic pumpkin pin was slapped haphazardly on her sweater, while, twisted around her wrist, an ominous-looking black leather, silver-studded dog collar served as a bracelet.

Twirling her car keys, Basinger stormed determinedly through the door, exhibiting a childlike curiosity that immediately took in the room.

"Shoot, I was beginning to believe that somebody made you up. I was beginning to think there really wasn't a Nancy Collins."

"Some days there isn't," I confirmed, and then apologized for our canceled appointments. Now I felt bad.

"Oh, that's okay—all that did was make me more determined than ever to talk to you. That's how I operate. I told 'em, I said, 'Listen, I'm only talking to Nancy Collins and *that is it.* I don't care where she is, I'll get there—even if I have to ride on the wing of the plane.' "

So it hadn't been press-agent blarney. "This is all very flattering, but have you ever read my interviews?"

"Nope," she admitted. "I'm here strictly on word of mouth. Which is how I get most places. Your name just kept coming up. First, Greg Gorman was taking my picture and he said you were the one to do the interview. Then, once I got your name in my head, it came up again and pretty soon it became pretty obvious that it was you I was going to *have* to talk to. It was all intuition, and my intuition never lets me down."

Intuition, when paired with prominent cheekbones, is damned near unbeatable. Spontaneous, funny, feisty, honest, naïve, Basinger turned out to be a gorgeous hayseed, Judy Holliday with a drawl. Her beauty had surely been her passport, but she'd gone farther than a mere face could carry her. This was a woman who knew what she wanted—a film career or an interview—and was damn sure going to get it.

Having, myself, come from a long line of southern women who Got It Done, our rapport was instant. As Basinger wound herself into an armchair, her feet curled under her, the two scheduled hours stretched easily into seven. This girl, as Mama might put it, "had sand." Grit. Numbers and dates were her enemies, instinct her friend. More than laugh, she hee-hawed, talked in a rush, frequently interrupting herself to digress, only to circle back again, sum up the point of her conversation, and strike, with typical southern acuity, at the core of the matter.

Finally, around ten, the phone rang. It was her husband, Ron Britton. [They have since divorced.] As she talked, Basinger eyed my address book, which was lying by the phone. A year of wear and tear had left it dog-eared and bereft of its leather cover, its pages exposed on the spiral binder, awaiting transference to a new volume.

As she walked toward the door, Basinger shot me a sly look. "Well, if I ever play a reporter, I'll know now what to do," she announced with satisfaction. "It's all about being—all the time—busy, isn't it? Always on some deadline, always in a hurry. Your address book tells the whole story."

"What do you mean?"

"No front, no back, no time."

Indeed.

——

What interested you in 9½ Weeks *in the first place?*

I wasn't interested. *I hated it.* Thought it was laughable. I read the script and said, "I've been handed some scripts on my doorstep but this is the pits."

If you hated the movie so much, why did you finally take the role?

My agent talked me into at least meeting the director, who'd been seeing girls from Europe, New York, L.A.—everywhere. I met Adrian [Lyne] in a trailer on a studio lot one day and we talked about everything but the movie, which was a relief, knowing, as I did, that I didn't want anything to do with this film. Afterward, Adrian kept calling my agent, asking when I'd meet with Mickey. I said, "Never." I didn't want the part. Meanwhile, my husband, Ron, read the script. We read it, reread it, and reread it, and then we would look at each other funny. We found ourselves going to the beach, which is something we seldom, if ever, do, except in wintertime, when we like to walk on the beach in the late afternoon and think—usually when we're not feeling right about something. Well, we found ourselves migrating to the beach every single day, walking for hours, 'cause in our hearts, Ron and I knew it was *that* time in life. And yet, I resisted. I knew what I had to do to play this role. This wasn't just a going-to-work-every-morning kind of movie. I knew I'd have to come apart at the seams in every way, shape, and form—mentally, psychologically, physically. And nobody was gonna do that to me—nobody, meaning me. I wasn't going to do this to myself. But finally I met with Mickey, which was one of the worst days I've ever lived through. We did a scene on tape for Adrian that turned out to be not a scene, but an experience. It was one of the heavier scenes in the movie, where we play a game—I crawl around on the floor picking up money. At one point, Adrian said, "Do you have on hose? Do you mind taking them off?" I got very defensive and said, "Fuck you, man, I'm not taking off anything! What the fuck are you talking about? I don't go to test for a part and take off my hose and roll around on the floor with people—what the fuck is this?" But little to my knowledge, Adrian knew that *that* was Elizabeth, that Elizabeth wouldn't have done it either. I'd heard many girls had come in to test and were quite sexually open to doing anything to get the movie. Well, I was just a hundred percent defiant. I just said, "Fuck you, you asshole. I'm not having anything to do with this." I was just out of my mind, and as we went through the scene I just came completely apart emotionally. I couldn't deal with it. I cried and cried, out-of-my-mind wrecked. But, again, that was also what Elizabeth would do. When I got home there were twenty-four roses sent from Mickey and Adrian. I called up my agent and said, "Listen, you son of a bitch, don't you ever call me again." I called him all kinds of names because I was out of my mind with fear. Just that one day, that one little scene, was so emotionally, electrically freeing. I was gone. I knew that I could do anything if I could let myself go that far. But I was also afraid of how much further than that I could go. So we went through about three or four more weeks of me saying no. I couldn't sleep at nights for fear I was going to do the movie. Adrian went to New York to do more casting, just taking for granted that I was going to do it. When Adrian came back to California, my agent said, "Why don't you have lunch with him to work things out?" I said, "I don't want to have lunch with him—I don't want anything to do with this movie, so stop calling me." But, really, what I was saying in my mind was I didn't want to have anything to do with *me;* I wanted to leave me behind, wanted to run in any direction away from this whole idea. But I ended up having lunch with Adrian and he said, "You're doing the movie, aren't you? You know you have to do it, don't you?" And I said, "I guess I am."

How did Ron react to your playing a role that required so much sexual explicitness? A lot of husbands wouldn't have liked it.

He knew I had to do it. My work wouldn't be what I think it is and is gonna be, and I wouldn't be feeling as good about myself, if it hadn't been for the release of this part. After that movie, I knew there was nothing I couldn't do. I decided a long time ago that I'm not gonna let myself off easy in my life. I want to feel it all. I want to see it all. Me and myself agree on that but sometimes we fight each other. [*Laughs.*]

You said once that you had to do 9½ Weeks because "I've been through a 9½ Weeks myself."

Very true. I didn't mean the *9 ½ Weeks* experience solely, but, yeah, I've had my "9½ Weeks." I went through a lot of this story.

With your husband, Ron?

Yes. And it has nothing—well, that's not true, it has something—to do with sexual liberation, but I don't mean *just* sexual liberation. We went through nearly two years of a very strange relationship like this. See, I am very quiet, very shy to the world. And when somebody finally figures you out and shows you your inside—on *their* face—it can be quite scary, especially when they reveal your past and hidden fears. But it took time. At first I didn't want anything to do with Ron because it's scary to be opened up like that. But when all of that is out, nothing can be more liberating, nothing can be more coveted than love in a relationship that has liberation. Then love takes on a whole other meaning than all those things written on Hallmark cards. Once you've met someone who turns you inside out, it's another whole ball game. I'm a very lucky human being to have—

Met Ron?

Absolutely. Because I just don't believe there are thousands of people out there for everybody. I've always believed there's that one person, and I don't think you should settle for less. Now, most people in life never, ever, will meet that person. Never run into them. But the key to that is your dream. If you just go forth with your dream, those things are going to happen. I always just figured that I'm gonna go get what I want because in this life there isn't anything that's so hot it's ungettable. If you want to climb Mount Everest, go climb it. Follow that dream, and along the way there are so many gifts you'll get. That's what little pieces of heaven are all about. Of course, it's not going to be wonderful all the time, just because you believe so strongly. I don't believe in the idea of working at a marriage; I believe in working on yourself . . . just being pals with yourself, being strong, strict with yourself, and fun. You also have to be very tough, fiercely smart about outsmarting anything, any entity that might hurt your whole existence.

What attracted you to Ron?

He's the person with the least bullshit I've ever known in my life. He tells the truth all the time—even to himself about himself.

Was it love at first sight?

It was mutual admiration at first sight. We've been together six years. Ron is so smart. He keeps his mouth shut about most things, but he listens, which is one of the finest qualities that anyone can have. If you want to win, listen. He's listened his whole life and won over and over again. People always say they can never figure him out, but there's nothing to figure out. It's just him. There couldn't be anybody who's more supportive of me than this person. And he loves animals so much. We have nine dogs and seven cats. Right now my work is beginning to mount up and mean something. I'm finding out the meaning of a career. Before now it's really been hit and miss . . . some money or no money. We've gone through some hard and some great times together. I've been supportive of him because we do this together. We work on life. Right now, for instance, he's completing a screenplay, but he doesn't want to be a writer, he wants it to all go through me. He just wants to get it done. He doesn't need to be up front.

Believing, as you do, that there is only one man for you in the world, you must have felt an enormous relief when you finally ran into Ron.

Absolutely. It was like a vacation in the park. Like a day off forever. I swear to God. [*Laughs.*]

Do you think you and Ron will be able to make your relationship work for the rest of your lives?

Oh, yeah. We . . . *are*. We just *are*. [*Laughs.*] Toys "Я" Us and we are *it*.

Switching gears, you also starred with Sam Shepard in Fool for Love, *taken from Shepard's play and directed by Robert Altman. Again, it's a psychologically interesting piece in which you and Shepard play lovers who discover they have the same father. Shepard, of course, remains something of an enigma. How would you describe him?*

I think he's a plain guy who just likes to ride horses. In fact, I think he is a horse. I think he's a horse, and when he picks up that pen he has to be a person because they don't allow horses to write. I mean, he knows more about horses than anybody I've ever met. And I grew up spending half my time on a farm, so I was around horses a lot. Sam would much rather be riding polo ponies than anything, I think.

Is he smart?

Yes. He's incredibly, instinctively smart about one blocked-off area. It's like an unnamed town. He built it. He's the ground, all the animals, and all the characters who live there. He was born with that, I do believe. And he's incredibly smart about that town. Plus, he's truly a sweet guy. Some parts of him are very volatile, but he's got a great sense of humor and he laughs—a big laugh. I like that about him.

Despite doing such films as Hard Country, Never Say Never Again, The Man Who Loved Women, The Natural, Fool for Love, *and* 9½ Weeks, *you've given almost no interviews, so there's really very little known about you. You grew up in Athens, Georgia, one of five children, right?*

I was in the middle. There was Skip, Mick, Kim, Barbara, and Ashley.

And your father was a musician?

That was way before any of us. My daddy played with bands all over Chicago and really had quite a wild existence. After World War Two, when he came back, there was no work, so he went to school, got his master's degree in business, and worked in finance companies until he was president of one himself. He's a frustrated musician, but he's proud. He never let it kill him. He doesn't live in the past. He lives for tomorrow, which I always thought was a great quality, because if you live in the past, it will kill you. It is a cancer, and it can truly turn into the disease itself.

Your mother was once a model, wasn't she?

She modeled for years, went to New York, which she hated, and then did some underwater films during the Esther Williams time. Sometimes I'll go to Florida with my daddy, and in these old sundries I'll pick up a postcard and my mom will be one of those women holding a beach ball. And that tickles the hell out of me. My mom is really a very, very beautiful woman. She had a lot of chances to do a lot of things, but then you get married and you bog yourself down with five kids—and if you're a perfectionist, which she is, that doubles the problem. She was an incredible mother. The neighbors always thought my mom was wild. She wore short shorts and mowed the grass in her bathing-suit top and was always real brown. She could have been my sister. She was the kind of mom who ran with you in the woods and picked pumpkins and loved Christmas. She's like a child in the *Twilight Zone.* But I always just loved her so.

Where did your parents meet each other?

They were both from Hartwell, Georgia. Her family were all farmers. She met my daddy in a drugstore in Hartwell. She walked into the store and my father said, "You see that girl over there? That's the girl I'm going to marry someday." There's quite a bit of difference in their ages. Daddy's sixty-one, I think, and I can never figure out how old my mom is. [*Laughs.*]

Do they have a good marriage?

I don't think any two people could've respected each other more than they did. My father totally loves my mother for what she gave up to go through his life with him—bringing up five kids, not having it easy. [Kim's parents are now divorced.]

Did your family have any money?

We were okay, but that's all. A lot of that had to do with my mother and the way she never spent a cent on herself. She gave up a lot of things just so I could have ballet lessons. We didn't have money; we just spent it on living—on waking up, eating, and going to bed.

My mother was from Alabama, and I think there's something extraordinarily unique, not only about the relationship between southern women and their daughters in particular, but about women from the South in general.

Southern women are very strong-willed and intuitive. But sometimes being southern can be incredibly strangling. I was determined to beat that rap. Ever since I was born I said, "This is bullshit." I didn't want to have anything to do with it. I knew I was going to California. I didn't know how I'd get out; I just knew I would, and as long as you know that, you will. And ever since I was a teeny, teeny little girl I was very intuitive. Almost scary intuitive, almost too much for my own good. It can scare the hell out of you.

Until you can balance it with some life experience.

Or use it. God, if you can use your intuition, make it across the finish line, it's almost like going through a tragedy and coming out all the better for it. It's like having your own diamond mine or air mine when nobody else can breathe. But as a child, it made me much more nervous—to the point where I couldn't breathe. For instance, I hated school, hated going in every way, shape, and form. School scared me every day.

Why? Because you were shy?

Oh, the worst in the world. They never called on me to read aloud because if they did, I would faint. Pass out. So every summer my mother had to call up my new teacher two weeks before school started and tell her never to call on me.

What caused your shyness, Kim?

I don't know, because at home I was a wild clown. At home I was very safe and very secure. I always knew I wanted to entertain, wanted to be a singer, but the older I got the more petrified I got of ever standing up and walking toward a stage. It still scares me today.

How did you plan on overcoming this shyness in order to entertain?

Well, my daddy made a bet with me. They had these things called the Junior Miss pageants, and I was a good singer. So Daddy said, "I'll make a bet with you that if we find something for you to sing and you do it, you won't faint, you won't die up there." Now, I had no want to go through this pageant except for the talent part. But after I saw *My Fair Lady,* I learned to sing Eliza's "Wouldn't It Be Loverly?" and talk in a cockney accent. So Daddy helped me find a piano player; I rehearsed it for about three weeks and entered the pageant. And it was just the scariest, the greatest night of my life. Even if I think of my accomplishments now as an actress, nothing could have been quite like the thrill of having made it through that whole song. Well, that night everybody was in the audience and nobody had ever known that I could even open my mouth, much less sing. You could have heard a pin drop. It was magical. And I won. I won the whole pageant. So I went to the state pageant and didn't win the Junior Miss title, but there was a lady from Breck in the audience who asked me if I'd ever modeled. 'Course I said no, never really having thought much about modeling. But I came to New York with a bunch of other girls for the national Miss Breck contest (I'd won the Georgia Miss Breck), and I won it. They asked all the contestants to name two people they'd most like to meet. So I called my daddy and said, "Who should I say?" and he said, "Tickle them and say Mayor Lindsay and Eileen Ford." So I did, and I was invited to a block party at Mayor Lindsay's and met Eileen Ford, who asked me to sign with her agency that summer. But I didn't sign. I said I didn't know what to do. Eileen wrote a letter to my parents and asked them, but I said I'd have to go home and make up my mind. That fall I entered the University of Georgia, went for two semesters, and, of course, hated it. But by then I was becoming something I had never been. It was like a surge of strength had come to me during the summer, and by the end of that fall we called Eileen Ford, who said I could live at her house. So I left. I got on an airplane one Sunday afternoon with instructions to go to her house when I got to New York. But when I finally got there nobody was home. I beat and beat on the door and, finally, a Finnish gal named Suby came down the stairs. She couldn't speak English and I couldn't speak from fear, so we made perfect roommates. However, reality hit me at about five that afternoon. I just broke into tears . . . called Daddy and Mama on the phone and just said, "God, I'm here."

Did you like modeling?

Those were the toughest years of my existence, walking the streets of New York and modeling. It was the loneliest I've ever felt in my whole life. I don't care if I went out every night, which I did often, and modeled all day, it was so lonely. But I was very lucky, because my first week there I got a commercial and they took me to California—the place I'd always wanted to go. They took me out to Malibu and I couldn't believe it. I said, "This isn't the place. This isn't the place where they have surfboards and girls in bikinis and tons of cars. This isn't where the Beach Boys live." [*Laughs.*] Anyway, after that I got another commercial and things started happening pretty fast for me.

You must have sensed you were on your way, that you were on a roll.

I've always been on a roll. I don't think there's any other way to look at it. I just knew everything would come. But that doesn't mean that the roll doesn't roll off the table every now and then—or hit a bump—because I had my ups and downs in New York City. I just absolutely did not fit into that world.

Were you simply overwhelmed by the people you met?

I was never overwhelmed by anybody very much—by shows, by people, by New York, by California, by anything. I don't want you to take that the wrong way. It might sound corny to you, but the only thing that overwhelms me is the outdoors. Nature—now that's over- whelming.

Did you make a lot of money modeling?

I made an awful lot of money and I spent it all. [*Laughs.*] I swear to God. I'd never seen so much money in large checks in all my life. Models get paid through the mail and the agency will send you a check, so I just carried tons of these envelopes around in my pocketbook all the time. Once I carried a twenty-five-thousand-dollar check around for a week. Finally I'd get to the bank and just hand 'em over and say, "Put 'em in my checking account." I never had money and money had no importance to me. Now I want lots of money. Tons of money, because now I understand what it can do. But then, you see, I never wanted to be a model. I just thought, "This is almost like getting off before the home stop."

Still, you were very successful. What did your parents think?

I don't think they knew what was happening. They knew what I told them. But anyway, it was never enough. I always wanted it better. I always wanted to impress my daddy more.

Why did you think you had to impress him more?

I had this thing for years—we straightened it out four or five years ago—my father always wanted to be a singer. He knew I could sing but he never pushed me or helped because he feared it for me. He's very conservative and he thought it was a wild dream that I go and be a singer. But I didn't. When I was four years old, in my ballet class, I used to say, "I'm gonna be an actress. I'm gonna be an actress, singer, dancer; I'm gonna do everything. I'm gonna be the biggest movie star in the world. I'm gonna write. I'm gonna have anything I want." And everybody said, "Yeah, yeah, yeah"—but I was determined. If I'd wanted to be a country doctor, I'd have done it. But as it is, I'm practicing medicine this way.

How did you finally leave modeling and pursue acting?

One morning I woke up—I was living with a guy at the time—and said, "I can't take this anymore. I'm not going to work ever again as a model." Shortly after that, my boyfriend left his soap opera and I left modeling and we came to California, where we lived at the Holiday Inn with two dogs and a cat for four months, looking for jobs.

After you got your first feature, Hard Country, *there was a dry spell. Is that what made you decide to pose for* Playboy?

Playboy had asked me a million times to do some pictures, and this time when they called, I said, "Yeah, we can talk." I am very instinctual. I know exactly what, when, and how things will work—and my career's gone that way. I told *Playboy* I didn't just want to do a layout, I wanted to make a point with it. I said, "I need a film and I'm going to make this a silent film for me. I'm going to make Hollywood see something they've never seen in me." And since they sure as hell didn't expect it from me, it just happened to work. I knew it had no way of not working because I knew the shock value of it. As tasteless as shock value can be, it can also help. We shot it in Hawaii and Ron and I made up the text. The idea was to pick men in various businesses—Fellini, Bob Fosse, Sean Connery, George Plimpton—and show them pictures of this girl—me—and say, "What do you think of her?" They would see the pictures, have an interview with me, and write what they thought. Well, it just turned out like clockwork. It was a stupendous success. You can't imagine what happened to my career because of *Playboy.* Meanwhile, before it ran, I was called in to talk to people about this James Bond film, *Never Say Never Again.* I had never seen a Bond film and didn't realize the power of it. I didn't want to do *Never Say Never Again,* but I needed the money. I got the role and we lived in Europe and the Bahamas for over a year.

Was it a good experience?

Never Say Never Again was the worst experience of my life because [director] Irvin Kershner and I didn't get along at all. It was a long-drawn-out, disorganized shoot—not fun at all. Sean [Connery] really had a lot to do with us coming out with a film at all because he knows Bond better than anybody. I was chopped meat by the time it was all over. Anyway, Ron and I were in the airport coming home when I saw *Playboy* on the stands with me on the cover. I just stood there and watched all these men grab the magazine. It was hysterical. Ron was delighted; he thought it was so funny. When I got back to the States, I got tons of movie offers. I met with James Brooks to play Debra Winger's best friend in *Terms of Endearment,* but Brooks couldn't make up his mind and, meantime, Blake Edwards called and asked me to meet Burt Reynolds for *The Man Who Loved Women.* I love Blake; he doesn't fool around, and right on the spot he asked, "Will you do it?" I did and it changed my life.

Why?

Because I cut off all my hair. I had this real, real long hair and had become very attached to it because it was a big part of my confidence. It made me feel secure. When Blake asked me to cut it, he just meant trim it, but with my impulsive personality I'm either black or white—never in between. So I went to Julie Andrews's hairdresser—it was a Sunday and nobody was in the beauty parlor—and I said, "Cut it." The hairdresser said, "Kim, I can't cut it any shorter," but I said, "Shorter, shorter." So all of a sudden it's shaved—it's about that short. [*She indicates about an inch.*] Well, Ron, who loved my hair, walked in and almost fainted. I was even in a state of shock, but the most fun state of shock I've ever been in. I was the ugliest person you had ever seen! And I felt so happy to be that ugly. I was released. There wasn't anything I couldn't do then. I could act, I could do anything. I felt so much more confident 'cause I could just look ugly. I didn't have to worry about that fucking hair anymore. You know that fear I told you I had as a child and am still working on now? Well, I'm determined to rid myself of that bullshit—whatever it takes. Deep down, I didn't want to cut my hair. I wouldn't be pretty. People wouldn't look at me. But when I walked out of that shop and nobody looked at me, it was great.

What happened to your hair after you finished The Man Who Loved Women?

I wore a hat for a year. I wouldn't take it off wherever I went. I even wore a hat to bed—along with socks and long johns in winter—so you can imagine how sexy Ron felt. [*Laughs.*] It was terrible.

How was working with Burt Reynolds?

There is a side of Burt that nobody knows that he would like people to know, but somehow he's settled in one place and cannot get the push to show it. He's the nicest guy—funny as hell—and really down-to-earth, but very, very pained because he needs to show something else about himself. He's going to have to do it before he starts getting satisfaction.

Following The Man Who Loved Women, *you appeared with Robert Redford in* The Natural. *I must say you've had some very interesting leading men.*

I loved working with Redford. He's another challenge . . . a great guy. I mean, here's this man who everybody thinks is a hermit, living up in the mountains, probably snobby, and he's just a person. You can imagine how many people pull at him. It's a hard job being Robert Redford.

Do you think he likes being Robert Redford?

He's settled for it, but I don't think he's unhappy being Robert Redford. But there's an incredible part of him that's always trying to escape from himself, and I love that part of him. But, you know, this is all a game, anyway. It's a serious game. I don't take it lightly; it's work, but it's still a game—your relationship with the public—everything's a game. It's real but it's unreal because movies are unreal. Actresses are unreal, actors are . . . assholes. We're all assholes. You have to be a little unreal to be in this business.

So why are you in the movie business?

I tell you, between "action" and "cut," I know why. The rest of the time I don't. Between "action" and "cut" I just know that I love to pretend and force myself to keep my concentration that long, because that's very difficult for me. We could be filming right now and I'll be in the middle of a scene wondering if my housekeeper picked up the trick-or-treat candy, 'cause I get bored very quickly. Other times, I'm attentive and I'm very much there, and that I love—I love to really be *there.*

What about the attention you get? I once asked Sissy Spacek why she became an actress and she said, "Because I love being the center of attention," which I thought was a very honest answer.

Wonderful answer, but that's too simple this day and time because it's a fight to be the center of attention and it can be a dirty fight. We're an entertainment industry. So, let's entertain. Look, I love to be the center of attention but I'd have to love something more than that, 'cause I'd only last for about one second—until tomorrow morning, 'cause after you've won or after the reviews come out, there's always tomorrow morning.

You seem inordinately determined to overcome things that scare you. Has anything ever frightened you to the point of immobility?

One time I had an attack that crippled me. I was in the health-food store, reading a book, when suddenly everything seemed blurry, everything began buzzing. I started sweating profusely—my hands, my face. I couldn't breathe at all. I got weak—my feet, my knees. The only thing I could think of was just to get out of there. It was horrible. I finally made it out the door—left my basket and everything. I began shaking.

I finally made it to the car, and thank God I was close to the house, because I was sure I couldn't drive. But I did, two miles an hour. Whenever I saw a car, I panicked. I finally made it home, parked the car, and didn't go anywhere for four months. I thought I was losing my mind. It was the worst feeling. I'd rather have died right there than lose my mind. Anyway, I cried all day. I didn't know who to turn to. After about six weeks, Ron heard about a place in San Francisco called TERRAP, for phobias. We called and got Dr. Ronald Doctor—Dr. Doctor, can you believe that? [*Laughs.*] Ron drove me over and I started seeing Dr. Doctor. He told me I had agoraphobia, which is the fear of public places. Panic attacks. It's not a disease that you cure; it's an understanding you acquire. I learned to understand that my anxiety attacks weren't going to kill me, that they might help me as an actress, that nervousness is wonderful. Under it all, anxiety is the spice of life, but there are agoraphobics who haven't been out of the house for twenty-five years. It helped to find out I wasn't alone—that there are millions of us out there. I got relaxation tapes, saw the doctor, and exercised. I'd break out in tears from sheer release of stress. The first time I drove after all this I had to get on the freeway and go to Paramount—

Going to Paramount can make a healthy person panic.

That's true. [*Laughs.*]

You realize, of course, that a lot of people, especially men, find you devastatingly attractive and sexy. My guess is that you don't view yourself quite like that.

Right. Ron would roll laughing at that one. He's always saying to me, "Look at you," 'cause nobody would know the truth. I mean, I feel sorry for him because he hasn't had that. So, I don't know how to answer that question because I've always fought that all my life.

Why?

I think because I met myself real early. I did it when I was a baby. I met myself so early that I'm meeting myself on up the ladder. And I'm real outspoken about knowing myself. I wrote a song called "Birthmark" that I plan to record one of these days. Do you remember that song by Janis Ian, "At Seventeen"? It was about how ugly she was.

"Birthmark" is a song about the other half . . . about women who are beautiful. Having lived in New York and California, I've seen what happens to a woman who is born beautiful. It's a birthmark. There are a couple lines in the song that go:

> When blond hair grows darker, you hear them whisper that she's
>   lost it.
> With lines growing deeper, but not as deep now as the fear
> And the woman just gets weaker when the reason that they
>   seeked her, disappears.
> It's a birthmark.

"Birthmark" is a song about life going on at a physical level. And if you haven't met yourself before that happens, then you really got nothing. Still, I must say, Ron and I have big arguments about selling yourself a little bit for being what you look like. I read an interview with Sting where they asked him why he didn't wear a shirt under some of his things and he said, "Well, we're here to please and sex sells." And he's right. In 9 ½ Weeks and even in The Natural, I enjoyed the sexy part of myself being used for things. Enjoyed it immensely, in fact. Sometimes even at home I enjoy that. I don't want to be anybody but me, don't want to look like anybody but me, don't want to have anybody's problems but my own. But that sexy part has always been hard for me, although Ron's made it a lot easier. I like to be sexy for him, like him to be proud of me. I like him to be sexy.

Women are attracted to sex.

Everybody's attracted to sex. So I'm learning to use it a lot better than I used to, 'cause if we ain't using it, we're wasting it.

But then, intelligence and self-confidence are the sexiest qualities, aren't they?

Absolutely. Because everything else is at their command. . . . You know, women are so powerful it's frightening. Men are very strong, but women have this thing really wrapped up in beautiful paper and sold right from the beginning, don't they?

INTERVIEW

August 1986

**"[Hollywood is] the type of place
where people don't eat their young—
they put them on hold."**

—

Sometimes it's not that hard to get. Sometimes it just falls in your lap.
Sometimes it's just all in a day's work.

That's what happened with Robin Williams. On Friday I got an
emergency call from *Interview,* and on Saturday I was sitting in the
Helmsley Palace talking to America's funniest man.

The interview started late on an overcast afternoon. Robin and I,
illuminated only by natural light sliding through partially closed blinds,
huddled at one end of an obnoxiously ornate dining-room table in a
penthouse suite. In his Hawaiian-print shirt and suspenders, he looked
like a little boy stunned to suddenly find himself in the world of adults,
talking about grown-up things like marriage. When I asked how he had
managed to hold his together for ten years, he told me. In present tense
and detail. It wasn't until later that I found out he'd been describing
scenes from a marriage that was over. For even as we talked, he and

his wife, Valerie, a dancer, were in the process of splitting up. (Williams married Marcia Garces in April 1989. They had a daughter, Zelda, that July.)

As the light ebbed, Williams's face became less distinct, aptly reflecting that on all fronts, this was a man in transition. His film career, which had started so promisingly with *The World According to Garp*, had slumped in the wake of a series of silly movies. (It was subsequently resuscitated with *Good Morning, Vietnam* and *Dead Poets Society*.) And though he'd kicked the drugs and alcohol that allegedly absorbed his life in the seventies and eighties, you sensed he was still grappling with some cosmic black hole the stimulants had temporarily sated.

Still, Williams was unique, a person with limitless imagination. You had only to throw out an idea that intrigued him and, *whoosh* . . . he was scatting, improvising like a virtuoso. The Miles Davis of comedy.

—

How close do you think comedy is to craziness?

Sometimes there's no boundary at all. Sometimes it's legalized insanity.

Have you jumped over the line a few times?

No. Well, maybe once or twice. I try to keep a little distance.

How do you do that?

I stopped drinking. . . . That helped a lot, and my son, Zach [age three], keeps me grounded a bit. He has that look in his eyes, like "Oh, *Father*, must you do that?" Like Sylvester in the cartoons. He sometimes says, "Don't be funny. Don't say that. Don't say 'fuck it.' " We have those rules.

Were you in the delivery room when he was born?

Oh, yeah, "sharing the childbirth." Bullshit. You're not doing anything unless you're there circumcising yourself with a chain saw. My wife, Valerie, had to have a cesarean because Zach was wrapped up in the cord. Fun. They said, "You have Will Rogers inside there." Then they put up the little tent and gave her an epidural. So she was awake, asking me about the movie we had watched just before. "Well, how did it end?" "Don't worry—you're having a kid." "What happened?

Louis the Fourteenth—did he walk through the door?" "Yes, he did. Look! There's a baby!"

Did you go through Lamaze training?

Yeah, but what good did it do? It was like going through flight training and ending up in a glider.

Did they give the baby to you right away?

First they held him up. You could see him going, "What?! Whaaat? Why these lights? Some mood, some music." Then he pissed on the doctors and they said, *"Yeah,* it's a boy."

Did it make any difference to you whether you had a boy or a girl?

It made a difference because I got pissed on—a major difference because he can aim.

Do you find that having a child makes a huge difference in your life?

Well, first of all, you're looking at a little creature who imitates everything you do. That kind of cleans you up in one way. Everything that you do, they pick up on, and you realize how precious time is. I've been on the road now for a month. I'll come back and he'll be a totally different creature.

Is Zach funny?

Yeah, very. Very dry. It's like living with Oscar Wilde.

Is he like you?

A little bit. He has this look about him. . . . He performs. He works a room incredibly, the ladies especially. He's very driven and loves to move and to dance. One time I took him to the Improvisation in L.A., and there was music on. The floor was empty and he just started dancing. One day when he was here in New York he started break-dancing. He saw these kids, walked up, and started dancing. The crowd went crazy: "Oh, isn't that sad? Since he lost the TV show, he's got the kid working."

You were an only child, weren't you?

Yeah. It had wonderful advantages, but it's real lonely. You try to create a family, make brothers out of friends.

What's your father like?

A very elegant man with a powerful voice: He looks like a retired

English army colonel, except he's not. My mother is the one who has show-business tendencies, but she never exerted them.

Your childhood sounds almost ridiculously uncomplicated.

Very—it's the contradiction of what people say about comedy and pain. My childhood was really nice. My parents never forced me to do anything; it was always, "If you want to do that, fine." When I told my father I was going to be an actor, he said, "Fine, but study welding just in case."

I think an only child has a greater imagination, because clearly you live inside your head more than a lot of kids.

Yeah, but I didn't really start doing comedy until college. I was a very quiet kid.

How old were you when you discovered girls?

Oh, God, it was great. College—that's when I first moved away from home. "Let's make love in a car! I've got to have a bed with a stick shift right here." I had one or two steady girlfriends in high school, but then in college, it was three, four . . . I went crazy. At one point I had three separate girlfriends, running around mad. That was the second year of college.

Do you remember your first physical relationship?

Oh, yeah. It was in college. She was just wonderful, because she was like a deer. It felt like . . . California love. I just remember this tan creature wandering through brown California.

So you like women?

They're wonderful—they're amazing creatures. You can never learn enough. They're addicting in the most amazing sense. They have so many levels. There's the physical level, which is a lot of fun. There's the emotional level, which is extremely mercurial. Every twenty-eight days you have that massive mood swing, where nature's going, "Check, please." It turns your body into an Etch A Sketch, and then you start over. Men may have wars, but women have their period. Men go off and kill each other, but women say nasty things, which is even better. Women are incredibly intuitive. If anybody on the planet is going to evolve to the next level, that telekinetic thing, women will.

Are you able to be around people without performing?

Sometimes. Occasionally people say, "Why can't you just be you?" But this is part of being me, too, the performing. Then there are times when life's just real quiet and simple. I sometimes get tired of people saying, "Well, what are you *really* like?"

You first tried stand-up comedy at a place called the Intersection, in San Francisco. Did people immediately say, "Robin, you're so funny"?

No, they just said I was good . . . interesting. The place where I started was a coffeehouse. They used to have radical lesbian-feminist poetry readings and then comedy after that, so we had an interesting audience to begin with. It was in the basement of a Presbyterian church. It was such a rush the first time I did it! The fun thing was being out there onstage in the total silence. The performance was yours. If you died, it was yours too.

In retrospect, now that you've been away from Mork and Mindy *for a while, what do you think of the show?*

I think it was incredible. It was outrageous. The first year was really fun and exciting, the second year was *aanhh,* the third year was really bad, and the fourth year was great because Jonathan [Winters] showed up. But you know what television is like—it just sucks up everything. The third year was rough, because that year the networks were all trying to bust each other's balls. That was the year that television was accused of being heavily into tits and ass. Then they started to play with the format and get greedy. They started busting up the basic lineup and the simplicity of the show. It was downhill from there.

Do you think you stayed at that party too long?

Mork and Mindy? I had no choice—I was under contract.

Who advises you?

I have managers—there are four of them—and then there's one agent, Sam, if you can get him. "He's on the coast." "Well, I'm on the coast." "Well, he's on the other coast. He's in between coasts. He's in the Midwest. It's like the coast. No, it's a lake." "He's on a lake? Where?" "No, he's up north. He's out." "Who's on—" "Sam's on first. No, you're on second."

Which one of your movies did everyone advise against that you went ahead and did anyway?

The Best of Times, the one about football. Everybody said it was predictable, and I said, "Yeah, but I still love it." And it is a sweet film. Some critics said it was wonderful and others said, "Oh, what horse-shit." Sometimes you make a decision just because you love something.

What do you think the perfect Robin Williams movie would be?

God. It's out there somewhere. It's got to be. Something with spirit, with a character who doesn't drive people crazy. Mork was like that— Mork had total freedom, and yet people still found him sweet enough that they could tolerate the madness. It's a fine line. There has to be a story that's simple enough and strong enough to keep people going.

When you look at somebody like Eddie Murphy, isn't there just the teensiest bit of jealousy?

No, I'm very happy. I'm only jealous of his sense of knowing so strongly what he wants to do. I'm pretty vulnerable to people saying, "Gee, that sounds great." Eddie knows exactly what he wants to do— he'll turn down project after project after project, waiting until he's sure. I also admire Bill [Murray] because he's basically a straight-ahead cat who knows exactly what's coming. He started slowly and just worked his way through.

A lot of actors aren't as generous as you are.

What's to envy? Things are nice for me. What am I going to say—"God, I need more money than this"? Bullshit.

Do you have a lot of money?

Things are nice. All I need is books and more computer games. I don't want any more land.

What do you think of Hollywood?

It's very strange. It's the type of place where people don't eat their young—they put them on hold. I have wonderful friends there— people whom I've known for a long time—but I've also known people who have done some really nasty things.

When did Hollywood start to fade for you?

When the invitations started to cool off, when some of the movies didn't do well, or were critically nice but didn't make any money. Things started to get a little quieter, which was fine by me. It took the pressure off.

You've been pretty candid about your excesses. When did you quit drinking?

I quit *everything.*

Everything? No drugs?

Everything. You have to. To begin with, a kid forces you to do that. Like I said, there's the imitation factor, and besides, you don't need drugs when you have a kid. You're awake and paranoid anyway. Who needs anything else?

Were you doing drugs before you went to L.A.?

Very seldom, because I didn't have the money. Once you get the coin—

They give it to you for free.

Yeah, samples. I heard a great quote: "You have a drug problem? No problem. Everybody's got it." Everyone will pump you up if you're ready, because it also gives them some control over you. You'll tolerate conversations with people you wouldn't even *talk* to in daylight.

Did your drug problem ever reach serious proportions?

Who knows? I pulled out.

Were you so addicted you couldn't do without it? I'm talking about cocaine.

No one will ever admit that. Who knows? I stopped all of that shit at once—they all walk hand in hand.

How long has it been?

Four years.

Was it hard?

No. First, coke went, then drinking, then everything.

Did you think that coke made you funnier?

No, I never performed on it. That'd be stupid. I did it once and it was a *bad* time. It's the same thing with athletes. They can't perform when they have cocaine problems. The drug is a nerve deadener; basically, it's a local anesthetic. It doesn't give you that one-second delay you need to be quick. I have lots of comedian friends who still think, "Hey, I'm faster, I'm funnier." No, you're just faster. You're not cooking; you just think you are.

A lot of people think Richard Pryor is not as funny without it.

Yeah, that's sad. They're putting the pressure on him, too. It's hard, because even *he* feels sometimes that he's—

Not as funny. . . . What do you think, in retrospect, is the impact that the whole Belushi affair had on your life? [Robin Williams had visited John Belushi at the Chateau Marmont before he died on the night of March 5, 1982.]

He was a powerful personality and a powerful physical being, too. When someone like him takes the cab, it wises your ass up really quick. He used to sometimes sign autographs, "Wise up." John was on the frontier; he was out there pushing it. When that happened, it was like, "Look at you, you little frail motherfucker. You're small change, Jack." That was the main thing. That's all I'll say. It's time now that people let it pass, think positively of his memory and stop digging him up. Everyone's gone on now—Judy [Belushi] has gone on, everyone's going on—but the press and people keep bringing it back.

Didn't anybody ever say to John, "This is going to kill you, kid"?

People did. He had people who were supposed to watch, but he found ways around them. That's also testimony to the power of his personality. He could say, "Hey, come on, it's me."

When Belushi died—that must have been the nadir of your time in L.A.

I think that was pretty much the bottom rung. You don't get much lower than that. It was time to leave this unhappy watering hole—time not to wander down this canyon any longer.

A lot of people outside the business were surprised to learn of your drug use—you had seemed so angelic.

I think there was a little bit of a demystification. I couldn't keep that illusion up, anyway. Now I feel so much simpler. All I've come back to is what I was seven or eight years ago—just enjoying performing. . . . People say I even look younger now.

You looked much older the last time I saw you, in Hollywood.

It was the drinking most of all—it bloats you up. But you can come back. Your body says, "Okay, I'll rebuild the cells if you give me time. I'll put your skin back, I'll work on you, I'll deflate you. When you lose the weight and if you start running again, I'll get rid of as many toxins as I can." You get a second chance.

Are you ever tempted to go back?

I have no desire to go anywhere near drugs. People say, "Aren't you tempted?" No, because of the ridiculousness of it. I used to say this onstage: "Cocaine, a drug that makes you paranoid and impotent—mmmm, boy. That's a lot of fun."

Will you ever be in the position to talk about John Belushi?

I don't know. Maybe someday. It was nothing that exciting even then. It's what they described in the books—I was there for ten minutes and split. There was no great, wild madness. Nothing there.

Did you sense Belushi was as far gone as he was that night?

No. He was basically saying, "I had a couple. I'm out of here. I'm tired." He didn't want me there, obviously, because he had other intentions.

With this girl. [Cathy Evelyn Smith pleaded guilty to involuntary manslaughter and served half of her three-year prison sentence before being paroled.]

Whatever. Someone sent me there. No one seems to know who this guy was who was working the Roxy who said, "Go over there. They're looking for you." I got over there, and no one wanted to see me. I have a feeling it was some strange setup, that they wanted to catch a whole bunch of people and it didn't come through. I don't know. That's another thing that no one's ever gotten into. It's a whole other bag.

Smith was allegedly an informant for the police, wasn't she?

I don't know. No one will ever know, I don't think, because no one will ever open that whole bag. If they do, they'll get into a whole other thing.

You mean that there was a whole undercover operation?

I don't know.

When you went home, were you awakened by the police knocking at your door?

No, not at all. I didn't know until the next day. I was on the set of *Mork and Mindy,* and someone said, "You know John's dead?"

Were you surprised when you heard that?

Just a touch. [*Laughs.*] John wasn't doing anything out of the ordinary. He looked drunk. I'd seen him drunk before; I'd seen him *out there;* there's a whole mystique about that night. It's been portrayed as some incredible, dark evening. I've talked about it very openly, and still, people keep going, "But what *happened* that night at the Chateau Marmont?" Nothing happened. Wanna give me a lie-detector test? They keep making it into something else, and it's not. I don't know what else they'll find out.

Do you think that whole thing hurt your career?

No. Oh, God. It couldn't have hurt it any more than it was at that point anyway.

What do you think is the biggest misconception about you?

That I'm hung like a bear. I don't know what people's conceptions are, other than that I'm funny sometimes, wild and crazy. Beyond that, I don't know what people know about me. What they don't know won't hurt me.

How do you think your mind works?

In spurts. It works in compressions and bursts, compressions and bursts. You relax back a little. You're working, you pull back a second, and then this flood of things will come.

You have a very quick mind.

Yeah, but sometimes I can be facile. That's not the same thing as being creative. Being facile is using what you've heard and just reshuffling things. But when you really break through to something, that's when you get that *"Ooooh."*

FRANCIS FORD COPPOLA

TODAY

April 1989

**"I feel I'm a fabulous manipulator of money,
because not only am I here at the age of fifty,
having given my family a wonderful life and provided
for all their needs in a very fine way,
I've also gotten to take a flyer on absolutely
every hunch and dream I ever had."**

Okay, okay, I got to Francis Ford Coppola on a slightly false pretense.

I claimed to know something about wine.

I don't. I love it and I drink it, but beyond that, it's all Gallo to me. Which gave me only momentary pause when I got the call in February from a favorite *Today* show producer, Bob Brienza, wine expert extraordinare.

"How'd you like to interview Francis Ford Coppola?"

"Great!" I said.

"About wine," he said.

"About which I know nothing," I said.

"You've eaten grapes, haven't you?"

Armed with that expertise, I took off for the Napa Valley, assured by Brienza that he'd be there to cover me on any spirited questions.

"Don't worry—I'll take care of everything," promised my own personal reincarnation of Hugh Johnson. But, alas, my wine critic got stranded at Cape Canaveral. He called me from a cellular phone.

"Are you on the plane?" I asked.

"No, I'm on the launch pad. The shuttle didn't go, so I can't, either. I'm stuck here until I see rocket fumes."

In the interest of education, I put down the phone and drank a bottle of wine.

The next morning, armed with research headache, I drove with my camera crew the two hours from San Francisco to the Napa Valley, where thirteen years ago Coppola got into the wine business, more or less by accident. Looking for a country house outside of San Francisco, the Coppolas decided on a turn-of-the-century Victorian showcase located on fourteen hundred acres of the Niebaum estate. The Niebaums were former proprietors of the Inglenook winery, which was famous for growing some of the best grapes in the world. With resources like these in his backyard, Coppola decided to add "winemaker" to a curriculum vitae that already included Oscar-winning director, writer, and producer.

In 1979 Niebaum-Coppola produced its first vintage, a full-bodied red table wine. Ten years later, Niebaum-Coppola had been paid the supreme tribute of being served in not one, but two world-class Parisian restaurants. The retail sales (including the sale of Coppola grapes to Inglenook) had turned the winery, Coppola claimed, into a million-dollar-a-year operation, which the moviemaker now wanted to promote on *Today*.

When we arrived, Coppola was nowhere in sight. Neither were any grapes. It was, it turned out, the wrong season. There were acres of vines—just nothing on them. We'd have to punt, not stomp, to tell this wine story. I took one crew to a large multifunctional barn, whose three floors housed a screening room, an extensive library, and, in the basement, massive barrels of fermenting grapes, shelves of wine bottles, and a ruddy-looking wine master straight out of *Falcon Crest*. I told the crew to shoot everything.

The other men I directed to the main house, a spectacular white Victorian number with wraparound porches, cut-glass windows, and mahogany molding. We were greeted by Francis's assistant and a saucy, self-possessed toddler named Gia, the daughter of Giancarlo Coppola, Francis's twenty-two-year-old son, who died in a 1986 accident in a boat driven by Griffin O'Neal, Ryan O'Neal's son. (A portrait of Giancarlo hung prominently over the fireplace in the living room.)

The nerve center of the house was the kitchen, a sunny white room. A Coppola nephew and friend sat at a rectangular side table discussing film and drinking cappuccino. In the hallway between the kitchen and dining room stood a massive rack of gleaming copper pots and pans, obviously well used by Coppola, who is passionate about not only eating food, but cooking it.

Eventually a slim, unassuming blond woman in her late forties walked into the room and introduced herself as Eleanor Coppola, Francis's wife of twenty-five years. This stay-in-the-background demeanor was deceiving, I soon discovered. She was the linchpin. Francis Ford Coppola might dream up the show, but Eleanor ran it. As diametrically opposed as this couple appeared—she blond, he dark, he plump, she thin, he locquacious, she demure—this was obviously a marriage with legs, having survived a child's death, bankruptcies, and the making of *Apocalypse Now,* Coppola's controversial Vietnam movie, the tempestuous filming of which precipitated star Martin Sheen's heart attack and prompted Eleanor's publishing debut. In a book called *Notes,* she recorded in diary form her own apocalyptic saga of both movie and marriage, openly discussing her husband's infidelities.

Around two o'clock a station wagon pulled into the driveway and Coppola lumbered in the back door. His dark hair and beard were generously streaked with gray. Though he'd always been a big man, Coppola's girth had increased considerably, straining the seams of his sports jacket and khakis.

Since it was past lunchtime, Coppola speculated on whether he should cook and then do the interview. Talk first, eat later, I suggested, hustling him toward a chair. As the crew adjusted lighting and mikes, Coppola scrutinized himself in one of the TV monitors: "I look like the dictator of a small Third World country."

We started talking. Somehow we filled two twenty-minute cassettes with wine talk. (Did I really just ask him what year the first "brew" was sold?) Coppola, as expansive in conversation as in life, segued, with little urging, into his childhood, movies, money, and, ultimately, the death of his son. Two hours later we finished.

By now everyone was famished. Coppola doffed his jacket and headed for the copper pans. While Eleanor put together an antipasto and uncorked both a 1979 and a 1981 Niebaum-Coppola, Francis diced broccoli and threw pasta into a pot as the cameras rolled. Obligingly, the director hammed it up, pouring a glass of wine, holding it up to the light, sniffing the bouquet, tasting. Announcing he was preparing a pasta primavera from the northern part of Italy, he moved effortlessly, and within minutes spaghetti was being ladled into a gigantic china bowl.

Suddenly, three giggling teenage girls scurried through the door. Sophia Coppola, Francis's seventeen-year-old daughter (who would replace Winona Ryder in *The Godfather Part III*), stopped to talk to her father. A pretty brunette with translucent skin, Sophia plainly had her father wrapped around her little finger. Mentioning a story she had read, she eyed him flirtatiously.

"Can we make it into a movie next summer?"

"Sure," replied Coppola.

Since we were losing light, I hurried everyone outside. It was time for me to direct Francis Ford Coppola. With a scene from *The Godfather* in mind—Marlon Brando cavorting with his grandchild in the orchard—I instructed the director to meander through the vineyards with his granddaughter, Gia. As this giant of a man ambled through the naked bushes, gently holding the hand of the tiny creature who barely reached his knee, I hummed the *Godfather* theme under my breath. When the two finally walked out of camera range, I clapped and whistled.

"Terrific, Francis, terrific. But could we do that take again? And this time, just try and relax."

———

You once said that kindergarten was the happiest time of your life. Why?

Because life was just a great adventure every day. You got to go with the other boys and girls and just play and learn things. Everyone was nice to you, open with you; if you did something that was a novel idea, everyone was happy that you had that idea because then they could play, too. It seemed like an enchanted time. There wasn't a bad thing about it.

It was only later in life I began to be aware that people were building up protection for themselves, that they didn't live their lives with the attitude of "This is fun. Let's try to do and create and experience as much as we can." They seemed to be conservative about their energies, their feelings, and certainly their money. I never could understand why because it was clear you're not going to be able to keep it.

Your father, of course, is Carmine Coppola, who not only wrote and scored several of your movies, but won his own Oscar for The Godfather Part II. *Could you describe your relationship with your father for me?*

In an Italian-American family the father is, on one level, the top boss. My mother . . . was a homemaker, so in that sense it was a very traditional family. My father was very preoccupied with his career all his life. The kids always followed what was going on with it; we very much invested our feelings in hoping that Daddy "got his break." We would always say prayers for him getting his break—even when I thought the "break" was the one in the car. [*Laughs.*] We just felt he was talented and wasn't getting an opportunity.

At that time he was composing music, wasn't he?

Yeah, he was the solo flutist for the NBC Symphony under Toscanini; he was a very fine flute player. He always felt that that virtuoso instrument held him back, because if you're a violinist in an orchestra and you want the chance to compose or conduct, it's okay because you're just one of eighteen violins. But a flute player is a very exposed instrumentalist. There's only a couple of them. It's very hard to find one who's a soloist. The idea I got as a kid was that he wanted to go on to do other things in composition.

Your childhood sounds very warm and loving.

It was a very happy time for me. . . . My aunts and uncles always came over and I could see my father was happy to be with his brothers, and they'd tell stories, get loaded on wine, talk about operas, sit at the piano, and sing and say how great Puccini was.

And the women would be making all this great food. It just seemed to me that a family, with all the cousins and stuff—that was the happiest time of life. But I think families are really powerful medicine for all people. Every person probably has real strings to their family that they can't break.

You've done several movies about the relationship between brothers. Your own older brother, August, was a great role model for you, wasn't he? [August Coppola is dean of the School of Creative Arts at San Francisco State.]

Yeah. He was five years older. He was very handsome, very bright, interested in interesting things like novels and writing. He was very popular with his friends, always had girlfriends. I was more of a loner, so I clearly wanted to be more like him. The fact that, even at a young age, I got interested in writing and reading was just to imitate him.

Did you think you were talented as a child?

No, I didn't. I was in a family in which talent was the most precious commodity around. I was sometimes sad because I didn't feel I had a gift of any kind. They always took kids in our family and stuck them with an instrument. And in my case, they always said, "Oh, he doesn't get it." Or "He's not good at it."

I came from an extremely good-looking, talented family and I always felt homely, that I didn't have gifts like they had in music or writing. I wanted very much to have something, because talent was always held up as *the* big thing in our family. It was, you know, "Does he have talent?" So, if I had talent, I didn't know what it was, because it was nothing that, at the time, was valued by the family.

But you could sing, couldn't you?

I could sing. And that was one of the little edges I had with my father. When important guests would come and he wanted to play a song, he'd say, "Francie, come on, Francie. Let's sing the 'Subway Serenade.'" And I'd do it and then I'd get extra dessert. And for a while, I'd be "in." But the next day when they looked at my marks, I was out right away.

As a child you had polio, didn't you?

For a year I was essentially bedridden.

That must've been very isolating, because at the time there was no vaccine.

It was the most feared children's disease of the time. It was 1949; there was a big epidemic. I myself wasn't so worried about it. I remember more the effect on everyone else . . . seeing my father, who's a pretty vain kind of guy in his world, to see him crying . . . you know, see everyone around me crying. Polio is something that hits you for one night. But the damage done in that one night is what paralyzes people because it attacks the nerves.

So you were paralyzed?

Yes. The morning after [it hit] I woke up in the hospital and there were kids crammed everywhere, three high, in bathrooms, hallways . . . it was a big epidemic. I looked around, thought I'd get up, and ended up right on the floor. I couldn't stand up. I couldn't move my arms or anything. But my attitude at that time was like, "Oh, isn't this interesting?" It was seeing my family's reaction that really made an impact. After a couple of weeks in a hospital, they brought me home, where I was just stuck in a room. I had a television, a little toy movie projector, a tape recorder, and some puppets. But I never saw another kid . . . they just didn't want any kid to come near me. So for a year and a half I would just entertain myself in this bedroom. I played with my puppets and with trying to synchronize the sixteen-millimeter projector to the tape recorder—which I never achieved.

Were you just one day no longer paralyzed?

In those days people didn't know [about] or agree on treatment. One doctor told me I'd never walk again and that I should stay immobile in the bed. They literally pinned me in the bed with safety pins. But I hated the safety pins so I'd get out of my pajamas and crawl around the floor to adjust the television. Maybe it was the fact that I kept trying to be somewhat mobile that kept those links alive. It was only later, through the good graces of the March of Dimes, using the Kenney method, that they sent a therapist. And then one day I called my brother in and I said, "Look," and I went like that with my arm.

And everyone said, "Oh, look, he's improved." And then I just got better and [eventually] returned to school.

You must've felt very different from your peer group.

I wanted so badly to be accepted by the kids. We moved around a lot and I didn't tend to have a lot of friends. The school welcomed me back. My dream was to be a guard, like a monitor, with a yellow button. That was real status. So they made me a guard and I stood in the hallway for about three days. And then my teacher said, "Oh, they only gave you that because you were sick," and she took it away. But that's the way life is. One day they say how great you are and then the next, they take away your button and say you're not anymore.

Actually, that was good preparation for Hollywood. When did you finally realize you had some talent?

During the shooting of *Apocalypse Now.* It came to me that the things I was trying to be good at, struggled with, were not the only things, that there were things that I did very quickly and easily. And, in fact, that's where I was talented. It's like many of us. We want to see our talent in a certain area and then we learn, "My God, it's not here. It's over there." Understanding that one has talent is very often giving up some ideas of what talent is and accepting where you get it.

And what did you think your talent was?

My talent was in kind of almost instant conceptualizing, getting an idea, getting lots of ideas, and saying, "Hey, you sit over here and you wear blue . . ."—but not thinking that that's anything because everybody does that in their lives. But the order of doing that, the decisions I made, the ideas I had—that was my gift.

In many ways making Apocalypse Now *was a very painful experience for you, wasn't it? What was it about that movie that made you so self-aware?*

It just happened to be a particular conversation with a particular person. I remember it dawning on me, like, "I get it. You're not necessarily talented in the things you wish to be talented. But you are talented in *something.*"

When you were younger, you attended Hofstra University, where you got involved in theater, writing, performing, directing . . . it must have occurred to you then that you had some special gift.

I always had great gifts in inspiring other people to play—[being] a ringleader, [saying], "Well, why not? We can do it." I was always good at that. I did a lot of directing in college and that's where I really learned it was something I could do.

But I wanted to be a writer. And I always felt my writing was dumb. It never came out the way I felt about it. So directing for me was almost the next best thing. I could be with people and get some degree of approval. I knew I had a lot of organizational talent. But the talent I really wanted was creative writing . . . to create, to write, to make things that'd be beautiful.

You didn't think directing fulfilled that?

Well, yeah. But even my directing is usually greeted with controversy and misgivings. No one ever looked at one of my films and said, "Boy, this is beautiful."

They certainly did with The Godfather *and* The Godfather Part II.

Yeah, but if you look back you realize that all those pictures grew in stature with time. Even *The Godfather,* even the second *Godfather.* The first *Godfather* was a fabulous hit, but it was adapted from a fabulous hit of a novel. What made *The Godfather* really popular, I think, was Mario Puzo. The book was an enormous success. What I did was bring my experiences of being Italian-American, my attitudes toward families, and enhance it, do some good casting, for instance. Usually, my films go through some years before they find themselves in the audiences. But there's reasons for that.

Which are?

The film business is such a powerful industry that it's to the company's advantage to make films that are exactly what the audience wants because that's how they're successful. But if you always gave people, say, the kind of food they [wanted], then they'd never have tried Japanese food or they'd never have tried all those things that people say, "Oh, yuck" about, and then after they've tried it, say, "Gee, I didn't think I could eat lamb's brains."

Given the rash of Vietnam films made in the eighties, how does Apocalypse Now *look to you in retrospect?*

Apocalypse wasn't ever meant to be a war movie. It was always a curious look at morality, using the great masterpiece *Heart of Darkness* as though it's *Hamlet* set in cowboy clothes. I very much admired Joseph Conrad's work and thought there were some relevances to Vietnam. So I just went on that adventure. I think *Apocalypse* is . . . *something.* It's there, it gives you something when you see it, it's going to be something that you'll want to maybe look at years from now. With art, you're really just looking for life. You just want to have something that has a little life in it.

The first movie you ever made, in 1963, was called Dementia 13, *a low-budget movie made for Roger Corman, the king of Hollywood B movies. You've said that this was the only film you enjoyed working on.*

I may have said that because I was twenty-one and it was exciting to be in Ireland, which is a wonderful place, with my friends. But I've enjoyed my other movies, not necessarily the ones that were successful. So much of whether you enjoy working on a film has to do with who's putting the screws to you. Because a director is in a very tough position. It's no different than making wine. When you make wine, you get up one day and see the sun has gone out of whack and you have to rush and be ingenious and figure out what to do. Well, in a film there's always like big, big, big, big problems every day. And if someone's being real mean to you, then you tend not to be very happy. Or if you're in a place you don't enjoy. So many other things determine whether you enjoy a movie, not just whether it's going well or not.

What movie did you enjoy making the least?

The Cotton Club was tough because I was brought in by Bob Evans to help out. He was going to be the director. I didn't even want to do it. But he just begged me to take over because it was going to crumble. And then the second I took it over, he started attacking me. When he realized he couldn't attack me by coming to the set, he just went to the press, and it became a big deal. Every day we were trying to make the thing and there were these big articles.

You've said that, on balance, Hollywood has been very good to you.

I think it's because they like someone who tries doing things. They have the studio system. They really consider themselves picture makers. They're not intellectual about it; they're not trying to compare this or that to some great Polish director. They really are picture makers. You know, there is something called show business. And whether it's movies or Broadway shows or the circus or, even in a way, opera, show people do have certain characteristics that are, in my opinion, very, very beautiful. A certain kind of loyalty and family.

Back to The Godfather *for a minute. When that movie opened you became, overnight, a mega–star director. How was that period for you?*

To have great success is as traumatic as to have sudden failure. It's a big change; it puts you in many situations where you've no precedent to know how to behave. Consequently, everyone who's become wealthy or famous overnight has probably repeated the same dumb mistakes. I always wanted to be successful as a writer, so I was shy about claiming so much credit for *The Godfather*. Certainly, I made the movie. But I didn't write the story.

You wrote the script.

I wrote the script. But to write a script based on a good novel is like having great grapes on your property. . . . All you do is care for them and try to let them tell you how to make the wine. In the case of a movie, it's the same thing. You let the book tell you how to make the movie. But some part of me always wanted to have a great success with something I'd written, that was mine from the beginning to the end. I've had that in a modest way, but that's more and more on my mind as I get older, to try to spend more time trying to write the stuff before you make it.

As a professional director, I feel I'm a pretty good director. If you gave me some fabulous book or story that the public was disposed to be interested in, I can go out, cast it well, and do a good job on it. I feel confident about that. Usually, however, I don't choose the kind of thing that the public's necessarily interested in.

When I saw Peggy Sue Got Married *and realized you directed it, I must admit I was surprised. It wasn't the kind of movie I associated with Francis Ford Coppola.*

Peggy Sue wasn't my kind of piece. I thought it was the typical fare they give the public, same story, same situations over and over. But there was something about *Peggy Sue* that reminded me of Thornton Wilder's play *Our Town*. And I said, "What was it about *Our Town* that made you cry?"—when Emily went back and saw her family. I thought, "Maybe I can make *Peggy Sue* in that style." But you give me a job and I'll do my best. I'll try to find some reason to fall in love with it.

I like all my movies because I know I always tried some experiment, always tried to get some lesson out of each picture that I could use in a new phase of my life when I wasn't so much a working guy and had served my apprenticeship. That's why they're so different, one from the other.

In 1983—the early eighties—you had another metamorphosis. You opened your own movie studio, the Zoetrope. But it eventually went bankrupt and you were millions of dollars in debt. Were you afraid?

I knew that I didn't have the money to really carry off the dream I had. I was just hoping that if I started it, maybe someone would look and say, "That's a good thing" and help me or be a partner, or that we'd get lucky and something we did would be successful. I was pretty sure we were going to lose all the money from *Apocalypse,* because that was our own dough. *Apocalypse* was thirty-two million dollars of my money. And I said, "Well, it's going to take five or six months before they get the news we lost it. So maybe in that time I'll do something else that will be successful." But the irony was *Apocalypse* was very successful and we made a great deal of money. The joke was that the studio wasn't, and we lost it.

I was more like a kid wanting to have the studio, rather than having really worked out the practical considerations, that if you open a business you ought to have enough money on hand to run it for at least three years to give it a fair start.

But then I thought, "Well, if I wait until I have enough resources to do it, I'll never do it." And more than anything, I wanted to have my own little film company. I've always wanted that. One way or another I'll always have something like that, because that's where I really get my pleasure.

That's your kindergarten.

Yeah. That's it. And all the activities that we do, whether it's making films or writing or doing creative projects or making wine, are really all the same thing to me. It's all something that brings people together and they have a good time.

Money. You and money seem to have a very complicated relationship. You either have none or you have a bunch. You either seem to be handling it well—or, as perceived by some people, are blowing it hand over fist. Do you feel comfortable with money?

I feel very comfortable with money. I think that may be what separates me from other people; I have no regard for money. I don't value money other than what you can do with it. The idea of having a lot of it means nothing to me. The idea of building things, instigating projects, making ideas come true, is very valuable to me.

I feel I'm a fabulous manipulator of money, because not only am I here at the age of fifty, having given my family a wonderful life and provided for all their needs in a very fine way, I've also gotten to take a flyer on absolutely every hunch and dream I ever had.

You realize that a lot of people in the movie business wouldn't agree that you handle money well, that you have the correct attitude toward it.

There's been so many misconceptions about me. I made over twenty movies. Only a couple of them were big, overbudget films. With the exception of *The Cotton Club*, where I was one part of a big, big picture, the movies I made that went over budget were my own films and my own money. I made the decision to go all the way with them because I was interested in the projects more than my bank account.

So I never was irresponsible with other people's money. It was only *Apocalypse Now* and *One from the Heart* that were considered these big-budget films. But, once again, those films marked a new era. If you were the first in your neighborhood to buy a thirty-thousand-dollar Mercedes, when two years before they cost eight thousand, everyone said, "God, he bought a thirty-thousand-dollar car." But then the next year they're all buying thirty-thousand-dollar cars. Well, after *Apocalypse,* all movies cost that much. So we were just a little ahead of our time. But the important thing is that *Apocalypse Now* was my money. We made hundreds of millions of dollars on that picture.

Not right away.

No, it took a year. But *Apocalypse* is one of the biggest-grossing pictures in history. But *Tucker: The Man and His Dream* was made for budget, *Peggy Sue* was made for budget, *The Outsiders* and *Rumble Fish* were made for budget. *Godfather* was made for six million dollars. The great majority of my films, the money has been managed very well.

It's been reported that during the filming of Apocalypse Now *you had a nervous breakdown. Is that true?*

I don't think it was a nervous breakdown. When you make a film in which you're out in the jungle for a year . . . and all the pressures that means on yourself and your family . . . and your actor [Martin Sheen] gets a heart attack and you're financing the film yourself and the people at home are making fun of you as though you're some kind of crazy person who's just lavishly spending money on some silliness when, in fact, you're working on a project that had some value and you're being courageous . . . well, you hoped the people at home would say, "Good—we have people like that."

Anybody would get pretty down for a while. I got pretty depressed because I thought I was trying with all the energy I had. But the perception of what I was doing wasn't what I thought was really happening. I was incapacitated all of a day. And I was back working the next day. So I was just pretty sad, is all.

You and your wife, Eleanor, have been married for twenty-five years. I'm sure this hasn't been a boring marriage. How would you describe your wife?

She's a bit different than me. I'm very much what you'd call an Italian personality; I'm always in a state of enthusiasm. I want to do wild things, like, "Let's make wine. Let's have a wine business." My wife is more, "Well, really should we do this? Can we do this?" I'm a little more impetuous.

Family—your family—the idea of family, is really the beginning and end for you, isn't it?

Well, I think everybody's like that. We all love our mothers and fathers. It's hard for me to imagine someone not having some kind of bond with your parents, your brothers, sisters.

When I think of people who get divorced, I think, How could I ever go up to my brother and say, "Well, Augie, I don't want to be your brother anymore. Here, this is Joe. My new brother." I mean, that's what you do when you get divorced. Although I could see there are people who are tough to live with.

Are you tough to live with?

I don't think so. I think I'm a lot of fun to live with. Because my sad moments I try to do alone. Even my temper, which is spectacular, has not happened very often. There probably aren't many people who've really seen it. The ones who saw it were enough. [*Laughs.*] I haven't lost my temper on a movie for ten years.

You say you have lots of good ideas. Do you have good follow-through?

I have great follow-through. I always finish everything I start.

What has been the most painful time in your life?

Well, obviously, the loss of my son. My son was extremely caught up in the world of cinema, entertainment. He'd chosen that as a profession. And he left school at a very young age to be my apprentice. So he was like an apprentice, a companion, a co-conspirator. A lot of my family always says, "Francis wants to do what? Make wine? What's he going to do *now*?" But my son said, "Oh, what'll we do? What will the bottle look like? What will the label look like?" I really valued that collaboration with him.

I was happy to have a baby when I was in my early twenties, because I figured, "When I'm forty, I'm going to have a twenty-year-old son who's going to help me, work with me, and we'll do things together." And that was the way it was.

I was very satisfied with my children. I got the children I wanted. So, obviously, to lose him was *the* event of my life. I have to mark everything as "before" and "after" that.

How do you cope with losing a child? It's got to be the hardest thing in the world.

There are no words I could really get into with you that could express . . . the only thing I'll say is that he died at twenty-two years old. And even though he was only twenty-two he had an extremely great life with parents and a brother and sister who were crazy about him. And we did great things. He got to fall in love, he got to direct, he had a little banana [girl] who runs around here. He got to do so many things that I have to say he had a very happy, complete life. It just was shorter than other people's.

My wife and I were in Greece before the accident happened. We saw a statue of old parents with their son. Obviously, the son had been killed in the wars and was coming back to say good-bye to them in that statue. And I was very struck by that. This is certainly something we share with parents from the beginning of time. This is what makes a human being. I'd rather be a human being than be a rock and feel nothing. The fact that we are human beings and have this extraordinary love and emotion is a privilege.

Giancarlo was killed in a boating accident. The boat was driven by Griffin O'Neal [who was subsequently found guilty of "reckless boating"]. Do you feel any bitterness toward Griffin?

None whatsoever. There were two boys and now there's one. I wouldn't want that boy to suffer. Although I know it was his recklessness, I know it wasn't the kind of accident that would happen to someone who was a little more prudent and a little more responsible. Griffin is a kind of wild, irresponsible kid. But he did not want to hurt my son.

Just the day before the accident, when I was talking to my boy about Griffin, because Griffin had been in a lot of trouble, he said, "Look, Dad, Griffin's a good guy. Griffin's all right." And that's what I say. I have only a kind of feeling of love for Griffin because he was my kid's friend.

My kid was kind of a loner—with children, people his own age—because he was so identified with adults. And I was happy that there was a friend, a friendship. But, of course, he picked another loner. And that wasn't a good mixture. But Gio wouldn't want us to penalize Griffin for what happened. I take my cue from his feelings.

You've said you no longer look upon yourself as a director. What is your job status these days, anyway?

Well, I'm a wine grower. I really look at the time up until now as a kind of apprenticeship. I've done many, many things. I was smart enough in my life to make everything I did also be an experiment. So I have the results of these experiments in my head, things I did on movies. People said, "Why did he do that?" Well, they'll find out someday. Because I intend in this latter part of my life to do things with the results of those experiments. If then I was a professional, now I'm an amateur. But the word *amateur* comes from someone who loves what they're doing and does it for love.

What kind of things might you do for love?

Well, I'd do anything for love. But I would write.

Books? Screenplays?

I'm in love with the cinema. I'd like to try to write a little more in the tradition of the great novelists, say, in the beginning of the twentieth century, who were really experimenting with narrative, time, tense, and internal consciousness—the interesting things that could be brought to storytelling. But maybe try and do that for the cinema. I feel cinema is probably the most free thing there is in the world.

In 1989 you turned fifty years old. How do you feel about that?

I think a fifty-year-old man is in the prime of his life, the time when he might think about tackling the toughest enterprises or projects. And I like that.

At fifty, do you think you finally have enough talent to satisfy your family?

[*Laughs.*] You know, it's funny. You go your whole life, they'll never say once, "You know, I'm proud of you." You hear it through other people—"Oh, your dad's proud of you." But he always tells me, "Oh, that film. I couldn't understand that film you made." Or worse, my father won't even *go* to movies that he didn't write the music for, that I made.

So your dad's never said, "Francis, I'm proud of you"?

You'll never get what you want from your parents. You have to just imagine it.

ROLLING STONE

August 1984

**"I had one quality of someone
that everyone knew in the seventies."**

▄▄▄

Here it is, right up front: Corny, sentimental, whatever you want to call it, but I love John Travolta. To me this guy is one of the world's great human beings.

Here's why.

In January 1985, my mother, diagnosed with pancreatic cancer, checked into the National Institutes of Health in Bethesda, Maryland, to undergo a strenuous ten-hour operation. In order to divert Mama's focus from the two days of painful preparation, my brother and I tried to fill the hours with as much life, glamour, pizzazz—everything Mama loved in healthier times—as we could manufacture.

Flowers, cards, letters, and phone calls from old friends, new friends, and our friends came rushing in. My brother, Pat, then the Undersecretary of Energy and hip-deep in Republican politics, called on senators, congressmen, and politicos to phone and say hello. President Reagan sent, not surprisingly, a preprinted card reading "Nancy and I hope you're feeling better." Vice President George Bush, on the other hand, personally wrote a touching note so full of praise for my brother that it almost cured Mama on the spot.

While Pat covered politics, I took media and show biz. Gloria Steinem, Helen Gurley Brown, Liz Smith, Joan Rivers, Nancy Friday, all friends, weighed in with their own calls. In between the syringes and thermometers, Mama took it all in stride—much more so than the nurses, who, by the end of Day Two, were overwhelmed by the hoo-ha going on in the Collins room.

Still, I wanted to surprise Mama and deliver a real live movie star. But if I had one ironclad rule it was: Never ask a celebrity for a favor.

That, however, was under normal circumstances. And there was nothing typical about this. Screw the rules. But who? Then I remembered. John Travolta's mother had died from cancer, as had his girlfriend Diana Hyland. He knew the drill. I'd interviewed him twice, for *Rolling Stone* and *Today*. We'd gotten along well. He was a sweet man. Perhaps . . .

I got on the phone to Los Angeles and his press agent, Gary Calkins. My determination on Mama's behalf overcame the awkwardness I felt about my mission. "Listen, Gary, this is an enormous favor and John may want nothing to do with it, but . . ."

Gary didn't hesitate. He wasn't sure where Travolta was, but if he could find him, he would relay my request. I thanked him and left Mama's phone number.

By 9 P.M., Mama, sapped but oddly game, had finally finished readying herself for the following morning. The phones were silent, the hubbub quieted, as I sat in the waiting room. Suddenly, a wild-eyed young nurse came hurrying toward me. "Nancy, is it possible that John Travolta is calling your mother?"

"It certainly is. Please transfer the call."

By the time I got to Mama's room, she was deep in conversation with the star. "Now, John, I just know your career is going to soar again," she counseled. "All the girls in the bridge club loved the last movie. And remember, honey, you're so young. You've got plenty of time."

And his time was what Travolta graciously gave. Fifteen minutes later she handed the phone over to me.

"Was that all right?" he asked.

"Wonderful, John. I can't thank you enough."

"Well, I've been there. I know what it's like."

Unfortunately, we both did.

—

How do you behave with the women in your life?

I find myself covering my bases. To be really honest, I'd have to say I'm afraid of committing to one person, so I have maybe three or four people on the line. But it's very uncomfortable to me now.

Is having a relationship as important to you as your work?

Probably not, because love always seems like an alternative. With a career, you're depending on your own ability—not someone else's—to get you through. Love takes two; your career takes one. And with love, there's always another fish in the sea.

What attracts you to a woman? Do you have a physical type?

Your traditional well-built woman, meaning large breasts, small waist, good hips, good butt, good legs. That's my sexual ideal.

What other qualities do you like?

I have such a high opinion of women that my expectancy level is also high. I expect them to be intelligent and very career-oriented. If they want a family, fine, but that doesn't mean giving up goals. Bottom line, a woman's gotta be stimulating, which would then provoke a continuous sexual appeal. I have less tolerance with women than I do with men. I can tolerate a man's not being bright or ambitious, but not a woman's.

Where did that come from?

It began with my mother and sisters. I grew up around women who were colorful, exciting, inspiring. I have an innate understanding of what women do. I allow them much more grace than most men would.

You mentioned that you're currently seeing several women. Do they all know about one another?

Pretty much. But I feel I have to come clean about my situation because it can come apart at any minute, and I don't like that feeling. I like everyone I'm involved with, and I never want to lose those friendships. Romance has a tendency to confuse friendships, and I don't want that.

With all this multiple dating, don't you think you've broken some hearts along the way?

Yes, but never to a big degree, because I'm much too honest with a person I'm involved with. There's a minimum of heartbreaking I can do, because from the start I say, "Hey, look, this is the situation."

Surely the tables must occasionally turn and you get nailed?

Sure, but as I said, I was very much loved by my family. And when you're very much loved, it takes a lot to convince you that you will not be loved. Because even if you don't love me, I would never equate it to mean that everyone doesn't love me.

Sounds as if, theoretically, you'd like to commit to one person.

That's what I want. But to be honest, I am always more open, loving, complimentary, and adoring to the person who comes with built-in barriers—someone I know there's no future with. When I know there's an absolute future, I get more restrictive. I don't let that person know how much I care, because it could develop into something more serious and permanent, and I'm scared of that.

You didn't seem afraid with Diana Hyland, who was eighteen years older than you. You lived with her before she died of cancer in 1977.

That's true, although her being eighteen years older was certainly a built-in barrier. I was incredibly mad for this woman, and the age thing, because it was awkward in society's eyes, only made the relationship more titillating to me.

You said, at the time, you would've married her.

I felt that and openly admitted it—after the fact. But it's a complicated statement. Who knew what that would've led to, especially with her sister being older and ill. In my heart, I felt I wanted to marry her, but again, there were those barriers.

What attracted you to her?

On the first meeting, I was just incredibly attracted to this woman. I saw the whole picture in her first ten words—depth, intelligence, beauty, perceptiveness. She had gone through a rough marriage, a lot of career ups and downs, and had come out at peace with herself. It was very sexy. The most important things were the relationships in her life. She really savored the people around her. At the time, I was open, just fooling around with a couple of little affairs. I had almost decided to quit looking for anyone special, and then she came along and was so dynamic, I knew I had to spend time with her. She broke my heart from the start, but it took a month before I decided to be with her.

What made you decide to be with her?

When she said it didn't matter whether or not we were together romantically—that she could have me either way, sexually or just as a friend. That was the deciding point, when I realized she appreciated me as a person rather than just as a young stud. Then I said, "All right. I can do this." At that time in my life, I was in the middle of complete hysteria, so she was quite an influence. The relationship gave me a calming quality I haven't plugged into since. Since then, I haven't run into anyone who had that.

So it's been six years since you've fallen that much in love with a woman?

On that level, yeah. But I've begun to realize there are different— maybe even more practical—ways one can love. Diana and I were together only seven months. It ended on a peak, and because of that, my feelings were heightened. I'm not necessarily looking for that again.

Have you actually lived with a woman since then?

Not particularly. In my life-style—and I think it's the same with other people in my profession—you travel and work so much that you never really end up living with anyone. People live with you where you are at the moment. It's truly gypsy-style.

What's your definition of love?

I don't mean to sound whimsical or neurotic, but I've discovered that because my life is malleable and gypsylike, I have the ability to feel like I'm in love with a few people at the same time. It's not as if I'm a farmer. If I were, I'd have no problem being with one person, committing to that life-style. But I'm in a business where I find it very hard, at this point, to be monogamous. So, yes, I could say I'm in love with [actress] Marilu Henner, even though that doesn't mean I'm not in love with other people on some level, too. The one thing Marilu and I have in common is that we know each other so well that she could even hear this conversation and it would be okay.

Quite frankly, this I-can-love-everybody business sounds like an excuse for playing around.

Like I said, I've wanted to come clean about my situation for a long time. The only voice bothering me is the one that says, "You're going to lose everybody." If I have a sexual attraction for someone, I can keep it for years. Whatever it was about them that got me turned on usually continues to keep me turned on. I'm very committed to my sexual desires.

Do you want to get married someday?

I don't know. Every day it's different. I think I'd like to get married, but mainly to have children. If I weren't having children, then I don't know how compelled I'd feel to get a piece of paper.

Could you stick with one woman?

By nature, I don't think man is monogamous, even though by agreement he tries to be. By nature, I am not monogamous, but by agreement—and ideal—I am.

Do you think of yourself as having a strong sex drive?

Yes. But it needs to be unleashed by someone who likes it. Otherwise, I tend to inhibit it. I like being with women who have the same sexual appetite. I get frustrated if they don't, because it's very difficult for me to be with someone I have to coach. You know, "Okay, honey, I'm the sex master here, and I'll get you through the paces, and together we will solve your psychological blocks." I can't do that. So I'm usually attracted to women who have big sexual appetites and fewer sexual hang-ups.

Besides Marilu Henner, most people would be hard-pressed to name any of the women you've dated.

Many of them are famous, but I just don't go places where we're photographed. Besides, I don't stay in one place very long. I am never home more than two weeks in a row. A lot of the reason you don't hear about what I do is that I'm on the road doing it.

How about Jane Fonda? You once said you had sexual fantasies about her.

I had a recurring dream about her, which I won't describe. Jane's a woman I feel has a reserve sexuality she tries to temper. I think she's probably a wild woman in bed.

You know, of course, that your own appeal is androgynous. Why do you think your sexuality appeals to men as well as women?

I really don't know. My characters have always been very masculine. If I am androgynous, I'd say I lean toward the macho androgynous.

You also know one of Hollywood's favorite games is to claim that all leading men are secretly gay.

Oh, yeah. That's a notorious rumor.

Then you know that people say that about you—that you're gay?

They say that about me, Marlon Brando, every male, especially the first year you become a star. It wears off after a while, but I've heard it said of just about everybody.

Did it bother you the first time you heard it about you?

Not really, because the rumors about me were so extraordinary. The gay rumor about male stars is such a classic that it didn't surprise me to hear it about me, because I'd heard it about the others. All I thought was, "Oh, I see the game now."

So, would you like to set the record straight right here?

Sure, if you'd like.

Are you gay?

No.

You once mentioned that your personal style has been highly influenced by blacks. What did you mean by that?

All the qualities that make me uniquely appealing to the masses are the black qualities I have as a person—my sense of humor, my dancing, my openness, sexually, with my movements.

Where did you pick up those sensibilities?

It started in the fifth grade, when I transferred from a Catholic school to a public school that was predominantly black. Right away, I loved the black people, and they loved me because I could dance and was funny to them. The white kids never laughed at me, only the black kids. So it was the first time I was accepted by the masses. Like the blacks, I simply called things as they were.

How did they influence your sexuality?

As I said earlier, I was always attracted to women with an open sexuality, and it was the same with blacks. I sensed their strong sexuality, and it made me feel comfortable. They'd always say, "Hey, Travolta, get your fine ass over here. You wanna fuck me?" It was always real open. And when you danced with a black girl, you could grind and get down without necessarily meaning you were going to have sex with her. It simply meant you could move seductively and enjoy it. So I felt very safe with them expressing myself verbally and physically. In fact, the first girl I ever kissed was a black girl.

How old were you?

Twelve, and she was sixteen. She introduced me to reefer. She said, "Did you ever soul-kiss?" And I said, "No, I don't think so." And she said, "Well, come on over here and let me try it with you." So we kissed. I loved her because she was so complimentary; she thought I was fine, and I thought she was fine, too. I loved talking with my black friends about sex. They'd go into vivid descriptions without any shame at all. I loved it because it satisfied my voyeurism. Actually, I wish now I could talk as freely about sex with white people as I do with blacks. See, I love talking about sex in detail—I like talking about what I like to look at, what I like to feel, what I like to experience—but I find I always edit myself around white people.

How old were you when you first had sex?

Thirteen.

A black girl?

No. But I don't think I better say her name.

Being Catholic, were you guilty about it afterward?

It was more Irish guilt than Catholic. My father was very open about sex, but my mother, who was Irish, was more reserved.

Did your parents have a good marriage?

They really adored each other. My father thought my mother [a drama coach and actress] was the living end, that she was the best actress, the best director, and had the most style, presence, and personality of anyone he had ever known. They had a very hot relationship. Even after they'd been married twenty-seven years, you could walk into their bedroom in the morning—like I sometimes did as a kid—and there they'd be, nestled in each other's arms, their bodies totally locked together. They were really into each other.

Pretty exciting after twenty-seven years. Don't you want that with someone thirty years from now, too?

Sure.

Evidently, you got into trying drugs early. Do you use any today?

No. From sixteen to eighteen, I did marijuana, but it always made me sick—physically ill. Then, when I was eighteen or nineteen, I had trouble sleeping for six weeks and took some Seconals, but that was short-lived. I tried cocaine, too, when I was about seventeen, but it didn't take either. I know I have this image of being antidrug, and I am if it hurts you, but really, I don't care what other people do. It's none of my business. The reason I don't do drugs is because I don't have good physical reactions to them. It's the same thing with drinking. I'll drink once a month, and then it's just to get high or drunk.

Are you still involved with Scientology?

I haven't had any auditing for about a year and a half; auditing is a technique where you have a trained listener, an auditor, prepare questions for you, and you sit opposite and answer them. Every answer is registered by the E-meter, which reacts according to the energy masses in your body. The questions are designed to give you relief about whatever subjects are bothering you.

Then, despite all the negative publicity about Scientology, you still believe?

Yes. I think it's pretty brilliant. I try to separate the material and the organization, because I don't agree with the way the organization is being run. I believe that the material is more worthy than the individuals who are handling it.

How much money have you put into Scientology over the years?

I don't see it as giving money; you're exchanging for services.

Ten thousand dollars? Twenty thousand?

Maybe in that ballpark, yeah.

Scientology uses your name a lot in promoting its cause. Do you feel it has used your celebrity for its own purposes?

I've been something of an ostrich about how it's used me, because I haven't investigated exactly what the organization's done. One part of me says that if somebody gets some good out of it, maybe it's all right. The other part of me says that I hope it uses some taste and discretion. I wish I could defend Scientology better, but I don't think it even deserves to be defended, in a sense.

What is the biggest misconception about John Travolta?

That I'm insecure and uncertain. I think people misinterpret my sensitivity or perceptiveness as insecurity and indecisiveness. I'm given less credit for being a strong individual than I deserve. No one could've gotten to the place I am and survived it this long without being strong.

What drives you?

A lot of it is my family—especially my mother when she was alive. If I didn't have my family to motivate me, then it'd probably be my friends. You're always driving yourself because you get all the rewards, but secondarily, it's for the people you love. Beyond that, my driving force is maintenance—maintenance of a career. [*Laughs.*]

*Your last few movies—*Blow Out, Urban Cowboy, *and certainly* Moment by Moment—*weren't in the category of* Saturday Night Fever *and* Grease. *People in the business seem to think you need another blockbuster in order to get your career back on track.*

The truth is, I don't need another blockbuster for my career. *Urban Cowboy* did a hundred million dollars. Now what's wrong with that? If it had been my first movie, I'd have been a big movie star. It keeps on being compared to the first two movies, which are so mega that if I had only done one of them, I'd still be okay. I was offered *An Officer and a Gentleman,* which I turned down, basically because I felt the girl had the best part and because I'd just finished *Blow Out* and wasn't ready to go right back to work. Anyway, after the movie came out, I said to Warren Beatty, "Do you think I should have done *An Officer and a Gentleman?*" And he said, "Why?" And I said, "Because it was a commercial success." He said, "You have two of the biggest movies in movie history. Why do you need another one? Just do good movies, John." And Warren, who I happen to think represents the ultimate show-business viewpoint, was right. In the list of the ten top-grossing movies of all time, I was the only actor the public came to see as an actor. The rest of the top grossers were all special-effects films—*E.T.*, *The Empire Strikes Back*, *Jaws*, *Raiders of the Lost Ark*. I may be the only actor the public went to see instead of a shark.

In retrospect, are you sorry you made Moment by Moment?

Only because I get asked about it so much.

Did you ever see the film?

Only once. I didn't like it, but I didn't mind my performance.

Why didn't the film work for you?

I didn't feel Lily and I had good chemistry. As people, we had incredible chemistry, but onscreen it didn't work. I learned from that one—that you have to have chemistry as well as the script. I can't understand why it's still getting rehashed. I almost feel I need something like it again so the attention gets off it.

You mean you need a new bomb?

[*Laughs.*] Right.

How did you and Sly Stallone end up working together on Staying Alive?

I'd seen *Rocky III* and said if I ever did a sequel of *Saturday Night Fever*, I wanted it to have that kind of pacing and excitement. Last year, my agent put me together with Stallone, and we were instantly in sync about the story line. We both wanted *Staying Alive* to be all about show business, the story of a kid who goes to New York, becomes a jazz-dance teacher, wants to make it on Broadway, gets rejected, and finally does make it.

Rocky in ballet slippers, huh? *How did you like working with Stallone?*

I miss his energy right now. He has so much unique survival energy in him that he makes everything matter. In my life, I tend to make things matter and not matter, in order to keep a balance. If things work out, fine. If not, I'm not disappointed. With Sly, everything matters. It's fun to be around someone who creates that illusion—you know, "This is going to be a *great* movie"; "This is going to be a *great* dance number"; "We're going to get you in great shape." It's very exciting to have someone other than yourself care about you. A lot of times, that kid in you wants to think that someone will take responsibility for you. Sly always makes you think you're responsible for yourself but is still there to give you the kind of energy a parent does.

Speaking of getting into great shape, he certainly helped you there. How long did the Stallonization of John Travolta take?

About seven months, five of which were prior to the film. Every day, I did two and a half hours of weight lifting and anywhere from three to eight hours of dancing. Now that the film's done, I'll probably maintain with an hour of weight lifting three or four times a week, plus an hour of cardiovascular—running, dancing, walking.

When you see yourself up there on the screen, do you think you're attractive?

I know what to do to be attractive, and I have confidence in my appeal. Sometimes when I see myself onscreen, I wonder what people tune in to, because I find myself more interesting than traditionally handsome. But I've been told it's not just the handsomeness, anyway— it's the acting ability, the sexuality, the singing and dancing, they like—so I take it all as a package.

Do you enjoy being a movie sex symbol?

At first I loved it . . . in fact, I've always loved it. However, after you're pegged one, you learn—mainly through journalists—that maybe it's not such a good thing, that it has a shallow connotation. But in order to be where I am, you have to be a sex symbol in some fashion or another.

What do you think is your best feature?

The transparency in my eyes. I have the ability to think a thought and it's seen. It's my biggest asset as an actor.

What is your biggest drawback as an actor?

I can be a sponge and pick up on people very quickly, but sometimes I pick up stuff I don't want.

What are your obsessions?

Airplanes. And on the physical side of life, sex and eating.

Do you think you're smart?

Yes. Bottom line. I don't know whether it's an appropriate thing to admit to, but I do. Now, that's different from being well read and

having a wide vocabulary, although both those things are easily handled—just pick up some books and read a dictionary. So I'm not
concerned with that because, basically, on any particular subject matter, I feel I can usually give a good rumble.

*Stallone said of you, "John walks that fine line between being a very
young man and a very vulnerable old man." How does that strike you?*

A brilliant perception. I never thought Sly was tuning in to that part
of me, but he picked up on something that's been a problem for me
ever since I was a kid. See, I was the youngest in my family. My mother
and father were both forty-two when I was born, so by the time I
started really picking up their vibes, they were already fifty. I started
looking at life through their eyes, but life through fifty-year-old eyes
may not be as chipper as a kid deserves to see it. What I observed was
fifty-year-old parents and their anxieties, their blues, their sensing the
third chapter of their lives. That's never left me, and as a result, I have
always had an older person's point of view on life. In other words, I
sense the end. I get blue more easily because I'm not always appreciat-
ing the youth I have.

*Your mother, who died of cancer in 1978, was a tremendous influence
in your professional and personal life. What do you miss about not
having her around?*

Her relentless, undying interest in my well-being and career. There's
nothing like it. No one is more interested in your career and your
well-being than your mother. *No one.* And I miss her being able to
enjoy all of this. We came from a neighborhood where you had dreams
of having what I have. And she always did. She got to be here at the
ranch for a couple of weeks, and she went to the Oscars and Europe,
but being able to really have lived this life-style would've been something else. I would've really gotten off watching her enjoy it.

*The moment you found out your mother had cancer, do you recall how
you felt? Perhaps somehow cheated . . . helpless?*

I had a particular problem, because I disagreed with the doctor about
how to treat my mother. My turmoil was more than just my mother's
being at the fates of her life. It was really, "Are we doing the right
thing?" Her blood was not coagulating enough to cut into her anyway.

But she didn't have the healing abilities, the stamina to bear up. She should never have been opened up, and I feel I let them do it because the doctors made me feel it was okay.

So you feel guilty?

I feel responsible for that, yeah. The doctor persuaded me to have the operation, and then, when it was over, he said, "Hey, man, we're only a practice." I said, "Well, you didn't say that three weeks ago. Three weeks ago it was a demand. She must have this operation. Now, suddenly you say you're just a practice?" We had a big fight.

With Diana and your mother dying within eighteen months of each other, what questions did that raise about your own mortality?

It was a rude awakening that we are always right next to death. It's a cliché, but it gave me an ability to appreciate life more and to do things I want to, within reason. Like the time I bought my plane. Financially, it was a little steep for me, but I said, "Man, flying is one of the passions of your life, so do it." And I savor people more. I anticipate how much I'm going to miss them if they or I go. I'm less afraid of dying because I accept it more as a part of life.

Does the fact that you've done films that will live after you help you accept the idea of dying?

Definitely. When I was a teenager, I remember thinking that I did not want to leave this world without its being marked by my presence in some fashion. That was a compulsion for me. So my achievements have enabled me to be a little less afraid of death on the one hand; on the other, they also make me not want to leave because I have so much to live for.

Have you always been ambitious?

Yeah. I always wanted to do well, although I don't think I knew from being a movie star. Doing well to me meant having a series of Broadway shows and always being able to work. I think I had a lot of presence onstage, and I was good, but I don't think I had the technique to carry a serious stage career. I never had the projection to get to the back of the theater. You had to be three aisles away from me to get my performance.

Saturday Night Fever *turned you into the sex symbol for the seventies, just as James Dean represented the fifties and Steve McQueen the sixties. What was it about you that bespoke the seventies?*

Being a child of the sixties and a seventies teenager made me understand my own generation, even though I was probably more career-oriented than most. But it was really through my performance that I became an archetype. Everyone could identify with me because they had a friend either like me or like one of the characters I played. I had one quality of someone that everyone knew in the seventies.

That probably says a lot, considering the fact that the seventies was such a lackluster decade.

You're telling me? [*Laughs.*] I was king of it!

PLAYBOY

January 1983

**"I like a woman passionate and focused on me. . . .
I don't want a woman who has anything of magnitude
or devastating interest to say. . . . I want
someone to have a good time with."**

I couldn't believe his answers.

I couldn't believe my questions.

But, then again, this was *Playboy* and Dudley Moore—I should've seen it coming.

It was 1983, and Dudley and I were sitting in the living room of his oceanfront house at Venice Beach. Having just come off *10* and *Arthur*, Moore was America's favorite British export. Everybody wanted to interview him, and he was only too happy to comply. Talking about himself came quite naturally to Dudley, since he'd been doing it for over twenty years on the shrink's couch. Much of that time he'd spent trying to get over, come to terms with, or learn to live with the fact that his mother was a cold, distant figure who alternately acknowledged and denied that her son had been born with a debilitating clubfoot.

The way Moore coped with this cornucopia of hang-ups was through sex—wanting to have it, having it, and then talking about it. Sex was the way Moore kept score. God had dealt him a cruel and unfair blow with his mangled foot, but he could still get even. He could play piano, be funny, act, get famous, and get laid.

Dudley used sex to keep reporters at bay. If you're uncomfortable discussing orgasms, you'll get nowhere with the tiny Oxford graduate. To be a good interviewer, you have to recognize your subject's lingo, adjust, and go with it. No matter what he says, you cannot blink, you cannot lose your sangfroid, you cannot appear shocked. And you can never sit in judgment—even when, as in Moore's case, he shares with you a romantic ideal vapid enough to make your teeth grate.

When people sign up for the *Playboy* interview, they assume they'll be asked—and must tell—the intimate details of their sex life. They feel some First Amendment imperative to own up to their lust à la Jimmy Carter. But *Playboy* interviews aren't necessarily about sex at all. What they're about, as in any interesting discussion, is the primary concerns of a person's life. Sex becomes the dominant theme only if sex is the subject's dominant preoccupation, although, over the years, I've found novelist Ayn Rand's observation to be chillingly correct:

"A man's sexual choice is the result and the sum of his fundamental convictions. Tell what a man finds sexually attractive and I will tell you his entire philosophy of life."

Thirty hours of tape later, Dudley Moore on sex . . .

—

Let's start with the important stuff: You're perhaps the only man on this planet to have been in bed—onscreen, anyway—with both Raquel Welch, in Bedazzled, *and Bo Derek, in* 10.

Well, Raquel played a tempting creature known as Lillian Lust. Holy shit, she really has a great body! When she was supposed to seduce me in the bed scene, I wore three pairs of underpants, thinking, Christ, if I get an erection, maybe three pairs will help. I was thinking of tying my cock down with Band-Aids or something—literally! I thought it was going to be very embarrassing. But that kind of scene ultimately turns out to be unerotic, because you're thinking of something else.

And the scene with Bo?

Well, I had to do both scenes with both women twice. Hmmmmm, I think a little pattern is emerging here. [*Chuckles.*] We were both naked, but they lighted it so you couldn't see a damned thing. I was nervous, but Bo wasn't. She had to get up from the bed and walk over to the hi-fi and then go back to the bed. Let me tell you, it wasn't easy for me.

The sacrifices you make . . .

Indeed. But it *is* embarrassing to have everyone staring, saying, "What's she got? What's he got?" You feel more stupid than turned on. You're thinking about your lines, your timing, your camera angles—not about sex.

But did you find Bo sexy?

Bo is basically cool. I didn't think of her as a sexy person. I don't mean that as an insult. I just mean she doesn't farm it out in public. She's not like Bardot, who used to flirt with the world; nor is there a sensuality as you have with Anna Karina or Sophia Loren.

Movie scenes aside, sex appears to be a pretty important theme running through your life.

I think sex is the most important part of anybody's life.

The most important part?

The ability to enjoy your sex life is central. I don't give a shit about anything else. One's desire for another person is the most flattering thing you can take from that person. The best sex you can give anybody is what you take from her with the utmost enthusiasm.

Are women, then, more important to you than your work?
Absolutely.

Are they the obsession of your life?

Totally. What else is there to live for? Chinese food and women. There *is* nothing else. Actually, I sometimes hate women for having such an effect on me.

That comes through from time to time. Some of your humor—especially the early stuff with your former partner, Peter Cook—seems to have some anger toward women in it. Are you secretly a little hostile toward women?

No. I just want to do everything to them. I want to murder them

and love them and embrace them and die in them and live in them
and *all* that stuff. *Everything!* Just go through the dictionary, and that's
what I want to do: I want to aardvark them, Afghanistan them, blender
them, demarcate them, Zulu them, I want to do *everything*!

Have you ever been to bed with more than one person?

Yeah, with two women. But just once.

Did you like it?

Yeah, it was fuckin' great. I also tried it once with a male friend and
a woman, but we just ended up laughing. I mean, it was like choosing
ends: "Which end do *you* want?" It was so exhilarating we couldn't
do anything.

When did you realize you were going to be such a prisoner of sex?

When I was about eleven. I looked at girls, and suddenly, all I
wanted to do was to love them, have them kiss me. I even remember
their names. Joan Harold and Shirley Powell and Louise McDonald
and Jean Dabbs and—oh, fuck . . . Yeah, sex really had me by the ears,
but it wasn't until a couple of years later that I focused on doing
something more with girls.

As a teenager, I found the idea of intercourse completely frightening.
I do remember the first breast I ever fondled. The girl wasn't exactly
attractive, but she did have a fair pair of knockers. Anyway, we went
behind her house, where I stood on some bricks so I could reach her.
Then, as if by remote control, she guided my hand to her breast. I
remember feeling this thing and thinking, Oh!—as though I'd put my
hand on a sheep's eye or something.

And how did you feel about it afterward?

Totally disgraced. I thought, That's it. I've done it now. I've blotted
my copybook. That went on for some time—girls and very passionate
snogging and smooching, a bit of breast fondling. But nothing very
much of a south-waist nature. I remember once at a party sitting frozen
in a chair with a girl on my lap. We were both pretending we were
asleep, but I felt the sexual electricity just whipping through us. I didn't
actually get into any heavy petting until I was about sixteen or so and
met a French girl. She terrified me. But I still used to visit her in Paris.
She had a little garden house where we'd go, and I would venture to

insert part of my disgusting body into her, only to withdraw as if we were magnets with equal, but like, poles meeting.

And then, of course, I used to wank myself to death over my father's magazines. He had quite a collection. Come to think of it, he's probably also the reason I've always fantasized about women with big tits. I mean, show me a fire hydrant and I'll come on the spot. But I also like a nice ass and legs. In the end, of course, none of it makes a damned bit of difference, because it's just pounds of flesh. Besides, basically, I just want the same things *all* men do: Rice Krispies and sucking.

How old were you when you got around to having intercourse?

Oh, about forty-five. [*Laughs.*] No—twenty-two, twenty-three. Technically, that is. What is that Chinese saying? To walk a thousand miles, you first have to walk one foot. Well, to fuck a girl, you have to put one inch in. And although I'd gotten that inch in now and then from the time I was fifteen, I was too afraid to leave anything as valuable as my penis in that cavern of no return.

What did you think was going to happen?

I didn't know. Maybe pregnancy. I was just terrified; my repression had been so long and continuous.

Was part of that terror knowing that in order to make love, you'd have to undress and expose your clubfoot?

No, not necessarily. Although I was quite attuned to the possibility that I would have to make love in my duffel coat and snow boots, with just the offending member emerging and splurging. Emerge and splurge: the wisdom of life.

No, my dread was more general: that of allowing myself to be out of control with someone I hardly knew. Which is why masturbation is always very safe, because there you not only control the person you're with but you can leave when you want to. [*Laughs.*]

You've mentioned your clubfoot in public, usually briefly, but what exactly is your handicap?

When I was born, both of my feet were turned in. The right one apparently righted itself, while the left one was more severely damaged. As a result, my left leg is one half inch shorter than my right and is shriveled from the knee down. If I look at it dispassionately, I realize it looks like a sweet child's foot. I've learned to see it that way because of the people who didn't throw up when they saw it.

Were there a lot of people who did, figuratively, throw up?

When I was a child, yes. I was constantly made aware of it. I didn't realize my foot was different until I went to school and got laughed at. My leg was an object of ridicule. Kids used to shout, "Hopalong!" and mimic me. I always wore short pants, so the greatest day in my life was when—at thirteen—I was finally allowed to wear long pants and cover my leg.

Wouldn't it have been more humane to have put you in long pants sooner?

Of course. But my mother didn't want me to feel there was anything wrong—and yet she did. On the one hand, she was very anxious about my foot, and on the other, she pretended it didn't exist, which made me very confused. She either overinflated me or underinflated me. It was either "You're perfect; there's nothing wrong with you" or "You're a complete cripple." So with that came the idea that I was either a genius or a piece of crap.

How did your leg affect you socially?

I had a very isolated youth. I was withering in the hospital, being operated on, or at home, sitting in splints, recovering. I spent so much time in the hospital, where the distance between me and another person was six feet, that when I finally got out in the world and was only two feet from a kid who was alive and kicking—not depressed and waiting to get well—it was suddenly very frightening. Any sense of humor I might have had was severely limited by my enormous fear of being out there.

And I have some ghastly hospital memories. During the war, I was on a ward that was loaded with soldiers. I was the only kid. One night, there was a soldier across from me who, when they drew the curtains around him, kept screaming, "No! No! No! No!" I was very frightened.

Later, I was wheeled into a darkened operating theater, where I was left alone. I stayed for what seemed like two hours before anybody knew I was there. I was dying of thirst, but nobody gave me water, because nobody saw me there. Finally, this guy came in—this prick of a doctor—and said, "It's the right leg off, isn't it?" I said, "No, no, no, no. It's the left!" As it turned out, that asshole was trying to be funny.

Another crucial thing occurred when I was left in a hospital for about two weeks without visits from my parents. My mother said she just couldn't get there, bless her heart. But I gather from psychological studies that kids up to the age of five who are institutionalized or left on their own for more than two weeks generally freeze up. They never quite crack out of it. I'm not sure that happened to me, but even today, I'm afraid of family life. I like to be on my own, basically.

Your own family was English working class; did that mean you grew up poor?

We were poor. But so was everybody. My father was an electrician for the Stratford East Railway and, as such, he never made more than fifteen pounds a week—that's about forty dollars. We didn't seem poor, but we didn't seem rich, either. Richness to me was having a bike with three speeds rather than a fixed wheel. When I did *Beyond the Fringe,* I earned in one week what my parents had managed to save in twenty years—one hundred pounds.

Did you get your sense of humor from your parents?

They enjoyed humor very much. But my father was a quiet, hidden man whom I dearly loved but also despised because he wasn't stronger than he was. He was also a Christian Scientist, so his life was his church—apart, of course, from the steaming repressed sexuality that was locked inside him.

And your mother?

An irredeemably repressed ball of floating anxiety.

Sounds as though they were well matched.

Yes. [*Chuckles.*] My mother was a complete fucking mess in terms of knowing who she was and what rights she had. She felt she didn't have any right to her body and, in fact, was disgusted by it. Yet, with all that, there was a humor and brightness that just kept her nose above water. That—and being incredibly defensive—kept her going until she was eighty-one.

Were you funny as a kid?

No. Quite frankly, I never had any sense of humor. I was a very pompous little boy who was *driven* to humor.

As a defense against your clubfoot?

Yeah. And my height. I got funny so I wouldn't get beaten up anymore.

Were you actually brutalized by other children?

Bullied and pushed, mostly. See, I also liked schoolwork. I was a hardworking kid who used to ask teachers for more work in front of other kids. I just loved to work. But, as a result, I got punished by my peer group. Once I started being funny, making fun of the teachers as they did, I was accepted.

Did you keep up your studies?

No. I stopped reading when I started clowning. I always had a vivid imagination and read like a maniac, two or three books a night. So I very much resented having to clown, because it stopped me from learning and developing. Sometimes I despise the fact that I make people laugh. But being funny is a way of drawing blood without revealing where the arrow came from.

It sounds as if you and your mother had a complicated relationship.

We did. I was very attached to her—but very angry with her, too. She made me feel that if I made one false step, she would die. You must understand, I don't blame her for it. I don't have any bad feelings toward her now. But then she was constantly worried about my foot.

Worried or embarrassed?

Both. My mother was obsessed by my foot and, because of that, made me obsessed by it.

Why that obsession?

She had wanted to produce something perfect. My mother had a brother on whom she was quite fixated. He was a missionary in Africa and died of some disease. When she lost him, she longed to have someone replace him. But instead of producing the perfect brother, she produced this *leg*.

Are you sure you're not reading into her motivations?

No. She told me she felt that way. She said the pain I was going to suffer was unbearable—but obviously it was the pain *she* was going to suffer, feeling, as she did, that she was on trial for producing a hunchback.

Was she warm or affectionate with you?

No. There was nothing from her, no hugs or anything. Her excuse was that I shouldn't be touched because the plaster might break on my leg. So I often felt as if I were stuck on the mantel with a sign reading DON'T TOUCH HIM.

My first intimation of the effect that physical affection, particularly from a woman, had on me came from a nurse in a convalescent home. When I went into the home, I was terrified. It was my first night, and this nurse said, "Should I kiss you good-night?" I said no. But then, as she was going, I said yes, and she bent down and kissed me, so loving and gentle and sweet. That kiss affected my whole life. A friend said to me, "You've looked for that tenderness throughout your whole life." And I have. It haunts and sustains me. Which is why, I suppose, I live for touching and being touched.

When you got older, did you and your mother ever talk about what she'd done to you as a child?

There was one moment, the last time I saw her before she went into the hospital. I think she had intimations that she was about to bum off. She started bringing out photographs of herself as a young girl. And she said, "I don't know why you say you were unhappy as a child. Look at this picture of you." And there was this picture of me smiling.

Anyway, one Sunday afternoon, I remember saying good-bye to her, and I remember her doing what she often did: She looked at me in a peculiar, obsessive way, as if she had to put everything into it because that was the only way she could express it—nonverbally. That particular time, I looked at her and we just nodded at each other as if to say, "Yeah, I know what we feel for each other and I know there's no way of unraveling it or somehow making good the bad parts." But in that thirty seconds, I felt as though the whole of the thing had been straightened out. And that was the last time I saw her before she went into the hospital and had an operation from which she never fully recovered.

Do you still feel inadequate?

I'll always be enraged and humiliated by my handicap, except now I can deal with it without being persecuted.

Since you link your foot to your sexuality, what happened once you started having sex with women? Did you tell them about your foot beforehand?

Oh, I always felt I had to bring up this odious skeleton, as if somehow it would fly out of bed and hit them on the head if I didn't. I always had to say, "I have to tell you something. I've got this . . ." and go through great agonies. I felt they had to know they were going to bed with this deformed fish.

Was there ever any woman who was unkind about it?

Never. Never in my life. Some women, in fact, couldn't understand it at all. You know: "What are you *talking* about? So you've got a bent finger or a bent ear. What's that got to do with anything?" But even then, I wasn't convinced. I still felt I had to come up with this prologue: "Hello, I want to stick my foot up you."

Let's stay with your sex life for a while. Who first told you about sex?

Kenny Vare. I was about nine or ten, and Kenny came running into the playground as if he were bearing the news of the Vikings' landing. "Do you know what you have to do when you grow up?" he asked. "You have to put your winkie in a girl."

Well, by that time, having already masturbated myself into the ground, I thought, My God. I've done it. I've ruined myself for this ghastly task. I really thought there was something wrong with me.

I gather that your mother didn't know about your preoccupation.

God, no! But I've got some hilarious stories about masturbation. In fact, I've always wanted to do a film about it. I remember, through sheer fear and lust, coming six times in one evening when I was supposed to be doing my homework. I just sat there masturbating, with my parents next door. That always made things a little more titillating, you know.

See, I had a carpet on my bed. And I used to come all over the carpet and then rub it in. The carpet became like sculpted grass. I'll never know why on earth it was never discovered, except that my mother would occasionally say, "This carpet got all funny. Very strange, isn't it?"

But the actual idea of masturbation never got brought up at all. Except once. Well my mother, my father, my sister, and I were all sitting around in the living room, the only room in the house, besides the bathroom, where you wouldn't freeze your balls off in winter. Anyway, Mother was sitting across the room, darning socks, while I sat on the sofa, hand in my pocket, having a nice, quiet feel. The only person watching me, as far as I could tell, was the Virgin Mary, who happened to be in a picture above our fireplace—and I knew *she* sure wasn't going to blow the whistle on me. Anyway, on the radio came a coloratura soprano, singing some Viennese piece. [*He breaks into an operatic aria.*] Suddenly, she hit an extremely high note, prompting my mother to say, without missing a beat, "This-woman-is-singing-the-highest-note-that's-ever-been-sung-don't-do-that-dear."

Well, the moment was frozen, because my mother had discovered me. And from that night onward, I could be found in the early hours of the morning, frantically flipping the radio dial to find a coloratura to masturbate by. I could always come on the top note.

Who was your first real love?

A very beautiful actress.

Thus beginning an unalterable preference in women.

Shit! I hadn't even thought of that, but you're right.

What is it you find so compelling about actresses? You've married two and you're seeing another one now.

It's the fact that they compel you to look at them. Beautiful women are generally the most insecure about their looks, so they're sometimes like flashers in Central Park. They may not want to have *sex* with the whole world, but they do need to be *attractive* to the whole world.

Okay, back to your first actress.

Well, this girl was intrigued that I was a virgin.

Did she seduce you?

I don't remember how it came up, but I told her I'd never had an orgasm inside a woman. She said, "Oh, I think you *ought* to," and we agreed to meet in a hotel in Oxford. She came up from London on the milk train, arriving at five A.M. after having missed the eleven P.M. train. I was sitting on the platform waiting for her, trembling with fear, shame, anticipation, and cold. We went to the hotel and got into bed. I recall her looking over my shoulder at something on the wall while we were doing it. You can imagine how heartening that was.

How did you feel?

I found the whole thing not very exciting at all. As I came—and I'm surprised I did—she said, "Oh, I forgot to put my thing in," meaning her diaphragm. Well, she got pregnant. She told me later but said she'd deal with it and did. I saw her a couple of times after that, but it didn't work.

So after all those years of silent lust, reality was a disappointment.

I felt a great fear in my loins—a traction of fear that shriveled me spiritually and organically. I cringed with fear and shame and disappointment. Eventually, however, I came out of that theological funk.

And became even more obsessed with women?

Shortly thereafter, I was doing *Beyond the Fringe* in London and by that time had decided that what I wanted to do with my life was perform onstage, make people laugh, and play jazz because it attracts women. So I did that; I started playing jazz in the basement of a club called The Establishment, which Peter Cook had founded. Each night, after the performance, I'd go to play jazz and [*giggles*] stroke girls.

Were women the sole reason you started playing jazz?

Yeah. You ask any jazz musician why he wants to play jazz and he'll tell you the same thing.

What is the correlation between jazz and sex?

Jazz is very up front, if you'll pardon the expression. A visceral, unambiguously sexual sort of music. There's an excitement to jazz that, if you understand it enough to play it, manifests itself in other areas.

In other words, if you can improvise well on the keyboard, chances are you can improvise well in bed. Onward. Have you ever considered yourself an intellectual?

I'm a performer. And there is an intellectual exercise in that. I am as intellectual as any of them in an area they don't know fuck-all about—music. To write music is an intellectual activity. Anyway, my feelings about an intellectual life are that it's the by-product of an emotional life. The intellect is the muscle growth on top of the emotional roof, instead of the other way around.

Do you think you're a good musician?

I think I'm a terrific musician. I think I'm hot shit! I also think I'm a terrific actor and a terrific comedian.

But you still care more about your music than about your performing?

Absolutely. Always have.

How did you get started in music?

I started studying piano and singing in the church choir at the age of six. From the age of eleven to eighteen, I used to go to London to the Guildhall School of Music every Saturday morning to study violin and organ. It was actually the headmaster of Guildhall who suggested I apply to Oxford for an organ scholarship.

Not many working-class kids applied to Oxford in those days. Did you think you'd get in?

Well, in those days I wanted very much to please, so it seemed like a distinguished thing to do, and I did. I competed in an organ-scholarship competition and won a scholarship to Magdalen College. As a working-class boy, I was, indeed, greatly surprised to have been accepted. I remember the day we got the notification, my mother went absolutely wild with ecstasy. She ran down the road like Archimedes, screaming, "My son's going to Oxford!"

The thought of Oxford must have been pretty frightening.

I was very frightened. And when I got there, I felt very ill equipped. Everybody spoke so factually. I had the feeling I was in the presence of very superior beings. I felt they'd all had a classical education, were older, and had done national service, which I hadn't because of my leg. I felt *very* inferior.

What was the toughest part of that first year?

Not knowing how to open my mouth without having it sound like an old saw, because, coming from Dagenham, I spoke in a very lazy accent—not cockney, but sort of suburban. I went through a terrible stage of trying to imitate other people's voices, so I ended up with a peculiar voice, very untidy, with vowels lurching in every direction. I still talk that way today.

I was also at odds with the place because it was too beautiful. Magdalen College is breathtakingly beautiful. And there I was, this clubfooted wanker sitting on the organ seat, playing this beautiful organ in this beautiful chapel. I felt I really didn't deserve to be there.

How long did you feel that way?

For two years.

Then what happened?

Comedy. My third year, I started doing cabaret, and it was like being the school clown all over again. I found a niche and became rather well known around campus as a cabaret performer, a guy who improvised and generally made a fool of himself. After that, I started acting in sketches and doing revues, which ultimately led to *Beyond the Fringe.*

Do you have a favorite sketch from Beyond the Fringe?

I really liked the war sketch, about the so-called romance of World War Two. A lot of World War Two stories involved pilots who never returned. So in that sketch, there is one scene between Peter Cook and Jonathan Miller in which Jonathan says, "It's up to you, Perkins. I want you to fly up in a crate, take a shufty [have a look] over Bremen, and don't come back!" Peter says, "Well, thank you, sir. Is this *au revoir?*" "No," replies Jonathan, "this is good-bye."

Did the four of you ever use drugs to write or perform Beyond the Fringe?

No. None of us ever used drugs then. Ever.

Do you use drugs now?

I don't like drugs. I have no temptation. Now, I do eat a lot of sugar and salt—masses of salt. I was reading an article in *Time* about people's salt consumption, and I eat twice as much as the person with the largest intake. It's probably just eating away at my balls, replacing all the sperm with sodium chloride. One day, I'll come and there'll be this little puff of salt out the end and I'll give birth to Lot's wife. [*Laughs.*] I did read once that salt intake gives you hardening of the penis. Now, in that case, I may double my already excessive salt intake—though, let me hasten to add, I have never had a problem with hardening of the penis.

If you say so. But what's more difficult to believe is that you've never tried *drugs. A little marijuana, maybe?*

I have sucked on a marijuana cigarette about a dozen times, and once it did give me an orgasm that lasted for three days. But then, I don't need pot, because my orgasms normally last that long, anyway.

Undoubtedly. And have you ever tried cocaine?

I've had one minor sniff of cocaine, which I did under protest, because I didn't even want to try it. Well, nothing happened. Of course, that's what everybody says, but [*he breaks into swinger jargon, like his character in* Foul Play] "Hey, I'm no different. I've just had seventeen snorts of cocaine, but nothing's different, baby."

Fact is, not only do I fear being out of control but I get a buzz from a cup of coffee; so if I took cocaine, my ass would fall to the ground, my cock would explode into a thousand stars, and a breast would turn into a cantaloupe—you know, the usual humdrum stuff.

When Beyond the Fringe *went beyond its modest beginnings and opened in the West End of London, how did you celebrate? With limousines, caviar, more salt?*

I continued living the same way I always had. I was living in a small room that cost me ten shillings a week—that's about ninety cents—and I stayed there. I drove a silly little car, a 1935 Austin box car, that I finally had to abandon on the side of the road, whereupon I bought another car for forty pounds—that was a hundred dollars.

When Beyond the Fringe *broke up, you and Cook teamed up, off and on, for the next fourteen years, doing movies, another stage revue,* Good Evening, *and* Not Only . . . but Also—*a hit TV series for the BBC. What was* Not Only . . . but Also?

Not Only Peter Cook . . . but Also Dudley Moore. Basically, we did the same type of comedy sketches, the same eccentric humor with some slightly smutty jokes thrown in.

Slightly smutty?

Well, it *was* the BBC.

Do you have a favorite Cook line?

My favorite line was one that Peter came out with one afternoon. We were talking about his wife and he said, "My wife does all the cooking . . . *and* all the eating. She goes down to the well every morning, but she is not a well woman." And then I said, "How did you meet your wife?" And he said, "I met her during World War Two. She blew in through the window on a piece of shrapnel and became embedded in the sofa. One thing led to my mother, and we were married within the hour." There's such a marvelous thoroughness about the whole thing. Very British. Somehow, he'd summed up colonization, the empire—everything—all in one go.

How would you describe Cook?

Basically, a fucking cunt. [*Chuckles.*] He's an enormously softhearted/hard-hearted, sweet/sour, vulnerable/invulnerable man. He lives on the edge of two poles.

You two had a pretty volatile relationship, didn't you?

I always enjoy Peter on my own, but if I'm with somebody else, we always get into an argument. There's a videotape coming out of an album we did titled *Ad Nauseam.* It's really a documentary about Peter and me, showing the irritability that existed between us. I mean *real* irritability. We've always gotten pissed at each other. Peter's always pissed off with my nitpicking, logical mind. And I used to get pissed off at his lack of directness in dealing with people.

Obviously, the irritation worked as a creative catalyst.

Yes, and it also endeared us to each other. Although we never speak unless we bump into each other.

Both in this interview and in some of your work, you show a preference for the scatological. You really do have a fairly dirty sense of humor, don't you?

Oh, sure. I have a very ribald sense of humor, what is conventionally known as obscene. It's always there and it's always been there. It's just my way of thinking. People always wonder how, with this ribald outlook, I can also write such emotional, moving music. They can't put together the feeling swings. Not to make a comparison, but Mozart had a very scatological sense of humor, too. He was always talking about farting and cunts and asses. He had a very *basic* sense of humor. I don't find anything wrong with that. I just love having a fun time, cocking a snook, as they say.

Have you always talked dirty?

From the time I was about thirteen. But there's a misconception that if you talk dirty, you're not a serious person.

Is Dudley Moore a serious person?

Of course. Very, very serious, indeed. Gosh. Absolutely. Profoundly serious. Very, very, very serious. Phew. Gosh. Golly again. Fucking-A serious.

Some people also feel that way about Wholly Moses.

It wasn't as farcical or as romantic as it should have been. But when I was approached by the producers, I found them so nice and friendly that, even though I thought they were nuts to do the material, I said yes. In retrospect, I was nuts to have done it.

We're showing a dangerous tendency toward drifting away from your crucial subject—sex. Let's get back to it quickly. What do you find sexy in a woman?

I love romanticism in a woman, even though in many ways I strongly disapprove of it. I like a woman passionate and focused on me, without, of course, drifting into cannibalism. I look for someone who's huggable, has a sense of humor, a lot of feeling, and can talk about the crucial things in life: enjoying yourself, dying, enjoying yourself. [*Laughs.*] You know, "Oh, God, oh, God, I'm coming. Bang, pop . . . ah, done." That sort of thing.

What about brains?

I don't want a woman who has anything of magnitude or devastating interest to say. Basically, I want someone to have a good time with. Fun!

So your women don't have to be smart?

Not in the slightest. Or only in the very slightest. If I want to be stirred up intellectually, I have my books and my films. It's not important to find that with the woman I'm with.

You do seem to have a definite physical type—tall, blond, Gentile. Are you sure you're not Jewish?

[*Laughs.*] Well, I married two blondes and am with one now. Actually, I go for women with an overbite and flared nostrils, an aggressive, slightly hostile look. I love the looks of Bardot and Marthe Keller, both of whom have that vaguely toothy quality. And, of course, Susan Anton has enough to feed the world.

Are you the jealous type?

Very.

How does it manifest itself?

Murder and shoving Steinways up people's assholes.

What was the most difficult part for you of being married?

Just *being* married. Just the notion of being married is such anathema to me that it colors my whole life. I feel starved. I feel as if I'm not available to the rest of the world—as if I have to curtail my feelings. I think being on such a monogamous level with my mother made me feel that I don't want to be married to her—or to anybody else. I've already experienced the horror and anxiety of feeling I can't move.

Why do you think you got married the two times you did?

Oh, that's not available.

To whom?

To the world. You can't expect me to talk about my marriages.

You're so open about the rest of your life; why not about your relationships, since you say they're the most important part of your life?

Because there's a real distinction here. I want to love people and have them love *me*. So why should I sound off against my ex-wives, whom I love?

Then let's just talk about Tuesday Weld the woman. You know, she's a near cult figure to a lot of men. What attracted you to her?

I was very attracted by her waywardness, her devilishness, her unpredictability, her unbelievably aggressive humor. When I bantered with her, she always won. That was half the attraction—trying to win with her. But there was no winning, because I was afraid of her.

Afraid of what?

Of being rejected, and I think she knew that, even though she didn't reject me. I've always been afraid of rejection. That's been the primary fear of my life; and, therefore, it's easy for me to feel in an inferior position a great deal of the time. Tuesday is very sweet and soft as butter, really. But she has weapons that she uses quite devastatingly. Anybody who responds to them is finished. The main reason we finally parted was a constant locking of horns. But we're good friends and, of course, share our son, Patrick.

How did you feel about becoming a father? Did you want children?

No. I've always been terrified of them. It's not so bad now, but, frankly, I really don't want children. Now I'm glad as hell that I have Patrick, but for me, the first years were not massively attractive. I'm not that sort of person. And before he was born, I was worried to death that he'd inherit my foot.

There are some men who are wonderful fathers. They enjoy the years of seeing a child grow. But it's not my cup of tea, to put it in a banal way. However, now that he's six, it's increasingly delicious. I used to think children were mainly enjoyable to women, but Patrick—well, he came, he saw, he conquered.

You don't live lavishly. Without large family obligations, what do you do with your money?

I invest. I don't buy anything, because I have everything I want. As long as I eat well, have an occasional bottle of good red wine, and do my work, I'm content. I get my pleasure from everything that's free.

Needless to say, you're romantic.

I'm romantic in a way that's unreachable. My romance is out there in the dust of the galaxies. That sounds so cheap, doesn't it? My God, I can even smell ghastly perfume! My passion and romance are buried in the deep past of my youth—longing to be loved. That's the inspiration of my music. The other is sheer jest and joy.

In some ways—your height, for instance—you're an unlikely romantic lead. Does being short still bother you?

On occasion, though not that much. It bothers me if I am overweight, because then I look like a fucking tennis ball. That neurosis has really faded, because every leading lady I've had has been taller. When we were doing *Six Weeks,* the first scene Mary [Tyler Moore] and I had was a party scene. She was wearing heels that none of us liked. She said, "Well, I didn't want to wear flats, in case anybody thought I was trying to accommodate Dudley's size." She didn't give a shit! Julie Andrews, on the other hand, hadn't wanted to act with me in *10* because she didn't want to act with somebody who was smaller than herself.

Your role in 10 *was that of a guy having a midlife crisis—*

I've been having a midlife crisis since I was two weeks old. I went right from a midwife to a midlife crisis. I've been in therapy since 1964.

Summarize your psychiatric experiences, if you don't mind.

I started in England, going to a therapist twice a week. When I went to Australia, I couldn't do it, but I made a lot of progress by reading books on analysis. When I came to New York in 1973, I was with a woman who practices bioenergetics, an offshoot of Reichian therapy whose basic idea is that neuroses are reflected in a corporeal display of muscular spasms. I did Reichian therapy for a time but found it too studiedly self-conscious. When I got to California, I went into group therapy and found it one of the best moves I'd made. But I stopped therapy a year ago.

Is it a permanent halt?

I think so. I may go in to brush my teeth every now and again. But, basically, I feel fine.

Why do you think it took so long? Why so many years of therapy?

I just went at my own pace.

Vis-à-vis your therapy and your finding yourself, Cook once said that on your deathbed, you'd be issuing a press release saying, "Wait. I'm nearly there."

Yes, and he also said, "Dudley has been looking for himself for years. Why bother? *I* found him years ago." You know, I absorb all these swipes and keep on going.

What's your greatest strength?

I am very stubborn and very sensitive, but I also have the ability to put my hand in my chest and pull my heart out. And I don't mean wearing it on my sleeve or brandishing it above my head.

What do you think is the biggest misunderstanding about Dudley Moore?

My intellectual friends think I'm stupid and my friends who've had very little education think I'm a fucking brain surgeon. Actually, what I really am is a terrific musician and a terrific comedic actor.

Words for your tombstone?

That I want to read, quite simply, HE DIED AND ROSE AGAIN FROM THE DEAD.

PAST PERFECT

What these people all have in common is that they are now gone. When they were here, they informed, entertained, charmed, amused, and inspired us.

TRUMAN CAPOTE

New York, 1980

In December 1978 I convinced Truman Capote to do a "Twenty Questions" interview for *Playboy*. In November 1979, endless excuses later, he finally sent me a postcard in Washington: "I know your opinion of me must be very black but I have been writing against so many deadlines and plagued by such a variety of complications! However, when I am free I will call you instantly! Love, Truman."

"Instantly" never happened. Finally, I typed up questions and sent them to him. He returned his answers in writing:

Who are the five sexiest women you know?

"Kay Graham, Gloria Guinness, Lillian Hellman, Marella Agnelli, Mrs. Herb Caen."

Are the rich really different from you and me?

"Yes, they're more disloyal and they have better vegetables."

Define decadence.

"Decadence is deliberate cruelty."

People have always been interested in you. What is your appeal?

"I don't have any appeal. I just arouse curiosity."

At this point in time, who is the one person most responsible for pushing America further down the tubes?

"Sammy Davis, Jr."

Holly Golightly said she taught herself to like older men because she thought it was a good thing to do. Is this generally good advice for women?

"Indeed, it is. Older men are a passport that will carry you across all frontiers."

—

The last time I saw Truman, he was in a small, private Manhattan clinic, drying out, once again, from alcohol. Alone, sitting up in his bed, he looked fragile, lonely, and tired. But declaring himself cured, he said he'd had his last drink. He looked as if he meant it.

Thirty minutes into our visit, Truman suddenly asked if I'd do him a favor. He said he was having a terrible time sleeping, and the hospital medicine wasn't doing him a bit of good. Would I mind buying him some NyQuil? He looked exhausted and helpless. What, I thought, could possibly be wrong with NyQuil? I darted across the street, bought a bottle, and brought it back. It startled me when he immediately spooned some down; it was only five o'clock. After I left, I was walking down the street when it hit me. I went into a drugstore, picked up a

NyQuil bottle, and read the label: 25 percent alcohol. The Tiny Terror had struck again.

CLARE BOOTHE LUCE

Washington, D.C., 1977

I interviewed Clare Boothe Luce on my knees.

We ran into each other—or more precisely, I chased her down—one night at a black-tie dinner at the Library of Congress.

I spotted her across a noisy rotunda crowded with tables, and froze: my heroine, my idol, the impossible-to-get interview, sitting right there, furiously dragging on a cigarette and locked in conversation with the man on her right. Her dress was heavy brown silk. Her hair was chin-length, pale white with Dutch-boy bangs that brushed the top of her glasses, whose distorted thickness, a nod to cataracts, magnified and distorted her china-blue eyes. Though in her mid-seventies, Luce was still an imposing character.

Reaching the table, I knelt beside her chair to avoid disrupting her dinner companions. When I tapped Luce's arm, she turned to peer down at a pretzel-positioned blonde in a strapless black cocktail dress, notebook in hand, asking permission to chat.

"What about your legs? I'm worried about your hamstrings," she demanded.

"I'm fine. I do this all the time."

"What do you have in mind, then?"

Several hours plowing through her life. Short of that (and I was very short indeed), I simply started asking what I had always wanted to know: *How had she done it?* How had she pulled off a life that became a standard by which other women measured theirs?

"Luck, perseverance, genes—being pretty. It doesn't put a woman back, you know."

And men? They had certainly played a major part in her success.

"I still like men. And I still think they should be manipulated. That's the way to handle them."

The theater? "I am," she preened, "the largest employer of women in the American theater. Over three hundred thousand women have acted in my plays. By thirty-five, you know, I'd written four of them."

The Women? Had she really written it in only six weeks?

"No. A weekend. Although, of course, I did think about it for twenty minutes before I wrote it."

And if she had it all to do over again . . . ?

"I'd have finished college. Girls didn't in my day. We were lucky to get through school. And I'd have chosen a profession. I mean business or law—not the arts. If I were your age and TV were what it is today, I would've been tempted to try it. But it's really *en passant,* isn't it? Being recognized in the supermarket just isn't that big a deal."

By now my knees were going, her steak cold. One last question: What advice would she give a young female journalist on how to get ahead in her career?

"I would hope that your husband or father dies and leaves you a newspaper."

So much for feminism.

ANDY WARHOL

Washington, D.C., 1980

Andy Warhol, who founded *Interview,* a magazine devoted to interviews, hated giving them.

But in March 1980 he sat down with me in Washington. Warhol's favorite adjective was "great" (as in "Liza's great," "Misha's great"). His favorite topic was sex. "If you really want him to open up, tell him something about your sex life," suggested Fred Hughes, president of Andy Warhol Enterprises, who stayed in the bedroom of Warhol's hotel suite watching soap operas.

Andy was turning fifty. The face was round, the complexion the consistency of dough. His hair, bought in a store, sat atop his head like a silver divot. He was wearing Levi's with a white Brooks Brothers shirt, a tie, and a blazer. In his lap he fidgeted nervously with a paperback copy of his book *Portraits of the Seventies.*

Following Hughes's advice, I started with sex, but *his* sex life, not mine. Sex, sighed Warhol, was "too much bother." As was love. "The first thing I always tell my friends is not to fall in love. Love is too hard. You have to get involved with people. I don't think it's really worth it. It's never like it is in the movies."

So he had never been in love?

"No. I'm always fascinated by everybody. Besides, you can see love in the movies. It's easier."

How might he like his epitaph to read?

"Nothing. Just blank. And no name either."

ANDY WARHOL, A FIGMENT OF AMERICA'S IMAGINATION?

"Yeah. I like that." He smiled. "Let it read FIGMENT."

DIANA VREELAND

New York, 1979

"Every time she speaks," Jacqueline Onassis once said of Diana Vreeland, former editor-in-chief of *Vogue,* fashion editor of *Harper's Bazaar,* special consultant to the Metropolitan Museum of Art's Costume Institute, and one of the world's most brilliant eccentrics, "treasures are lost."

I was the recipient of those treasures one December afternoon in 1979 when I visited Vreeland in her offices at the museum in New York. She was preparing for her eighth annual Met exhibit: "Fashions of the Hapsburg Era: Austria-Hungary," featuring over 150 uniforms, costumes, related art objects, and paintings imported from institutions in Vienna and Budapest and hand-picked by Vreeland.

Vreeland's office at the Met was red—the color she most revered (a passion she also extended to bracelets, Jack Nicholson, Rigaud candles, unfiltered Lucky Strikes, Givenchy, straight backs, well-shaped skulls, and dollar bills—freshly pressed). She had a long neck; a patrician nose; black, blunt-cut, patent-leather hair; blood-red nails; scarlet lips; ruby-rouged cheeks; and a dancer's posture. She resembled an elegant, extravagant gazelle with a voice so basso profundo as to put Tallulah Bankhead to shame.

"My voice is hideous," she said. "It's tortured and tired, one that misrepresents me totally because I am not a tortured, tired person at all."

On the contrary. Mrs. Vreeland had always had a fresh perspective.

"Pink," she once declared, "is the navy blue of India."

And the bikini? "The most important thing since the atom bomb."

She was, I think, in her seventies when I got to her.

"Mrs. Vreeland, how old are you?"

"Oh, my dear, one must never tell one's age."

"Why?"

"Because no matter what you say, you're either too old or too young."

When Mrs. Vreeland died in 1989, her *New York Times* obituary stated she was "somewhere in her eighties." Bravo! She had won that battle, I thought, until, at her memorial service, her son Tim began his eulogy with words I found to be decidedly hostile: "My mother was born in August 1903, in Paris."

Mrs. Vreeland was not easy to interview. She was imperious, curious, demanding, polite, flamboyant, perceptive, and strikingly naïve. But she was never boring. I asked her to describe herself.

"That's kind of a tough question. Well, I would describe myself as a nice lady who gets up in the morning and gets cracking."

"In life," she concluded, taking a final drag on her cigarette, "one has one's crises, changes, circumstances, and opportunities—all that sort of thing. But you must just go along. Bash on! Don't look left nor right and never compete. Never. Watching the other guy is what kills all forms of energy."

BETTE DAVIS

Westport, Connecticut, 1976

She was not the hardest to get nor even the hardest to interview. She was simply Bette Davis. A star. A tough cookie. A dame with a male ego. A woman, at sixty-eight, still trying to figure out men.

"It's impossible for my kind of famous woman to be married. And there's nothing the wife can do about this. The man, my dear, is never going to make a marriage work. If it works, the woman does it. I made my movies work, not my marriages."

And, indeed, there had been four, three of which ended in divorce. Ultimately, Davis opted for what she did best and sustained her most: the Work. She died a week after showing up in Barcelona, Spain, at yet another film festival in her honor. She was eighty-two. Though her looks had eroded under the multiple invasions of age, cigarettes, liquor, cancer, and strokes, she was, until the end, driven by the same libido that had fueled her entire life.

"Sexy? My dear, I was born that way," she said, torching up one of the countless cigarettes she smoked during our eight hours together. It was 1976, and Davis had just co-starred in a TV movie on the life of Aimee Semple McPherson, played by Faye Dunaway. ("What do I think of M-i-s-s F-a-y-e D-u-n-a-w-a-y?" she roared, jumping to her feet and flapping her arms as if massive sails were attached. "Joan Crawford was an angel with wings compared to Faye Dunaway.")

"From the moment I was six I felt sexy. And let me tell you it was hell, sheer hell, waiting to do something about it. As it was, I ended up waiting much too long because I was raised badly on that score. I was taught you had to be married to a man to sleep with him, so it wasn't until I was married the first time at twenty-six that I did it. God!

"But you know"—she leaned forward, drilling her blue headlight eyes straight into mine—"I've always felt sex was God's biggest joke on human beings. If that urge gets to you, you don't know *anything* until it's over and then you look at what you've got beside you on the pillow and say, 'My Gawd, I don't believe what I've ended up with.' "

We started talking around two—Davis wearing "a simple little cotton dress," false eyelashes, a blond wig stylishly coiffed. At five sharp Davis stood and asked if I wanted a drink. I didn't, but she did, pouring herself a hefty Scotch. By the time I left at ten, she'd had several more. As the liquor opened up, so did she. Her deepest regret, she said, was the several abortions she'd had before giving birth, at thirty-nine, to her daughter, B.D. (B.D.'s scorchingly critical memoir of her mother had yet to be published). "Next to B.D. I'm still, emotionally, the child," she claimed. "Unlike me, she's been married to the same man for thirteen years.

"You see, I was always the breadwinner. I never, for instance, took alimony from my husbands and, in one instance, I paid him alimony. But even so, it's nevah, nevah, nevah going to be a woman's world. It's always going to be a man's world or else men are going to be miserable. Men always have to feel like they're winning—whether it's a director or a husband you're talking about—or else they cannot take it.

"Listen, I knew. I knew. My own mother warned me. She said, 'Ruth Elizabeth, you cannot have it all.' And she was right."

ACKNOWLEDGMENTS

"I believe we have two lives," Glenn Close mused to Robert Redford in *The Natural*, "the one we learn with and the one we live with after that."

This is a book about the one I learned with.

My most important teachers, not surprisingly, have always been my friends and family, starting with my exceptional parents and my brother, Pat, one of the smartest, kindest, funniest people I know. When I told him I'd written about growing up in Montana, he asked to read it because "I just want to make sure we had the same childhood." Though that is still up for grabs, at least we had the same parents, and because of that, or despite it, depending on the day and crisis, he has always been there for me, my biggest fan. I'd also like to acknowledge with deep love Peggy Ann Snyder, Ruby Park, JoEllen Beavers, Ecna Morris, Mary Sheahan, Margaret Brady, Mary Collins, Bill Collins, and Margaret Harley.

And then there is the Focus Group, that throng of friends-cum-kin who help keep my eye on the ball and tell me, in no uncertain terms, when it's off. Much love, respect, and appreciation to Helen Gurley Brown and Liz Smith, who believed in me before I did and kept assuring me they were right; and, in alphabetical order (Look—Woody Allen does it this way): Ernie Angstadt, Ken Bell, Carl Brenner, Linda and Arthur Carter, Lois Chiles, Ann Marie Cunningham, Suzanne DePasse, Suzanne Eagle, John Ellis, Connie Ferlito, Yolande Fox, Nancy Friday and Norman Pearlstine, Lynda Guber, Alice Harris, Stanley Hughes, Brenda Johnson, Ray Johnson, Michael Kaplan, Elaine Kaufman, Jurate Kazickas and Roger Altman, Deborah Leff, Patty Matson, Celia and Henry McGee, Robert Mundy, Lynn Nesbit, Marcia Nousamen, Sandy Socolow, Maurice Sonnenberg, Penny Stallings, and Dawn Steel.

For giving me great breaks when I needed them, thanks to Michael Coady, Barry Diller, Steve Friedman, Barry Golson, David Hirshey, Ed Kosner, Richard Leibner, Terry McDonell, Steve Randall, Bob Wallace, Jann Wenner, and a wonderful editor, Susan Murcko.

Special appreciation goes to Christine Pevitt and the fabulous Amy Gross, whose interest in my story—at different incarnations—made this book a reality. Beyond that, thanks to all the smart, witty, patient people at Random House who saw me through this experience and lived to tell the tale, most especially the talented and terrifying Amy Edelman, copy editor extraordinaire, Mary Beth Guimaraes, Carol Schneider, Kent Holland, and Karen Rinaldi. For special services, I'd like to mention Joan Dean and Margaret Lee.

Most important, for their brilliance and compassion toward my mother and the rest of our family during a most difficult time, I'd also like to acknowledge Dr. William Sindelar, Dr. Jason Gutterman, and Dr. Jerome DeCosse.

And much love to all my friends in Hamilton, Montana, my secret weapon and one of the warmest, most original places on earth.

Writing a book is a frightening and complicated experience. About a year into it, I said to my friend Barbara, "If I ever tell you I'm going to write another book, I want you to shoot me." To which she replied,

"You can do it again—you'll just have to find a whole new set of friends."

Indeed, nothing tests the limits of friendship, much less sanity, more than the words "I just got a book advance." For staying the course in both areas a very special mention to David Norris, a talented architect in every sense of the word; Colin Callender, my cherished confidant and soul mate; Leon Levy, the wisest, most treasured friend in my life; Maury Hopson, whose humor and sensitivity are matched only by his chivalry—one of the true gentlemen; Susan Kamil, smart as she is and more beautiful than she knows; and Julie Grau, who hand-held me through one of the most difficult birthing processes in the history of the printed word, and whose astuteness is matched only by her goodness.

Finally, my deepest gratitude and love to four extraordinary women without whom this book would not have turned out the way it did: Barbara King Brenner, a gifted editor and even more gifted friend, who, beyond her remarkable literary talents, has the best taste in jewelry of anyone I know; Ronee Gebrow Hoade, who endured every version, written and oral, of *Hard to Get* and took up where Elsie left off; the brilliant Norma Kamali, who shot my photograph and designed the jacket—I wrote the book, but she finished it; and, finally, to Joni Evans, who saw me through typewriters and computers, three summer houses, hundreds of Hershey's chocolate kisses and endless telephone calls explaining why I couldn't possibly finish this book. She always agreed and then sent me right back to work. Her consummate professionalism is surpassed only by her clarity, character, and unswerving friendship. Before I found my voice, she assured me I had one. Joni made me write this book and, now that it's over, I am deeply grateful to her.

Finally, thank you, David Rosenthal, for coming up with the Perfect Title:

Hard to Get.

To say the least.